D0846100

7. 200

LOVE
AND
FREEDOM

LOVE
AND
FREEDOM

My Unexpected Life in Prague

Rosemary Kavan

FOREWORD BY ARTHUR MILLER

INTRODUCTION BY WILLIAM SHAWCROSS

EPILOGUE BY JAN KAVAN

Hill and Wang   New York

A division of Farrar, Straus and Giroux

Copyright © 1985 by Jan Kavan
Foreword copyright © 1988 by Arthur Miller
All rights reserved
Originally published in Great Britain under the title
*Freedom at a Price: An Englishwoman's Life in
Czechoslovakia* by Verso, 1985
Printed in the United States of America
First American edition, 1988

Library of Congress Cataloging-in-Publication Data
Kavan, Rosemary.
[Freedom at a price]
Love and freedom : my unexpected life in Prague /
Rosemary Kavan ; introduction by William
Shawcross ; foreword by Arthur Miller.
— 1st American ed.
Previously published as: Freedom at a price. 1985.
1. Kavan, Rosemary. 2. Czechoslovakia—Politics
and government—1945–3. Czechoslovakia—His-
tory—Intervention,
1968–   4. Communists—Czechoslovakia—
Biography. 5. Communists—
Great Britain—Biography. I. Title.
DB2218.7.K38 1988   943.7'042'0924—dc19 [B]
88-9733

I would like to dedicate my mother's book to the memory of my English grandmother and of those of her generation who rejected Munich and selflessly tried to help the Czechs and others who suffer from injustice; and to my daughter Caroline and her generation, who, I hope, will understand, as my mother did, that happiness, freedom and peace are indivisible, that the fate of any one individual or nation concerns us all and that the future depends on people being able to direct their governments as much in Prague or Warsaw as in London or Washington.

August 1988   J. K.

Contents

Foreword

Rosemary Kavan's book is a direct and unpretentious account of the Czechoslovakian tragedy, from the high idealism of the immediate postwar years to the Prague Spring of 1968 and its suppression by the Soviet invasion. She has written it all from the inside, as the British wife of a Czech Party official, sparing neither her own foibles nor those of others, and it makes a warm and human witness to what amounts to the surreal transformation of a Western people and civilization into something quite different — perhaps a colony of not Moscow exactly but Istanbul.

The Czech experience, as pure form, is the utter triumph of a particularly mindless bureaucracy — little different from what Kafka foretold two decades before, including executions for reasons no one can really put a finger on. Indeed, it is in many ways a system prepared for by the old Austrian bureaucracy, which had long since thrown its net over the Balkan and Central European nations of the Dual Monarchy. Marxism and the monolithic rule of the Party simply added yet another net to the first one, much as it did in China, where the Party's regulations were in a profound way prepared for by systematic Confucian regulatory mores. What the Party added that was new, however, was a disconcerting pretension to rationalism and democratic legality. But this merely covered over a totally whimsical selection of victims, and indeed persecutors, too, who in so many cases were simply victims awaiting their turn. On top of it all was ladled the sweet fudge of the old anti-Semitism, perhaps the ultimate irony when so many Jews had yearned for the coming of socialism as the new enlightenment, which would end forever their ancient brainless persecutions.

Because Rosemary Kavan has kept so close to what she saw and felt, her account will introduce those who are unfamiliar with the Czechoslovakian situation to the individual Czechs and Slovaks who, like all people closely observed, escape simple uniform definitions. And this makes their fall all the worse. This is not some "Eastern" country with whose unfree habits of life we in the West are unfamiliar — Prague, after all, is farther West than Vienna — it is a nation which had possessed and cherished freedom before being forced to give it up. This may be why, until very recently, it has been all but impossible to talk about Czechoslovakia with even liberal Soviet individuals, for they knew that here was no backward fascism Russia had smashed but a democratic and technologically advanced society which had been thrust back into far more primitive forms of social discourse and government than it had already achieved through its history. And Czechoslovakia may just turn out to be yet another fork in the road ahead, for when Glasnost truly is permitted to work its liberating mission in Czechoslovakia, releasing people's energies and hopes, regimes described in books like this will probably seem hallucinatory and hard to believe. But it all happened, weird as it is to contemplate, and it needs to be remembered, like an illness which leaves the body strong and healthy, except for the loss of its capacity to speak truthfully and to make its own choices in a candid and open rather than surreptitious and mostly illegal way.

Arthur Miller

Introduction

To my regret, I did not meet Rosemary Kavan till the early seventies. It was during the cruel repression which followed, slowly at first, the Soviet invasion of Czechoslovakia and the destruction of 'socialism with a human face'. Rosemary, who felt by now much more affinity with Czechoslovakia than with her native Britain, had remained in Prague as long as possible. But her association with the men, women and youths of 1968, and with their clandestine resistance afterwards, was too well known. She was allowing her flat to be used as a meeting-place, she was typing *samizdat*, and she participated in the distribution of the anti-election leaflet campaign, launched by the opposition in the autumn of 1971. The penalty was several years' imprisonment, and interrogators from the fifties were back at work. Eventually, Rosemary decided that the time had come to go back to England — where both her sons now lived. She was refused a passport but managed, somehow, to escape through Eastern Europe to the West.

In London she started to work for Palach Press. This news agency, named after Jan Palach, the student who immolated himself in protest against the Soviet invasion, was founded by Rosemary's son, Jan Kavan. Since its inception it has provided an extraordinarily full and accurate flow of news from Czechoslovakia, and recently as part of the newly-formed East European Cultural Foundation from Hungary and Poland as well. For anyone trying to learn or write about Eastern Europe, in particular the resistance and the groups striving for change, Palach Press has been quite invaluable.

Working for Palach Press was in some ways an easy

metamorphosis for Rosemary since she had been so long involved in the Czech underground. She knew most of the people whose writing she was translating or whose arrest she was reporting. But if familiar, it was also very depressing work to do in London, for the information which seemed (and was) so vital in Prague excited little interest in Britain. By the early seventies Czechoslovakia was an old story, meriting only short paragraphs in the papers edited by people to whom it was once again a faraway place of which they knew little.

On the few occasions I met her, Rosemary seemed an extraordinary creature with rare courage, humour and vivacity which were remarkable enough in themselves. I wished I had known her long ago, particularly in Prague when I first visited there in the summer of 1968, just before the invasion. I cannot think of anyone who would have been a better guide to the intricacies of the city, which she adored, and its politics, by which she had understandably become obsessed.

When I did finally meet her, I did not know the details of her life in Czechoslovakia over the past twenty-five years. Having read her book and learned about what she had gone through, her resilience I find all the more remarkable. Her book is both moving and an extraordinary, invaluable account of life under Stalinism.

I do not want to summarize the book — the reader should enjoy to the full Rosemary's cocky and inimitable style — but perhaps I could just mention some of the highlights which seem perhaps best to symbolize both her own story and the torment that has been Czechoslovakia since 1945.

Rosemary Kavan was a middle-class English girl who married a Czech communist in Britain in 1945 and went home with him to witness at first hand the misery that communism plunged the country into. Not that she would have put it like that; in those days she was, as she would later acknowledge, a naïve and over-enthusiastic supporter of the Party's cause. Her husband, Pavel, was a hardline communist, not the sort of person she would like to have as an enemy. 'He took no account of inner conflicts and psychological pressures and subtleties of motivation. He was interested only in political unambiguities: for or against.' He changed later.

Pavel worked in the Foreign Ministry; they were posted to Britain, and in the Stalinist purges of the early fifties his British contacts proved very dangerous for him. Rosemary had applied for a job in heavy industry ('the heavier the better') in order to learn more about Czechoslovakia and communism. It enabled her to take her mind off the terror which was stalking the land. But not for long. The purges of the early fifties swept further and further through the ranks of the Party; for Pavel too came the 5 a.m. ring on the doorbell. She kissed him goodbye, and he was gone for years.

Pavel and others were accused of being part of a Titoist conspiracy to drag Czechoslovakia away from the Soviet Union. The arch villain was Konni Zilliacus MP who, through his contacts with Czech communists, had been 'directly responsible for Yugoslavia's defection to the warmongering West'.

Rosemary had the extraordinary experience of listening to the trial over the radio. She waited to hear him deny the charges and was horrified instead to hear him admit them. However, after he started answering one question before the prosecutor had finished asking it, she realised that he was making mechanical responses to a prepared script.

In order to bring up her two sons, Rosemary took a job in the railway design office. She has hilarious accounts of the frustrations and the fears of office life in Prague in the early fifties when the whole country seemed to be held together, just, by bits of wire, string, cardboard and scrap metal, everything supposedly done according to some ludicrous and ill-applied plan presided over by bureaucrats and policemen incompetent or malign. 'The more I knew the Czechs,' she writes, 'the more I understood the attraction of Švejk. Švejk is a symbol of the moral victory of the underdog over the tyrant. His very acceptance of fate becomes a form of passive resistance. Though outwardly submissive, he retains the inner right to consign his superior to hell. His loquaciousness breaks his opponent's spirit; his imperturbability renders him impotent. In every encounter, Švejk makes authority look ridiculous, which removes the sting from subordination.'

Take the moment when Švejk is told that the Archduke Franz Ferdinand has been assassinated at Sarajevo. Mrs Müller says, 'So they've killed our Ferdinand.' 'Ferdinand?' he asks. 'Really? But which one? The one who used to pick up dog turds? Or that apprentice hairdresser who once drank the hair lotion by mistake?' This, says Milan Kundera, 'is not ignorance or stupidity speaking, it is the refusal to concede History a value, to grant it seriousness'.

In 1956 Pavel was released but the Party would not rehabili-
tate him fully. He found a job and then lost it — for getting
paralytically drunk and seducing an office colleague. When,
shamefacedly, he told Rosemary about it, she laughed, invited
him out to dinner and suggested he seduce her.

Pavel had a bad heart and he died in 1960. By this time
Rosemary had become bewitched by Prague and passionately
interested in the country's slow de-Stalinization and reform.
Moreover the boys regarded it as home, and Jan was becoming
very active in the student-reform movement. She stayed on.

Jan became involved with one of the bravest of the student
leaders to emerge even before 1968, Jiří Müller. Long before it
was allowed, Müller urged some independence for the country's
youth organization from the Party line. Indeed, he suggested
the Youth League should act as a 'corrective' to Party policy. He
was expelled from university and forced to join the army. Jan
asked Rosemary if fellow students pledged to Jiří's readmission
to university could meet in her flat. She knew it would likely be
denounced as a 'conspiracy', but she agreed. The group formed
an important part of the student revolt which coalesced in 1967
and preceded the revolt within the Party in '68.

1968 was the year of Alexander Dubček, the unknown, en-
gaging and hesitant leader of the Slovak party, who was
suddenly and unexpectedly made leader of the Czechoslovak
Communist Party. In an extraordinary torrent, the past began to
be re-examined and the future replanned, in an infectious
atmosphere of hope and goodwill that was too good, too revolutionary to last.

'For me, Prague Spring was a justification for sticking out the
years of disillusion . . . intoxicated with the new freedom, I
attended every public meeting.' It was indeed an exhilarating
time. She quotes workers who said how wonderful it was to get
the truth from the Party at last. But many others believed that it
proved the Party could never be trusted.

The trials were investigated. Pavel was publicly cleared. But
the full enquiry was never published in Prague because of the
Soviet invasion. It was smuggled to the West and published
there; ironically, Rosemary helped translate it into English after
she too had had to be smuggled out. She married again and was
very happy until, in 1981, she died of cancer, mourned by many
people, especially in Prague.

In Czechoslovakia there has since been scant improvement,

as a glance at any of the Palach Press bulletins will show. The government still persecutes and harries the ideas as well as the people of 1968. Those who were brave enough to sign the human rights protest document known as Charter 77 have all been harassed, some have lost their jobs, and others have even been imprisoned. There is a constant war on ideas and on any concept of Czech independence. The battle against words and literature is especially severe — hence the continued need for the *samizdat* which Rosemary helped produce. Milan Kundera has pointed out that persecution of writers and literature now 'aims at nothing less in the long run than the death of Czech culture, to which . . . the existence of the nation itself is inseparably bound. Russian totalitarianism's cultural concept is absolutely incompatible with the spirit, the wager, of Czech literature.'

One must certainly include in Czech literature all the manifestos, statements, appeals and protests that Czechs and Slovaks have made against their predicament in recent years. And in that brave list Rosemary's name figures prominently as one who has done much more than most people's best to make sure the struggle eventually succeeds, despite all oppression. And certainly her Czech friends would agree that she embodied its extraordinarily resilient, independent spirit. Her story is a restatement of that spirit.

William Shawcross

LOVE
AND
FREEDOM

Chapter 1

A people with such a genius for creating chaos should go far, I thought. Subsequent events were to confirm this impression.

At the beginning of July, two months after the end of the war, Pavel had written to me in Leicester from Prague: 'Get repatriated. I am leaving for Yugoslavia . . . ' He had been assigned to the diplomatic service and Belgrade was to be his first post. The prospect of chasing him across Central Europe with an assortment of dictionaries and without any orientation goaded me into activity. I gave in my notice, sold most of my belongings, and was informed that my first step towards Prague was to undergo a formidable list of injections – against smallpox, typhus, tetanus, cholera, malaria and goodness knew what else. The Czech doctor queried the wisdom of administering them all at once and then the difficulty of selecting the one that would be the most useful and least upsetting. In the end he solved the dilemma by issuing me with a sheet listing the whole galaxy, and implanted upon it a huge rubber stamp. The deed was done. This was my introduction to the Czech bureaucratic magic wand, without which you can neither be born nor die.

A few days later, I reported at 6 a.m. to the Czech office in London to be transported to my new country. There was no sign of any official. Scores of women with children crowded the corridor, clutching their cases and their fortitude. We waited. For a long time nothing happened. At length an official emerged and announced that the flight had been cancelled owing to fog over Prague. We were asked to re-appear the following morning. The same performance was repeated, and went on to enjoy a long run. The officials stuck to their original story with admirable tenacity against appalling odds. A fog over Prague in the middle of a blazing summer! I was impressed by their audacity, compared with officialdom's usual colourless excuses: technical hitches, unforeseen circumstances. Having been told on the ninth day that we should definitely not be flying for several days, we were contacted on the tenth day and told to assemble on the following morning.

We took off in a Dakota that had been hurriedly converted for our use.

Many questions whirled through my mind as the plane left England behind. What would Pavel, my husband of four months, look like in civilian clothes? What changes had he found in his homeland after a six-year absence? How would I adapt to his country?

Our paths had crossed in August 1943. I had just gained my teaching diploma and after two years of educational text-books, I had felt a need to broaden my horizons. A conference on the post-war world offered a good starting point. Many nationalities and a wide range of political convictions would be represented there. Pavel happened to be the leader of the discussion group I found myself in. He was an ardent and articulate communist.

Since my early teens I had considered myself a socialist. I had been influenced partly by my parents who were armchair socialists, and partly by books. At the age of ten, *The Last of the Mohicans*, *Uncle Tom's Cabin* and a story about Wat Tyler aroused my sympathy for the underdog. A few years later, Dickens, Upton Sinclair, Zola, Howard Fast, Leon Feuchtwänger, Walter Greenwood and John Steinbeck fanned my interest in social conditions. I wanted passionately to improve the human lot.

Pavel assured me that the roots of social evil could not be eradicated without political change. First, he said, you had to abolish private ownership. Then you put industry into the hands of the workers and divided the big landed estates among the peasants. This would eliminate the exploitation of man by man. Profits would be enjoyed by those who toiled. A planned economy would ensure efficiency, decent wages and full employment. Poverty would be wiped out. A free medical service and social insurance, paid for by taxes and profits from the nationalised industries, would mean that people would need no longer fear impoverishment as a result of illness or old age. There would be no privileged elite: all would have equal rights and opportunities. Everyone would attain self-fulfilment and happiness. He made it sound quite simple.

Pavel never left my side during the conference. Soon afterwards he appeared on my doorstep and continued my Marxist education. Slowly my life began to centre on Pavel. He was my mentor, my short cut to the brave new world. Furthermore, he epitomised the struggle against fascism. I wept when he described his anguish at the Munich betrayal of his country. My sympathy was mingled with shame, for my family — ignorant of fascism and considering war the worst of all evils — had rejoiced when Chamberlain proclaimed 'peace with honour' at the price of Czechoslovakia's freedom. 'We should have fought when the Germans invaded,' Pavel cried. 'The army was well equipped and ready to a man. We could have held off a German attack for three months. We would not have remained alone. The whole course of history would have been different. But,' he concluded bitterly, 'the politicians decided otherwise.'

Pavel had joined the resistance movement. When the Gestapo discovered his track, he was spirited away by the underground. Without saying goodbye to his widowed mother and brother, he left Prague and was passed from hand to hand over the border into Poland, and thence to Sweden and safety. He had fought with the Czechoslovak Brigade until the fall of France, and then he had escaped to England. The Czechs had had no chance to strike a real blow against fascism: their troops had been employed to cover the French retreat. Gnawed by disappointment, Pavel was eagerly awaiting the Second Front. The constant delays enraged him because, as he said: 'Every day adds to the hardships and terrors suffered by my countrymen under the Nazis.'

Pavel was worried about his family: he feared the worst, since they were Jews. His Jewish origin was part of Pavel's fascination to me. I was deeply moved by the history of the Jews: their persecution, their wanderings, and, above all, their endurance and indestructible sense of identity. Now they were being subjected to atrocities in Nazi concentration camps and Pavel had faced a terrible dilemma. He had been asked by the BBC to broadcast regularly to Czechoslovakia. This would certainly have endangered his family, if they were still free. Nevertheless, Pavel considered it his duty to accept. This made him a tragic hero in my eyes.

He was also a very active hero. The Czechoslovak Brigade must surely have been the only army in the West where privates with two doctorates were not uncommon and leaves

were spent in political activity. Pavel divided his leaves between the Czechoslovak Union of Students, of which he was
vice-president, the International Students' Council, of which he
was also vice-president, the *Students at War* magazine, of which
he was editor, the Czech section of the BBC – and me.

I was thrilled to be involved, even peripherally, in these
activities. Suddenly my life as a teacher in a slum school built in
the nineteenth century had acquired a view of the wide political
world. On a Saturday afternoon in the office of the students'
magazine, he would say: 'There are a few jobs that need doing.
They'll only take you half-an-hour; then we can go and enjoy
ourselves somewhere.'

He would then present me with a pile of correspondence to
answer, or articles to edit and type, which would have kept an
electronic brain busy for a couple of days. Or we would drop
into the British–Czechoslovak Friendship Club for a 'few
minutes'. These would extend to hours as Pavel was accosted by
kindred spirits with whom he would go into a 'brief' conspiratorial huddle. After an hour or so he would remember my
existence. Among the many to whom I was finally introduced
was Pavel's friend and idol, Eduard Goldstücker[1], with whom
he had been involved in student politics before the war and
who was now employed by the Czechoslovak government in
exile. He was a charming and cultured Slovak with an attractive
voice and a slow, emphatic manner of speaking that commanded attention. He was also a droll and prolific narrator
of Yiddish jokes. There were two other Slovaks: Vladimír
Clementis[2] and Evžen Klinger[3]. Vlado was widely loved as a

1. Eduard Goldstücker (1913–) studied at Oxford 1940–43. He was attached
to the London Embassy from 1947–49 and was then posted as envoy to Israel.
In 1951 he was recalled and arrested. He was sentenced to life imprisonment
in 1953 along with Kavan, Dufek and Richard Slánský. He was released at the
end of 1955, working as professor of German literature at the Charles University,
Prague until 1968. Since then he has been professor of comparative literature
at Sussex.
2. Vlado Clementis (1902–1952) was a Slovak lawyer and communist MP 1935–
38 and 1945–51. He was expelled from the CP for criticizing the Molotov–
Ribbentrop pact and the Soviet–Finnish war, but was reinstated in 1945. During
the war he was the BBC's Czechoslovak service's most popular broadcaster.
He was Foreign Minister in Prague from 1948 until his arrest in 1951. He was
executed a year later.
3. Evžen Klinger was a communist journalist before the war. He was
imprisoned in Czechoslovakia from 1949–1956.

man and respected as a lawyer who had defended communists in pre-war political trials. After 1948, Pavel was to serve under him at the Ministry of Foreign Affairs. Evžen, a myopic, bear-like and humorous Jew, was later to collaborate with Pavel on a number of abortive projects. Then there was Otto Šling[4], a florid, forceful Moravian, married to a staunch British comrade, and Vavro Hajdú[5], a lawyer serving in the army. These men were all pre-war communists; yet they were to end up on the gallows or condemned to a lifetime behind bars in the Czechoslovakia of the 1950s.

I spent a lot of time at the Club. It was a unique institution; not an escape from life, like an English Club, but an important component of living. Members entertained their friends, polemicized, studied, played chess, wrote letters, drew up wills. There a newspaper was not something to be idly turned over for scraps of gossip, or something from which one totted up victories and defeats like a cricket score. It was a mine of heterogeneous information and as such was treated with respect. The reader smoothed it reverently over its bamboo frame, adjusted his or her position with the air of one settling down for the night, and proceeded to assimilate it from A to Z, reading in between the lines for good measure. The reader then read the same news over again in French, German, Polish and English, hunting for discrepancies with the zeal of a biologist probing for bacteria. There, conversation was not a bauble tossed from lip to lip, but a morsel chewed voraciously to the core, whether it concerned the intimacies of love or the imponderables of politics. The Club was, in short, a microcosm of Czech intellectual life.

But I was attracted by Pavel as a man as well as a symbol. He was not tall, but rather chunky in fact, nor was he particularly handsome. But he had good features: straight nose, high forehead, neat ears, stubborn chin, a mouth with a full, sensual lower lip and the upper lip drawn into a thin line. His eyes were

4. Otto Šling (1912–1952) fought as a Communist in the Spanish Civil War, spending the war in England. After the war he was appointed Chief Secretary of the CP in the Moravian capital, Brno, and elected a member of the CC. He was executed in 1952.

5. Vavro Hajdú (1913–1977) was a Deputy Minister in the Czechoslovak Foreign Ministry by 1950. He was arrested in 1951 and sentenced to life imprisonment in 1952. After his release in 1956, he worked at the Institute of Law of the Czechoslovak Academy of Sciences.

his strong point. Hazel brown, they glowed with golden fire: patriotic, political or passionate, as the occasion demanded. In the army he was known as 'poker face'. One could read his thoughts and feelings only from his eyes.

Perhaps it was his manner that fascinated me most. He swept through doors (he didn't open them like ordinary mortals) on a wave of energy that excited me. His whole bearing expressed the conviction that obstacles would dissolve in his path. Being a rather different person myself, I found this irresistible.

I had always exacted a Platonic code of behaviour from my few English male friends. Pavel bulldozed these inconvenient English rules. We became lovers.

At twenty-eight, Pavel was an experienced lover. Uninhibited, technically assured, he guided me gently down untried paths. After an initial panic, my response was avid. My parents had shrouded sex in veils of silence, giving the impression that it was a slightly sordid, if essential, adjunct to marriage. I had been prepared to tolerate it, not to fall in love with it. My awakened sexual passion shocked, excited and absorbed me. I imbued Pavel with special powers as the bestower of such delight. After a girls' school, a women's college and an all-female teaching staff, he had transformed my life.

Getting on with the English was one of Czechoslovakia's war aims, in the promotion of which a thousand or so Czechoslovak soldiers and airmen went so far as to marry English girls. Pavel, of course, did nothing so conventional as to go down on his knees and ask for my hand. He simply told me he intended to marry me. In my novel state of intoxication, love and sex seemed inextricable. I believed myself to be in love with Pavel. His unorthodox declaration: 'I will not vow undying love — what man honestly can? But one thing I promise, with me you will never be bored', tipped the scales, and I became engaged.

Caution, in the person of my mother, said: 'Wait until the war is over. Go and see his country. You may not like living there. You don't know what security he is offering you.' Romance, in my own person, replied: 'Love conquers all. Once the night-mare of death and destruction is over, what can possibly defeat love?'

I believed in the power of love. My parents were still romantic-ally in love (and they were to remain in love until their eighties); my many aunts and uncles were still happy after years of marriage. I didn't give a damn about security, having known nothing else. On the contrary, I abhorred the predictability of my parents' lives. I wanted adventure, stimulation, purpose. Life with Pavel promised all these. Separation from my family was my only concern; but Pavel assured me that as soon as international transport was restored, visiting England would be 'no problem'.

As a means of transport the Dakota left much to be desired. The passengers were seated on canvas chairs chained to the fuselage. Every nut and bolt shook with an unnerving clatter and the temperature in the cabin was zero. I returned to the past for comfort.

I remembered our wedding, eight months after Pavel had left for France when the long-awaited Second Front had at last been opened. As I kissed him goodbye, I pleaded: 'Look after yourself. If anything happens to you, it will be the loss of nine men — soldier, student, activist, official, editor, journalist, translator, broadcaster and lover.' 'Or a cat with nine lives — I'll preserve the ninth till last,' he joked.

When he was gone there were months of anxious mail-watching. I received snippets of news between what were, for Pavel, extravagant outpourings of affection. (There's nothing like damp, cold shelling and a diet of corned beef to soften even a hard-boiled activist.) The Czechoslovak troops had not been sent to the front, as he had hoped, but had taken over the siege of Dunkirk. In one letter Pavel wrote: 'One of my nine lives has gone . . . A jerry took a pot shot at me. I had absentmindedly picked up my beret instead of my helmet. Anyway, he got my badge instead of my brains, you'll be relieved to hear . . .'

Concerning his more spectacular role in the siege, for which he was decorated, Pavel was modest, even reticent.

When my father returned from his special duty trip, Pavel applied for compassionate leave. It was April 1945. On his way to Calais on a borrowed motorbike he had an argument with a Frenchman. This resulted in him losing his way and hitting a tree. Consequently he arrived in England one day late and the wedding had to be postponed by a day. We were fitted in between two other ceremonies by a reluctant and adenoidal clerk who did not hold with English girls marrying foreigners. He made a last ditch bid for my freedom, whispering hoarsely: 'Id's nod too lad to chage your bind.'

We were rushed through a chocolate-coloured door to the dim, cheerless ceremonial office. A thin man with the air of a funeral director gabbled the brief words with one eye on the clock. He fidgeted impatiently while Pavel searched his pockets first for his glasses, presumably to check the identity of the bride, and then for the ring which I remembered was in my handbag. I still had the price tab, £5.5s., dangling from my finger when we were bundled through the exit.

My marriage altered my status as well as my state. I found that I had shrunk overnight from an unassailable British subject, legatee of all the pink bits on the world map, to a desirable alien attached to a mutilated blob in the heart of Europe. I thus became immediately suspect and was required to report my movements regularly to the police.

True to type, Pavel spent the first half of his wedding night bringing me up to date with the political situation. The new Czechoslovak coalition government, formed at Košice in Slovakia, had mapped out a socialist programme somewhat on the lines he had already expounded to me. 'It's a promising start,' he declared. He was then ready to turn, with a light heart and high hopes, to the more orthodox practices of wedding nights.

The wail of a child and the sharp reproof of its mother set my thoughts on a new track. What would marriage with Pavel be like? During two years, the longest time we had been together was three days — our honeymoon — and those had been spent largely in taxis. Suddenly I felt I hardly knew my husband.

I shivered. The cold was aggravating my period pains. I began to feel sick and, as the plane descended, reached for a paper bag. After four hours in the air, the plane at last flopped to the ground and bumped to a standstill. The last to leave, I lurched uncertainly down the steps. There was Pavel, larger in diameter and looking clerkish and sedentary in horn-rimmed spectacles and a crumpled suit; the dashing distinction of his army days had been discarded with his battledress.

'What in the name of God have you been doing?' he asked, a greeting that hardly did justice to the reunion of the pining lover with his mate.

The airways bus was about to sneak off. Pavel urged his civilian limbs into a sprint and managed to stop it. The driver leaned out of the window and held forth at length on the impossibility of waiting a single second for incompetent travellers ignorant of the whereabouts of their luggage. He had his timetable, his obligations to the other passengers, to the new Republic and to his wife and children.

I was to find out later that officialdom's response to any request, major or minor, was invariably a point-blank *no*, accompanied by a pious invocation to the regulations. This precluded either decision or action, both anathema to bureaucracy. Experience soon taught me to disregard this negative, and either to remain polite but firm, or else to rave like a lunatic. Bureaucracy then tore itself to pieces trying to meet my wishes; it waived laws, rules and ancient customs and, with the air of risking its neck in my interests, furtively drew from a locked safe the required document, permit, receipt or stamp.

In this case, having wasted a good quarter-of-an-hour vigorously saying nothing, the driver suddenly jumped down from his perch. Once on the same level as Pavel, he came to terms with him, and even joined in the search for my case, showing a great interest in its make, history, contents and owner. He found it eventually in the west-bound heap and prevented it just in time from stowing away to America.

Within an hour I was in my new home, a two-roomed flat in a secluded spot with an all-night garage on one side and a printing works on the other. It was chock-a-block with heavy, frowning German furniture. Suits and shirts thrown carelessly over the backs of chairs proclaimed the absence of a female hand. Pavel, following my gaze, declared cheerfully: 'Thank goodness you're here at last. Now the place will soon be ship-shape.'

He showed me to the kitchen and left me to prepare a meal. A cursory search revealed only some stale bread and a knob of margarine. I took these into the dining-room-cum-lounge, remarking that I couldn't find anything to go with them. 'I don't wonder,' Pavel replied. 'We used up all our rations in a slap-up meal for your expected arrival last week. Eva even baked a cake, but in a few days it went somehow.'

Eva was a distant connection of Pavel's family, as far as he knew the only one, besides Karel, his brother, to have survived the war. He had seen Karel, who had fled from Dachau and, after incredible hardships, reached the Soviet Union. He had fought his way back to Prague with the Czechoslovak Eastern Brigade. After a few days in Prague, he had returned to his regiment to be officially demobbed.

'And your mother?' I could hardly get the words out.

Pavel shook his head. 'Oh Rosemary, I couldn't write to you. It was too terrible. Our unit liberated Buchenwald. My mind still reels from the sights we saw. Among the names of those who were sent to the gas chamber I found my own mother's, together with my aunts' and uncles' and cousins'. The whole family. For weeks I couldn't sleep picturing their sufferings.'

I sat stunned with horror and pity. I wondered if grief was made worse by a sense of responsibility. Although it was unlikely that Pavel's broadcasts had decided his mother's fate — all Jews were scheduled for the 'final solution' — the cruel question must surely have persisted. His face was twisted into tortured lines. I put my arms round him and he leaned gratefully against me. Then he straightened up and said firmly: 'So now I have told you. I don't want to refer to this ever again. We must put the past behind us.' Brave words, but Pavel was to bear the scars of the past for the rest of his life. It was months before he uttered his mother's name again. Then he spoke of her with pride, telling me how she had faced widowhood and greatly reduced circumstances with fortitude and had worked to support her two sons.

The door bell rang. Pavel went to open it and ushered in a woman of about thirty. It was Eva. She grasped both of my hands: 'So you are here at last! Welcome! Welcome! I hope you will be very happy here.' We sat down. In the absence of anything else, I offered her a cigarette. She accepted hungrily. Noting that the ashtray was full, I rose to empty it, but Eva stopped me. She picked out the stubs and popped them into a matchbox which she put into her handbag.

'There's no cigarette ration for women yet,' Pavel explained. 'And only two a day for men. So we all collect toppers and roll the tobacco into fresh cigarettes.'

'I can live without everything except a smoke,' Eva sighed.

'In the camp she bartered her belongings for cigarettes,' Pavel put in, 'Then, when she had nothing left, her soup, which was often the only food they got.'

'The soup was water,' Eva replied. 'Water for cigarettes is good business.'

She was an odd little figure. Her chapped hands and feet and a distended abdomen spoke eloquently of the concentration camp. Her camp number was tattooed indelibly on her arm. Her hair was just beginning to grow again after an attack of typhus. A few teeth were missing — a blow from an SS-man. But she had beautiful eyes, warm, wise, friendly and forgiving. She had seen humanity at its worst but she had never stopped loving people. She became a staunch friend who stood by me through the difficult times that were to come.

Her first good deed was to rescue me in the matter of warm clothing. I had been allowed one small case on the plane. The other four pieces of luggage, with winter woollies and sweaters, were to follow by boat. Here, however, was another example of the right hand not knowing what the left hand was doing. The right hand had informed me in writing that delivery would take three weeks; the left hand had no intention of performing miracles; so my warm things reached Prague in spring. In the meantime, I was in danger of freezing to death in my first Central European winter. The only solution seemed to be hibernation until Eva offered me from her meagre possessions a camp blanket to have made into a dress. Its mud-grey colour imparted a corpse-like hue to my sallow complexion, and its bulk and intractability made movement about as easy as the Ablative Absolute. In texture it could be likened only to a hair shirt; I passed the winter in it doing penance for Munich.

Chapter 2

'Bristly lot, aren't you?' I remarked to Pavel, on reaching home one afternoon. At the grocer's shop an argument had been started, as far as I could make out, by a customer who had been short-changed. This had grown into a slanging match between the grocer and his middle-class supporters on one side, and the affronted worker and his allies on the other, and had then developed into a fierce political debate. Farther along the street I had then witnessed a group of Czechs forcing two German women to lick a huge swastika chalked on the pavement. The tufts of peroxided hair strewn about indicated the punishment they had already received. Catching sight of me, one of the men grabbed my arm, brandishing his knife. Pavel warned me I might be mistaken for a German if I went around in a trouser suit with my hair up. I promptly produced my alibi: 'Nejsem němka, jsem angličanka.' ('I'm not a German, I'm an English-woman.') This secured my immediate release and a shower of apologies. Half-a-dozen bystanders rushed up to shake my hand.

'Bristly?' Pavel looked blank.

'Fiery, belligerent.'

'Can you wonder?' Pavel asked soberly. 'A small nation, from its early history menaced by powerful neighbours, its land devastated and its population decimated by all the major European wars.'

'But we have had our triumphs, too,' he added.

Pavel was a true Czech patriot. 'I am first a Czech and then a Jew,' he declared. (I was to remember these words with painful irony at his trial some years later.) He was intensely proud of his Czech origins. The Czechs had played a crucial part in European history, he told me. During the Middle Ages, the lands of the Bohemian Crown had extended from the Alps to the Adriatic. For centuries Bohemia had held the Germans at bay in their drive to the East. 'John Hus led the Reformation; Comenius was the founder of modern education.' Then he broke off. 'On Sunday I will take you for a historical walk through Prague. When you tread the same cobbles, touch the same stones, see the same skyline as our ancestors, you will feel and breathe our history.'

I assented eagerly. I knew so little about my new country. When I met Pavel I couldn't even place it on the map. I didn't want to remain an ignorant outsider: I wanted to belong. And I needed to know Pavel's roots in order to understand him, as a man and as a Czech.

Sunday was a golden September day. Walking towards the river, we soon reached the embankment. I stopped dead, astonished by the view.

Prague is a visual feast. Built on seven hills, it presents constantly changing panoramas, each one more breath-taking than the next. I was looking at Hradčany, the castle promontory on the far side of the river. At its foot flowed the Vltava, bearing kaleidoscopic reflections under its many bridges. Below the castle wall, hanging gardens and ancient roofs descended to the water's edge. The crest was dominated by the Hrad whose flowing horizontal lines and smooth facades created an effect of both solidity and grace, while behind it soared the Gothic spire of the cathedral.

This view is stamped for ever on my mind.

We walked along the embankment to the Charles Bridge. 'The oldest stone bridge in Central Europe,' Pavel announced as we passed under a medieval tower at the entrance. We crossed the bridge, flanked on either side by a parapet of gesticulating saints. 'Sixteen arches, 520 metres long,' Pavel went on. 'Held together by eggs — an innovation thought up by the architects.'

'The original eggheads,' I murmured.

'Pardon?'

'Nothing. A stupid pun. It means intellectuals.'

'Well, that would certainly apply to the Emperor

Charles IV[6] who built it,' Pavel enthused. 'He was a statesman, writer, scholar, linguist and builder. He rebuilt the Castle and founded the cathedral, the New Town and Prague university, the first in central Europe.'

At the far end of the bridge stood another massive tower, part of the old fortifications. These no longer existed, yet we seemed to pass through invisible walls — straight into the Middle Ages, as though through Wells' time machine. We were in Malá Strana (the Lesser Quarter), one of the three ancient towns that comprise historical Prague.

I was immediately enchanted. The narrow, winding, cobblestoned streets were lined with distinguished Gothic houses. In the sunlight their stone walls became amber and their tall, elegant windows were golden. I followed their concise lines upward and saw that at roof level restraint had been abandoned. Here was a medley of gables: single and multiple, arched and indented, decorated with stucco, or dignified by pinnacles, pillars and parapets; some had dormer windows, some were blind and had been added to give height like crests on Maya temples. From among these flamboyant forms a sculptured population of saints and sinners looked down.

Among the burghers' houses were also stately Baroque mansions and palaces. Grander, more curvaceous and ornate, they did not make a separate assertive statement but merged democratically into the whole. It was difficult to believe that they accommodated flats, offices and ministries. Gripped by the past, I almost expected to see knights and nobles emerge from them.

We climbed Neruda Street, winding steeply uphill. The tops of the houses leaned toward each other, exchanging silent communications. Over the doorways delicately wrought artisan signs brought to mind the crafts that had once been the city's pride.

At the top we ascended the New Castle Steps ('new' in Prague usually means fourteenth century) to the Hradčany heights. We crossed the square to a wall bounding the right-hand side, and looked down. Below, the full richness of the Malá Strana roofs lay revealed under their rippling sheath of pantiles. There were tall, steeply sloping roofs and short, squat

6. Charles IV was King of Bohemia and the Holy Roman Empire (1348–1378), and is a Czech national hero.

ones; there were hip-jointed and recessed roofs and roofs that flowed over inset windows like eyebrows over brooding eyes. Even the chimneys had individual characters. The predominant colours were warm: bright red, deep crimson and cinnamon, and the roofs huddled together like comfortable old women gossiping. Needle spires and buttressed towers, crenallated turrets and onion-shaped domes grew out of the riot of roofs.

Far below the river wound like a ribbon; beyond lay the Old and New Towns and the modern centre. The peripheral suburbs merged into misty countryside at the horizon. Looked at as a whole, the panorama was a huge, coherent canvas, its foreground painted in gold and burgundy, fading to a silvery purple haze in the distance. The quality of its beauty was indescribable. It brought a lump to my throat and vague thoughts of human mortality and of the eternity of art. At that moment I fell in love with Prague. It was a love affair that was to last a lifetime, and which inflicted sharp stabs of longing in my later enforced exile.

While I drank in the architectural glories of Prague, Pavel regaled me with its history. His intense emotional involvement in past events — in this changeless milieu — injected me with a sense of living history.

Having followed the serpentine twists of Karlova Ulice through the medieval Old Town, where names like Rybná (Fish Street) and Uhelný trh (Coalmarket) conjured up vanished scenes of urban life, we had come to a magnificent arcaded square. Standing under the statue of Jan Hus, Pavel described to me with pride and sorrow the heroic rise and eventual fall of the Hussites who had believed in freedom of faith, and for nearly two decades fought to establish a world of justice, equality and education for all.

Later I was to realize this was not a remote and irrelevant chapter in Czech history: its faith, traditions and strong moral sense had become part of the Czech character, just as its tenet, 'Truth Shall Prevail', had become the independent Republic's motto.

Pavel's mood then darkened. 'It was in the Old Town Square that the Czech leaders of the rebellion against the Habsburgs were executed. Two years later we were totally defeated in battle, and our country lost its independence for three centuries. In the face of religious persecution, the educated classes went into exile; German became the official language. Czech culture was virtually destroyed. The Czech language was kept alive only as the spoken tongue of the peasants and the poor in the towns.' I then understood the longstanding Czech hatred of the Germans.

Pavel insisted we retrace our steps to the Kampa district by the river. Among ornate gas candelabra in the streets and Baroque fountains tucked away in unexpected courtyards, he regained his exuberance. Stopping short, he declared: 'Here, light begins to shine again.'

We were outside a modest stone house, belonging to one Josef Dobrovský[7], the father of the National Revival. Pavel's eyes shone as he tried to describe to me this re-awakening of national feeling, which reinstated Czech as a cultivated language, established the Czech theatre, created a new literature and re-created pride in the past and hope for the future. Although a brief armed revolt by the students and workers of Prague was ruthlessly suppressed, the movement for national sovereignty was kept alive until 1918 when the independent Czechoslovak state was finally constituted.

Pavel communicated his excitement to me. Some of the names of the 'awakeners' were familiar to me from Prague's place names. The main Post Office stood in Jungmann Street[8]. The park opposite the main station was named after Vrchlický[9]. Jirásek's[10] bridge was a stone's throw from our flat. From there I could see the Palacký[11] and Havlíček bridges. These names would now have a greater significance for me.

But it was to Old Prague — Staré Město and Malá Strana — that my heart was drawn. Old Prague was to become my spiritual home. I returned there again and again. I would wander for hours alone. There I felt an affinity with the

7. Josef Dobrovsky (1753–1829) was a Jesuit priest who produced the first systematic study of the Czech language and culture.

8. Milan Jungmann (1773–1847) was a philologist whose work was vital for the development of the Czech language. His best-known work was a detailed Czech–German dictionary.

9. Jaroslav Vrchlický (1853–1912) was a Czech poet and a translator of Shakespeare.

10. Alois Jirásek (1851–1930) was a famous author of historical novels and the leader of the 'national school' of Czech literature.

11. František Palacký (1798–1878) was an outstanding historian and the political leader of 18th-century Czech nationalism.

spirit of the place, and a happiness that was rooted in its beauty and harmony.

Our historical walk was followed by a literary walk that took in the National Theatre, built by money contributed by the whole nation during the revival, the 'awakeners' Karel Mácha,[12] poet, Jan Neruda,[13] critic and journalist, and novelist Alois Jirásek, as well as modern writers such as Franz Kafka and Karel Čapek[14]; we finished up with a foaming tankard of beer at U Kalicha (the Chalice), the good soldier Švejk's favourite pub.

The musical walk included the Bertramka villa where Mozart composed *Don Giovanni* for the people of Prague, the Smetana Museum, the Dvořák monument, the two opera houses and the many halls and gardens where concerts were held.

Our educational walk ended up on the Vyšehrad height where Bohemia's famous dead are buried and the fifth-century Princess Libuše foresaw Prague as 'a city whose fame would reach to the stars'.

The geography of Prague had made it impossible to adhere to chronology, and I was a little confused as to the sequence of events (I rectified this later from history books). However, I had formed a picture of the Czechs as a freedom-loving, moral and cultured nation, courageous in defence of their ideals and skilled in the art of survival.

I was not interested only in past history. I questioned everyone I met on their wartime experiences. They were eager to talk. I learnt of resistance heroes and partisans, of quislings and collaborators; I spoke to survivors of slave labour and concentration camps, and fence-sitters who had avoided involvement and aimed at staying alive.

In reciprocity I, too, was subjected to interrogation. 'Is your husband Czech?' 'Was he an airman?' 'What is your occupation?' 'Have you any children?' A woman I talked to in a coffee house asked me to address a gathering of English-speaking ladies on women in wartime Britain.

12. Karel Hynek Mácha (1810–1836) was a well-known poet.

13. Jan Neruda (1834–1891) was a Czech poet, novelist and journalist.

14. Karel Čapek (1890–1938) was a leading inter-war Czech dramatist and novelist.

I had never spoken in public before. My nervousness took a not unusual form. Owing to the shortage of toilet paper, my notes were non-existent before the meeting opened. As I entered the hall the audience was turned towards the platform like poppies to the sun. The woman in the chair introduced me. There was a burst of applause, not for me personally but for Britain and the British war effort. I was reassured. From the anonymous mass I selected three faces and addressed myself to them, I forgot my stagefright. I talked to them as if they were friends. I told them how British women had spent the war: working in industry, serving in the forces or with St John's ambulance corps, eking out the rations, enduring raids, parted from husbands, sons, sweethearts and sometimes from children evacuated to safer areas.

I described my own experiences. I had been bombed out, barely escaping with my life; I had spent many tense hours in shelters with my charges, listening to the drone of the v1s overhead; I had grieved for pupils who had been killed, and comforted those who had lost relatives in the raids. Our school had later been evacuated and I had been made responsible for emotionally disturbed children abandoned by their mothers while their fathers were overseas. My audience responded with sympathy. Question time went on for hours; no one wanted to go home. Afterwards I thought how easy it had been to establish bonds: women have the same human interests everywhere.

This talk led to others at other clubs. But it was fringe activity. I wanted to be politically involved. I asked Pavel how I could join the Communist Party. He was discouraging. 'What can you do in the Party? Meetings and political school will be in Czech. First you must master the language.' Yes, of course. I intended to learn Czech anyway: without it I would remain a stranger in my new homeland.

My initial zeal was somewhat chilled by the discovery that the task would take at least a lifetime. To begin with, Czech words on their own are absolutely useless. You simply do not know whether you are coming or going, nominative or accusative, until you have learnt by rote an imposing array of inflexions. There are seven cases. On top of that every single thing is either animate or inanimate, masculine or feminine or neuter, and for good measure hard or soft as well. So beginners face 98 declension endings before they can think of saying (in Czech): 'The new pen of my old aunt is in the back yard.' They may then approach the rest of the 689 morphemes. Most of them jump out of the window or, a wiser alternative, throw their grammar book out of the window, before getting this far.

The undaunted may proceed to the conjugation of verbs, divided into six classes and cluttered up with aspects, so that if you want to run somewhere, you have to make up your mind beforehand whether you intend to run for a short distance or long, and whether you are resolved to make a habit of it, or get it over with once and for all. There are minor pitfalls even in connection with prepositions. For example, there is a divergence of opinion between the Czechs and the English as to whether pedestrians are *in* or *on* the streets and as to whether one goes *to* or *into* the theatre; the English tend to leave you in the vicinity; the Czechs take you right inside.

The last page of the grammar book in no way signifies an end to tribulation. There is still the business of pronunciation. Though liberal with its declensions, Czech is grudging with its vowels: the spoken language thus resembles a series of coughs, splutters and hiccoughs. It is my belief that the Czechs deny themselves an abundance of vowels in order to stress the stamina of their race. Only a nation of great stamina could survive continual utterance of such breath-depriving sounds.

'You must acquire a feeling for the living language,' Pavel insisted. After that, I was obliged each day to listen to one poem and an aria from a Czech opera, and to translate a paragraph from the Communist daily. As a result, I gained a mixed vocabulary. I could state — with some truth — 'I wandered in a strange land', voice somewhat outdated sentiments, like 'Man has the sower's yearning', and draw on a selection of anti-imperialist epithets.

Many were the misunderstandings. I went into a grocery shop and asked: 'Have you eggs?' The assistant looked at me doubtfully and beckoned me to follow him. We entered the back of the shop. I presumed I was being given priority treatment as a foreigner and was about to be introduced to some under-the-counter eggs. The assistant said: 'Please' and indicated a door. It was marked w.c. The Czechs having no *w*, call it a v.c., which was roughly how I had pronounced the word for eggs. I dispersed the veil of misapprehension with an imitation of a clucking hen. 'Now do you understand? Eggs?' 'Ah, yes, eggs', beamed the assistant. 'Yes, we have no eggs. Next week.'

On the way home, eggless, I paused to watch a group of

people clearing the rubble away from a war-damaged building. They were clearly not labourers. One of them called out to me teasingly: 'Don't stand there gawking. Come and join us.'

Me? I hesitated. Why not? Physical labour would be a pleasant change from teaching English, and it would certainly not require fluent Czech.

'Dobře, přijdu.' ('All right, I'll come.') I was handed a pick and set to with a will to the accompaniment of encouraging grins. Everyone seemed to be in a good mood. The ring of picks on stone and the squeal of barrow wheels were interspersed with jokes and snatches of song. I warmed to the atmosphere.

All too soon my hands were blistered. A young man bound them up with his handkerchief. 'Not to worry,' he said. 'It happens to all of us at first.' They were students, housewives, white and blue collar workers, who had answered the call for voluntary labour. Similar patriotic brigades had sprung up all over the country. In addition to their regular employment, the 'brigaders' worked in factories, cleaned schools and universities (which had been used as barracks by the Germans), repaired roads and helped farmers on the land. Now that their German overseers were gone, the whole nation was plunged into a fervour of constructive activity. The following days I hurried through my chores so that I could return to the site. I was enjoying myself. Sweeping away the ruins of the past was practically and symbolically the first step towards building the brave new future.

My conversations on the site improved my Czech. Thus emboldened, I resolved to see Prague on my own. My method was to start from the centre, take a tram, get off at a random stop, look around and return by the same route. This was not as simple as it sounds.

Until I became acclimatized, I considered myself lucky to survive a ride in one piece. In the first place, there were no queues. As the tram drew to a standstill, a mass of grimly determined citizens surged forward. Elbows were much in evidence, hats tended to disappear. Perfect equality existed between men and women, young and old. Having missed a tram or two, or having been swept into the wrong tram, by observing old-fashioned courtesy, I went native and acquired a certain rugger skill in dealing with scrimmages.

Boarding and alighting were carried on simultaneously, so that it was just as exhausting to fight one's way off as on.

Having touched down on the pavement, one often got carried back into the tram by the ingressing mob. The conductor usually possessed a peculiar sense of humour and started the tram moving while the oncomers and outgoers were still sorting each other out. Consequently, between stops the tram resembled a planet throwing off heavenly bodies at top speed. There was no limit to the capacity of these trams: they might be overflowing but they were never full. At every stop they picked up a few more satellites who hung on by toes, teeth and magnetism. No one ever dreamed of waiting for the next tram. The mere suggestion would have been taken as a sign of madness; just as the courageous cry: 'Eight standing only; the rest off the tram!' would have been a signal for lynching the conductor. I came to the conclusion that this mode of travelling was highly profitable for the haberdashery trade: one rarely emerged with the full complement of buttons, gloves and belts.

Many of the conductors were women, awesome women. If the London policemen were selected for their height, the Prague tram conductress was surely hired according to weight and pugnacity. With the waist measurement of a kettle-drum and the voice of a sergeant-major, she ploughed her way through the sweating bodies like an elephant in a nursery of saplings. The passengers bowed in her path: those not permanently deformed straightened up in her wake. If smaller and weaker specimens dropped out of the tram's open end as the pressure wave hit them, they went unnoticed and unlamented. These little trips introduced me to a quantity of Czech ribs as well as a number of Prague suburbs.

One morning as I set forth, a middle-aged woman pounced on me from a door on the ground floor.

'I'm Marešová, the concierge for this block,' she announced. 'You must be the English lady, Mr Kavan's wife?'

'Yes, I am Kavanová,' I said. 'How do you do, Mrs Marešová?'

'It could be worse.'

I reflected: English people, when asked: 'How are you?' give the standard answer: 'Fine thanks,' even if they have just lost their nearest and dearest. But Czechs never admit to being well off even if they have won a fortune. To a general enquiry their replies are in a minor key: 'Bearing up'. 'Mustn't grumble', or further down the scale: 'I just about keep from stealing.' The more guarded fob one off with 'Thank you for asking', or simply 'Thank you', to which one attaches one's own interpretation.

One may also be given enigmatic replies like 'As fit as an old slipper'; 'It's for the cat'; or just 'Oh well, you know how it is.'

Having cornered me, Mrs Marešová released a volley of Czech that went something like this: 'I suppose you've settled down by now. That's a nice flat you've got; but no one stays there long. At the beginning of the war a wealthy Jewish family lived there. They bribed the Germans and managed to keep in circulation for a bit but, in 1943, they were transported to Terezín. The parents and the little girl ended up in the gas chamber; the older daughter died of pneumonia in time.

'Your flat was taken over by a German doctor and his wife. He was at Buchenwald for a time doing medical experiments on the inmates. Most of them died, but them as didn't went mad or paralysed. Well, when the Russians came and he saw Hitler had lost his perishing war, he and his wife committed suicide. The police found them on that red couch in the lounge. All togged up in their best clothes and sprayed with scent. They probably thought they'd be a bit high by the time they was found. Seems like the flat's got a curse on it. Let's hope to goodness you'll have better luck!'

With this pious invocation Mrs Marešová gave me a friendly nod and let me go.

My spirit deflated, I crossed the park into Vodičková Street. An alert pedestrian prevented my extinction by an oncoming military vehicle. Well-meaning friends in England had warned me that Prague would be overrun by hordes of Russians terrorizing the population. I had kept a wary look-out, but among the many strange uniforms it was difficult to identify them. Eventually I discovered that the least impressive uniforms covered Soviet soldiers and that the Russian was square, flat-headed, short-legged, and genial. Only when mechanized was he a menace. The motorized Russian drove at breakneck speed with one hand on the steering wheel and the other on the hooter. This saved time and exonerated him from blame. On the whole the Czechs were genuinely grateful to the Russians and tolerant of excesses committed by the liberating army on its march towards Prague. Nevertheless, I had narrowly escaped the fate predicted for me by my English friends. I thanked my saviour and walked on with a philosophical shrug.

At the end of the street I turned into Wenceslas Square, which isn't a square at all but the main boulevard. Devoted to feeding, clothing and enlightening the populace, it was relieved from the prosaic by a colourful mural on the Wiehl House and rows of lime trees growing out of circular gratings. Its enchantment was revealed at night, when necklaces of white lights gleamed between the trees and the National Museum. But by day it was uncompromising and solid, like a hospital matron.

Rounding the corner I almost bumped into a ginger, freckled figure. A red-headed Czech is about as common as the edelweiss in East Anglia. He, in turn, saw before him a brown-clad beanstick with an Edwardian hair-do, by all standards a horticultural rarity. We had seen only photos of each other, but it was a fifty-fifty chance. We seized each other's hands and exclaimed simultaneously: 'My sister-in-law, isn't it?' 'My brother-in-law, isn't it?'

Karel, now demobbed, had nowhere to go. I took him home and allotted him the fateful couch, trying to ward off the ghosts. He was a full-time student, along with tens of thousands of other Czechs deprived of higher education by the war. By all accounts, the classes and lecture rooms were as crowded as the trams. Karel would have chosen to study drama (like his brother he had a flair for histrionics) but Pavel had decreed economics, and he had always obeyed his elder brother.

Feeding my two men became my main occupation. The initial problem was to discover which shops sold what. All the windows displayed photographs of Beneš, Stalin and other personalities, also pictures of the war and the May revolution and views of Prague. There was almost nothing to sell, except food, and that was limited in variety and quantity.

Under the circumstances one might think that catering would have been simplicity itself. Not a bit of it. Take the ration tickets, for a start. These had to be collected from the National Committee every month on a certain day, a different day for every month. This was a feat requiring time, patience and persistence. The National Committee dealt with all problems, from housing and the registration of births, deaths, marriages and repatriates, to vouchers for keeping hens or radios. All these offices changed their headquarters from month to month but not the labels on the doors.

The first time I went for our tickets I took my stand outside door No. 130 on the first floor at nine o'clock in the morning, as directed by Information on the ground floor. The door was locked. Time passed, so did many flying figures. I was to find that though officials dashed along corridors in a purposeful hurry, inside their offices efficiency was less marked. They invariably took some time to find one's card, or to find that they had lost one's card. This was the worst possible fate for no one believed that a person existed unless he or she could prove it on paper. This meant that people had to carry around not only an identity card but also a birth certificate and copies of their parents' birth certificates in order to prove not only that they had been born but that they had parents. If these documents had been issued in a foreign country, both the originals and Czech translations of them were necessary. If any of these documents had been lost, affidavits to that effect were necessary, suitably signed and stamped, proving erstwhile possession of them. And if an affidavit were lost, then another affidavit confirming the erstwhile existence of the original affidavit was necessary, and so on. A foreign wife was required to produce her marriage certificate as well, because no one credited that she would be in this charming chaos unless she had a very binding reason. Then there was the certificate of domicile, which stated that you had successfully proved your existence and identity, and were therefore entitled to live . . .

Eventually I was taken pity on and informed that ration tickets were now dealt with on the third floor, door No. 303, but that they were issued in the afternoon between two and six o'clock. In the afternoon, I attached myself to the crowd at No. 303, only to be told, after an hour's heaving and shoving, when I had at last got within sight of the door, that this month the districts had been sub-divided and I now belonged to door No. 305 or 306. At each of these doors I was mystified by the announcement that this door had jurisdiction over the area enclosed by the following roads. I didn't recognise any of them. My heart sank. Usually my attempts at establishing the whereabouts of a particular street met with responses such as: 'Barricade Street? Let me see. Ah, yes, formerly Heydrich Road and before that Beneš Avenue. It runs between 5 May Avenue, that was Linden Avenue and used to be Masaryk Road, and Liberation Square, before that General Syrový Square and before that Washington Square and in the time of Francis Joseph, Empire Square.'

Not very hopefully, I turned to a fellow ration hunter.

Wonder of wonders, he actually knew our street. My heart leapt, but sank again as he said: 'The other door, Miss.'

I took my place as directed. People arriving after me said something in emphatic Czech and pushed in front of me. Obviously they had priority. Nearly everyone had priority. I watched dispassionately while the priorities argued among themselves. Towards evening, when there was no one left, I tumbled into the room in a state of collapse.

The quantities represented by the main ration tickets were scaled according to occupation. I, as a mere housewife with no children, was barely suffered to exist. Pavel was slightly better off, though as a penpusher he was only in the 'light worker category'. Karel, as a student, fell in between. No such system as registering at a particular shop existed, therefore it was advisable to shop early. At daybreak you had to present a jug into which half-a-cupful of bluish milk per capita was ladled from a churn. By the time the sun was up, you had to have joined the crowd at the baker's, and for the rest of the day you had to emerge at hourly intervals in pursuit of pickled cucumbers, red peppers, sauerkraut or pig's blood, delicacies that you were usually told were coming later, coming still later or had come but had just been sold out.

I had never had so much of so little. We lived on a diet of be-whiskered carrots and multi-ocular potatoes with a knob of meat on Sundays. I found, though, that others enjoyed roast joints and home-made cakes. They had relatives in the country or contacts on the black market. We had neither. I mentioned this deficiency to Eva who promised to procure me anything I could pay for. I ordered a kilo of sugar.

That evening, stirring two heaping spoonfuls into his ersatz coffee, Pavel broke out: 'Buying on the black market during the occupation was a necessary act of defiance; now it is sabotage of the economy. How can we plan our economy when large quantities of every item disappear from normal distribution? Until the black marketeers are rounded up, the only way to thwart their racket is to purchase only goods over the counter.' He turned to me: 'I hope it would never occur to you to buy anything beyond our lawful rations.'

My gaze was rooted to the guilty sugar bowl. I said nothing, but proved my patriotism thereafter by supping on black bread spread with mustard and washed down by saccharine-sweetened ersatz coffee. From the bitterness of its flavour and the sparseness of the lawns, I assumed that this beverage was distilled from burnt grass.

Since my arrival not a word had been said about Pavel's posting; it came as a bombshell when he announced one evening in bed: 'We're leaving for Belgrade on Saturday.'

This was Tuesday. I sat bolt upright. 'How long for?'

'A couple of years.'

'But, couldn't you have mentioned it before? I mean I've got to pack, and, and . . .' I stuttered.

'Well, you don't have to start now,' muttered Pavel sleepily. 'Time enough on Friday. We're only allowed a small suitcase each. We shall travel by special bus with armed guards. We have to be prepared for bandits on the way.'

'Oh yes,' I said calmly, as though handling bandits had been a subject taught at college.

All Friday afternoon I struggled to fit the maximum number of belongings into two battered suitcases. I had just managed to close them — by sitting on them with kilo weights in my pockets — when Pavel came in. 'The bus has broken down. We can't leave until Monday.'

On Monday Pavel set off to ascertain developments. I waited in travelling clothes, swallowing a Kwell every hour and with my impatience rising every few minutes. In the afternoon he brought the news: 'A spare part has to be made, something for the cooling system. It'll take several days.'

'I'll take longer than that to repair my cooling system,' I told him lightly. 'You Czechs go in for spectacular delays on your continental travels.'

Pavel went on as though he had not heard, which was his way of treating remarks against which he had no watertight argument. 'In the meanwhile I hope I can persuade them to send Černý instead. He speaks Serbo–Croat and I'd like to finish my studies.' Pavel had a habit of bringing out important decisions, which he must have been turning over in his mind for some time, as though they had just popped into his head.

I dropped a kiss on the end of his nose and asked mildly: 'Darling, would it be too much to ask that, as one of the interested parties, I be put into the picture a little in advance of the actual moves?'

'What do you mean?' asked Pavel in hurt surprise. 'I always tell you everything. You know I couldn't complete my law studies before the war because I got involved in politics. But now I'm a married man with the responsibility of a family.'

I opened my eyes wide. Surely in that instance I would be in the know?

'Not now, but some time,' Pavel reassured me. 'I must think of the future. I'd be better off with a degree.'

Pavel's uncle, who had helped support him, had advocated law as a suitable career for a bright young Jew. Pavel did not intend to practice law but the title of doctor would confer higher status as well as higher pay.

On Wednesday Pavel phoned: 'Darling, you can unpack; they've given way. I shan't be going abroad for at least a year.'

With admirable control I refrained from comment both on that day and on the following day when the decision was reversed once more. The powers-that-be kept up this daisy-petal policy — you will, you won't, you will, you won't go to Belgrade — for a further fortnight. When the subject had lain dormant for several days, I ventured to ask: 'How's the situation now?'

'What situation?' asked Pavel, reluctantly withdrawing his head from an enormous tome.

'Our situation, darling. You know, the little question of to go or not to go to Belgrade.'

'Oh, that was settled ages ago. The bus left last week with Černý. Can't you see I've already started?'

'What?'

'International law. I'm taking my second State exam in December.'

Chapter 3

Among the pupils I had acquired while waiting for Pavel's posting was a Mr Filipovský. An ex-factory owner, he predicted the early collapse of nationalization and the return of his property. Our lessons allowed Mr Filipovský to polish up his English and me to sharpen my arguments in favour of Czechoslovakia's political course. I felt a bit awkward taking his money. After all, Pavel represented 'them', that is the people who had confiscated Mr Filipovský's factory. I consoled myself with the thought that I was relieving the class enemy of a few ill-gotten gains.

Suddenly Mr Filipovský stopped coming. I thought nothing of it, until one evening when Pavel raised his head from the newspaper and asked in ominous tones if I hadn't had a pupil called Egon Filipovský. I nodded dumbly.

'His name is quoted here among a group of dangerous reactionaries arrested for sabotage,' Pavel informed me accusingly. 'Mrs Marešová must have noticed him coming here; she's probably reported it.' He rounded on me. 'Don't tell me you didn't recognize his politics.'

'Yes, I did, but awareness of a person's political views doesn't mean sharing them.'

'People here don't take that attitude. This isn't England where no-one knows or cares about his neighbour's associates. Here your politics is everyone's business. And people would automatically assume that you sympathized with Filipovský, especially as you are from the West. I wouldn't like to lose my job through your naïvety,' he added. 'In future I shall screen your pupils.' There was a cold note in Pavel's voice and a steely, almost hostile, look in his eyes which made me shiver. I wouldn't want Pavel for an enemy, I thought.

In the meantime the Kavan brothers had their own problems. In our century of wheels and wings they yearned to be mechanized. But the motor industry was down to rock bottom and you had to be a miner or a minister to obtain a voucher for anything that could be defined as driven, apart from snow.

'If we can't buy a car, we'll make one,' they declared, and entrusted a large part of their army gratuities to one Olda, a friend of Karel's reputed to be an expert at throwing cars together from scrap.

Once launched on a course, Pavel was impervious to argument, the elements and ordinary human wants. When writing, studying or making plans, he would eat and sleep on the camel system: one huge meal and one long sleep and then nothing much of either for about a week. Every free Saturday afternoon and Sunday, he disappeared with Karel to the outskirts of Prague where parts of a wrecked jeep and a three-wheeled delivery van were being grafted into a mechanism that might in the misty future be pronounced roadworthy.

At last the day came when Pavel, as excited as a young lover introducing the girl of his choice to his mother, took me to collect what, under the theory of relativity, might be termed the Kavans' car.

It was a livid red monstrosity (the market hadn't run to overcoating) with a rectangular front that dwindled suddenly into an undersized tail sheltering one back wheel.

'It's a bit out of proportion, isn't it?' I observed.

'The body may have some blemishes but the motor is perfect,' Pavel retorted. 'As with a woman, one does not look mainly for physical charms.'

'But what about h.p. and durability? I shall call her Matilda,' I added gravely.

'Why?'

'Well, she may be good for a waltz but she doesn't look reliable for a drive.'

'Nonsense! Hop in, you'll see. Oh, hang on to the door, the catch hasn't been fixed yet; it may fall off.'

'And I may fall out?'

Pavel ignored this eventuality.

'Sit well to the right,' was his next instruction. I saw why. The lever positioned between the seats moved in jerky arcs that threatened the passenger with a broken rib every time the driver changed gears. Pavel applied his foot to the accelerator. Matilda muttered wrathfully and subsided. After several repeats Pavel kicked her with ungentlemanly force. She leapt into the air as though stung by a wasp and lumbered forward.

'You see,' Pavel beamed. 'Everything's working — except the horn.'

Fortunately this was hardly necessary, for Matilda was producing a pandemonium — a cross between a tank and a tractor — that could be heard a mile away. Pedestrians froze into immobility and other road-users gave us a wide berth; under the circumstances a wise precaution, for the reversed positions of the accelerator and foot brake were creating havoc with Pavel's driving.

After a few hundred yards, a report like a pistol shot made me let go of the door. It flapped madly like a hen having its neck wrung. The roof had left its moorings and folded up over our heads, giving free passage to a good proportion of the highway dust.

'Wonderful spring,' Pavel crowed.

'More efficient than the ones we're sitting on,' I ventured. After a while I remarked uneasily: 'The seat is rather hot.'

I glanced down and to my horror glimpsed flames in the gap between the seat and its back.

'Pavel,' I said, trying to keep my voice on a note of cocktail-party politeness, 'would you mind stopping; Matilda is on fire!'

'Rubbish!' replied the omniscient co-creator. 'The cooling system's faultless.'

'This is no time for academic discussion: you can see for yourself if you'll take the trouble.'

The evidence of his own senses was the only argument that carried weight with Pavel. He coolly induced Matilda to a standstill, seized an army blanket that was keeping out the draught under the rear window, tipped up the seat that served as a lid to the engine and quickly extinguished the cosy little fire that was burning there.

'No cause for panic! Must be a faulty connection in the wiring. Olda'll soon fix that — no problem.'

One evening we were invited to a reception at Pavel's Ministry. Pavel, with his customary disregard for the passage of time, started six jobs instead of getting ready and then announced: 'We're late; we'll have to take Matilda.'

'It will be quicker, safer and surer by tram,' I pointed out.

'By tram we shall be half-an-hour late; by Matilda anything up to a day late.'

'Olda has overhauled her, she's in perfect running order,' Pavel retorted huffily.

In the main street we were reduced to a snail's pace behind a platoon of soldiers. They were made visibly uneasy by the commotion in their unprotected rear. Pedestrians cheered ironically as we brought up the end of the procession. When the army at last wheeled right, Matilda decided to prolong the attention she was enjoying. She stopped dead. Pavel, trying to appear nonchalant, sprang out in his evening suit and inserted a yard-long starting handle. He swung it. The engine failed to ignite and the handle dropped with a force that seriously damaged Pavel's equilibrium. Straightening his trilby, he tried again. This went on for some time, with Pavel swinging on the end like an immaculate frog on a pendulum. The crowd roared its approval.

'Press the clutch when I say "now",' Pavel shouted.

After the third effort, Matilda pounced; Pavel sidestepped with agility, grabbed the handle and flung himself into the driver's seat while I fielded his trilby. This trick evoked enthusiastic applause from the spectators and they waved us out of sight.

After the reception, Matilda let out her usual dead-raising whoops and again refused to budge. Pavel recited all the defects that might cause lesser automobiles, like Cadillacs and even Fords, to baulk, but firmly rejected them in the case of Matilda who was a hand-made model and could no more be compared to the mass-produced item than a Dior to something from Woolworths. Discovering a lever by my left foot, I shifted it experimentally. Matilda advanced.

'There you are, nothing wrong with her at all. Perfect engine; it was cold, that's all. There's nothing to driving her.'

'I'm sure there isn't,' I murmured innocently, 'when you remember to take the handbrake off.'

Matilda grudgingly conveyed us as far as the middle of Charles Bridge and there, in defiance of the highway code, came to a final halt. Pavel lifted off the seat and peered inside, trying to look like a professional mechanic, but instead giving the impression of an anxious surgeon who had lost a swab. He gingerly removed and replaced all the parts that by design or mismanagement had worked loose, but this time Matilda won on all points. There was nothing for it but to abandon her to a fine for obstruction and complete the journey on foot. For me, in high heels and long skirt, this was hardly a pleasure jaunt. When we finally reached our street, Pavel discovered that he had left the key to the outside passage in his office suit. He was prepared to wait in the street until the concierge got up at five a.m. Not I. I divested myself of my cumbersome coat and started to climb the iron gate.

'Really, Rosemary, in evening dress,' Pavel protested. 'Don't you English mind looking ridiculous?'

'No,' I assured him blandly. 'We rather like it.'

I squeezed through the gap at the top and once on the other side bade him goodnight. 'See you in the morning,' I teased.

Pavel regarded this as a poor joke. When I returned with the key, he looked at me grimly through the bars. I shivered, as though premonition had laid cold fingers on my spine.

Matilda continued to behave like an elderly, ailing relative; she was always in need of some operation but was never much the better for it afterwards. She leaked oil like a haemorrhage, and frequent tell-tale clangs denoted that further bits of her intestines had hit the road. Pavel displayed a tolerance for Matilda's failings that was often lacking in his relations with people. The fault was in the stars, the quality of the spare parts or the petrol, but never in Matilda.

Looking back, I see Matilda as a personification of the Kavans — undaunted by odds, unshaken by disaster — as well as of the national economy that ailed for decades in spite of a variety of 'infallible' remedies.

Chapter 4

I was busy, life was interesting, Prague was beautiful. The only fly in the ointment was Pavel whose zeal for the 'tasks of reconstruction' left no time for the construction of his marriage. In fact, his communist principles were abandoned at the doormat.

In my position as helpmate the emphasis was on the help. The mate's existence was recalled only when Pavel came to bed. (At three in the morning this fell short of conjugal bliss.) The help was expected to be permanently forthcoming. I had to rise at five to get him off to a pre-work meeting; to serve a belated supper at midnight; to rush off an article at a couple of hours' notice; or to entertain a bunch of journalists with no notice at all. Before leaving each morning, Pavel would issue a list of orders, and would phone addenda at intervals during the day: Do this, Do that, Go here, Go there, Buy this, Collect such and such, Bring x, y or z to the office. How I missed the disarming English preface: 'Would you mind!'

My regular duties included gathering up the newspaper cuttings that littered every surface, filing carbon copies of Pavel's own articles and letters, removing dirty shoes from under the furniture and sundry articles from behind cushions, and replacing books on shelves.

Living with Pavel was like living in a whirlwind. Constantly searching for mislaid items, he would scatter the contents of drawers, sweep piles of miscellanea off table tops and empty the waste paper basket on the carpet; then he'd dash out, half-an-hour behind schedule, leaving me to restore order.

On one such occasion he was brought to combustion point by the disappearance of a report on British foreign policy. As it was impossible to concentrate when Pavel was on the rampage, I joined in the hunt, and located the report tucked between the pages of a discarded newspaper. Instead of a shower of thanks, this sparked off an explosion of wrath: 'If you'd stop meddling with my things, I'd damn well be able to find them myself.'

Stung by injustice, not to say inaccuracy, I left Pavel's private devastation to its own devices and devoted an extra hour to the devastation of war. As soon as I returned home, agreeably exhausted, the phone rang. It was Pavel to announce that he was bringing a colleague home for coffee. *Force majeure*, I had to tidy and clean the flat at record, not to say, neck-breaking speed. With Pavel you couldn't win.

Well, I told myself, he has more important things on his mind: the Ministry, his studies, Party and trade union meetings. The war robbed him of six years of his life; he is anxious to make up for lost time.

It wasn't the neglect I resented, but the feudal assumptions. Every night my lord and master shed his clothes along a trail from desk to bed, expecting his handmaiden to retrieve them. Every evening he strewed the pages of a dozen newspapers around him, expecting his handmaiden to gather and fold them. When I protested mildly, he exclaimed 'But you have nothing to do all day!' And this was the man for whom I'd given up family and homeland, not to mention marmite and marmalade! Not that I demanded special treatment on that account; but even if I had been Czech, I would have appreciated a little appreciation.

I re-read Pavel's love letters from the front. I had to remind myself that the present preoccupied stranger was the romantic soldier and passionate scribe of the war years. I shook a little romanticism out of my system. You don't marry a man in a vacuum. You marry his upbringing; you marry his doting mother and Slovak maid, and out-dated theories about male supremacy. Laws can be changed over night, but not attitudes. That will take a generation. You must have patience.

All might have been well but for *mariáš* (pronounced as the French do marriage). Pavel devoted all of his limited leisure to this Czech version of poker. I sat through hours of it, a social smile pinned to my aching jaws while the other wives whispered in Czech, isolating me for much of the time. If I could have stayed at home with a book I wouldn't have minded but Pavel protested that this would be anti-social (sic).

But people, like Irish stew, boil over if left simmering too long. One evening, after an interminable card session, Pavel caught me sniffling into the pillow. It was just before Christmas, a treacherous time; Christmas undermines one's defences.

He was immediately concerned. 'Darling, whatever is the matter?'

'I'm bored, lonely and I miss my mother,' I gulped.

Against all my resolutions I poured out a childish torrent of sobs and reproaches. It produced a moment of silence. Various emotions skittered across Pavel's face: surprise, bafflement, aggrieved innocence, injured pride. It was hard for a man who had acted from the noblest motivations, having the welfare of his family and country at heart, to be accused of ruthless egotism by an overwrought wife. He drew a deep breath to refute and contend, then paused. And in that pause his communist conscience prompted 'self-criticism'.

'H'mmm.'

Again, the shifting phases flickered across his features: doubt, retrospective probing, a glimmer of admission. He promised to make amends. We declared an ecstatic détente and got into bed to cement it.

For a week or two Pavel picked up his undies and dailies and prefaced his demands with 'please'. Instead of *mariáš*, he spent the odd hour in conversation with his wife. He even took me to see Čapek's *Insect Play* and Smetana's *Dalibor* (which has remained my favourite opera). The improvement was short-lived. Pavel soon slipped back into his old ways. However, he had ensured that our reconciliation would have one lasting consequence.

I had just returned from the doctor in a state of shock and was pulling myself round with some of the precious coffee my mother had enclosed in a letter (the overseas parcel service had not yet been restored), when Eva dropped in on her way home from work. She was putting in a twelve-hour day, and frequently a forty-eight-hour shift, at the National Bank, sorting out the country's chaotic finances. Her little free time was devoted to her friends. She baby-sat, mended, advised and cheered. I was her most indulged beneficiary. This time she had brought some home-made biscuits. I scraped a little more coffee out of the envelope for her and we sipped in reverent silence.

After a few mintues Eva asked: 'What is the matter, Rosemary, my pet? You have a cloudy look today.'

'Lots,' I gulped. 'I'm pregnant.'

'How lovely.'

Lovely? I was not so sure. The thought of giving birth in broken Czech appalled me. 'I should have preferred waiting a while,' I said guardedly. 'Life is so difficult here. I can't imagine coping with a baby on top of everything else.' And I couldn't imagine producing a healthy infant on a diet deficient in fresh fruit and vegetables, proteins and cod liver oil.

Eva kissed me. 'Birth is a beautiful thing. In a modern hospital with doctors and nurses there's nothing to fear. In the camp it was worse, but even there it was an occasion for rejoicing.' She looked at me through the shadows of memory; the past was always just below the surface of her mind. 'Marie came to us in September 1944. She didn't know she was pregnant — in the camp what with the hard work and poor food, the woman's thing stopped. Even when her belly swelled, she thought nothing of it. We ate mostly soup and the liquid blew us out like melons. Then one night she woke me up. 'Eva, there are stirrings of a child in my womb.' 'Rubbish,' I replied. 'It's more likely to be hunger pangs.' 'No, no,' she whispered. 'It is movement. Feel!' She laid my hands on her middle and I felt the kick of the tiny being. I put my arms round her, for she was trembling. I promised that we would conceal her from the guards as her condition became plainer.

'We answered roll call for her so that she didn't have to stand for hours morning and evening. We stole for her from the kitchen. Marie did not know whether her husband was alive or dead. We never mentioned him; it was our baby, for there was not one of us who had not risked her life for it. The time came for her delivery, and freedom was still round the corner. Marie was brave. Her labour was long — two days and two nights. During the day we had to leave her under our bunk covered with rags. She could not scream for that would have brought the *kapo* to the spot. The baby was delivered on a pile of newspapers. He never uttered a cry, as though he knew that his life depended upon silence. On 3 May we were liberated. Marie and the baby survived, though his father did not. Today he is a fine boy with four teeth, and still he never cries.'

She hugged me. 'But enough of such talk. Your baby will be

born in great style.'

Pavel came in. 'Hullo, Eva, hullo darling. Where's supper?'

Eva sprang to her feet. 'I'll get it. Rosemary must rest. From now on you must take great care of her.'

'Why, she gone down with TB or something?' Pavel asked conversationally.

'No, she's going to make you a happy man.'

'She's done that already,' Pavel stated through a mouthful of biscuit.

'She means I'm going to make you a daddy,' I butted in. 'You know, the man behind the pram.'

'A father, eh! So I fixed it! What do you say to that?' cried Pavel prancing up and down.

'It's not a particularly remarkable achievement.' I tried to sound annoyed but Pavel looked so idiotically pleased that I had to laugh. Besides, I was already feeling more cheerful: if Marie could bring forth a bonny baby on scraps a dog would have spurned, Nature would doubtless manage on carbohydrate.

'Ah, what a son he'll be — with your looks and my brains! We'll make a physician of him or an archaeologist. I always wanted to go in for archaeology but my uncle thought there was more future in digging up legal evidence than fossilized remains. How many did the doctor say?'

'How many what?'

'I mean, you couldn't make it quads, or at least twins could you? Anglo–Czech quads — what a striking example of international solidarity that would be!'

I had no such political ambitions. 'One will be quite enough for me to start with,' I said apologetically.

'Oh well,' Pavel magnanimously dropped the subject of numbers. As an afterthought he added: 'How are you feeling? Okay? That's right, the modern woman takes that sort of thing in her stride.'

Eva returned with rolls, butter and salami on a tray in time to overhear this patently masculine remark.

'That's as may be, but she is to have some help in the flat. You must get her a char.'

'I do what?'

Eva immediately saw the impossibility of this suggestion. Pavel would sooner have found a four-leaf clover in the Antarctic than a char in Prague.

'Well, Karel will. And you will see that Rosemary does not

over-exert herself. You will carry the heavy shopping. And you must give her breakfast in bed to settle her morning sickness,' Eva went on, resolutely rubbing the gilt off fatherhood. I was beginning to enjoy the situation. Pavel chewed his salami in reflective silence. After the meal he trotted tamely into the kitchen to help Eva with the washing up. I put my feet up on the couch and languidly reached for a novel.

The brunt of Pavel's fatherhood was borne by Karel, to whom he delegated his domestic responsibilities. On the excuse that Rosemary must be spared, Karel was ordered to take down the garbage, bring in the potatoes and run Pavel's errands. Finally he was told: 'I'm studying late at night. You can take over this early morning stunt; and make it for two.'

At length Karel found a char; a triumph indeed. Private charring was frowned upon by the authorities and disdained by women, who were being enticed into industry with equal pay opportunities.

'She'll start tomorrow and will do the washing. She'll require a meat lunch and snacks in the morning and afternoon, and you will pay her 40 crowns an hour, that's roughly the salary of a high-ranking government official.' (Far more than Pavel was earning!)

At 7.45 a.m. the door bell rang. I opened it. A smartly dressed woman of about forty introduced herself as Miss Hertzigová. We descended to the laundry room, and Miss Hertzigová's steely eye fell on my pile of sheets, pillowcases, towels and teaclothes.

'What? Are they not soaked?' she exclaimed in horrified tones.

'No,' I replied in a small voice.

'Good heavens, they should have been soaking in soda all night! How do you expect me to get them clean?'

'They are going to be boiled.'

'I am aware of that. Oh well, I'll have to do the best I can, but have the goodness to soak them next time.'

I slunk out of the laundry room and returned upstairs to my typewriter. A few minutes later the internal phone rang. 'Madam, will you bring me some more soap, please.'

An hour later it was: 'You haven't forgotten my mid-morning snack, have you?'

I made tea, buttered three slices of bread and carried the tray down four floors. The lift was not working. No Czech lift ever works in an emergency. Foreigners, I was told, assumed the word *'nejede'* to mean lift, when in fact it indicated 'not working.'

Half-an-hour later there was a request for a scrubbing brush. I took it down. Miss Hertzigová heaved the sheets out of the huge wooden sink, spread them on a large trestle table and administered a ruthless drubbing. I ventured to suggest that as they had been only slightly soiled in the first place, a good boil was surely enough. The good lady withered me with a glance and the words: 'Madam, if you employ someone to wash your linen, they must assume you want it spotless.'

Miss Hertzigová had a healthy appetite. At lunch she consumed ten potatoes, half a cauliflower and the meat ration for two for a week. I toyed with a lettuce that brought forth the comment: 'You English don't eat enough; that's why you're so thin.'

My morning sickness showed no signs of abating: Miss Hertzigová remained a necessary tyranny. She was equally thorough about the cleaning. My vague instruction: 'Just run a duster over the furniture and the cleaner over the carpet' was treated with the contempt it deserved. The carpets must be rolled up and carried down into the yard; there they were slung over a wooden roller and belaboured with a bamboo beater. Dust flew up in clouds, doubtless settling on recumbent carpets in neighbouring flats, to be returned to us through the same process.

Though excused from hard work, I was never free from the continual: 'Madam, would you just pass, push, assist . . .'

We were rescued by Mrs Panská. A pupil had cancelled a lesson and I was enjoying a walk in the sunny air. An enormous backside ahead of me suddenly doubled up in the pursuit of apricots escaping from a burst bag. I swiftly joined the hunt, forestalling a small boy. The owner of the backside straightened up. Her round, jolly face, purple from exertion, was cupped by three chins descending in geometric progression to a magnificently convex bosom which rested on a dome-like abdomen. All these separate bulges rolled from side to side as she moved.

'Thank you very much Miss — er, young Missus', she gasped, catching sight of the future Anglo–Czech archaeologist. 'You're a foreigner, aren't you? You met your husband during the war?'

'Yes, he was a soldier.'

'Ttt, tt.' Romantic cluckings greeted this confession.

'And I see you will be nursing. Are you having any trouble?'

'Only with my char: she eats me out of house and home.'

'And you expecting! She ought to be ashamed of herself! I could do with a bit of extra money myself, my husband's only a railway guard. I'll willingly come and give you a hand. You don't need to worry about feeding me. I'm too fat as it is!'

On the appointed day Mrs Panská arrived with a bunch of sweet peas for the young missus and ten fresh eggs from her sister in the country for Kavan junior.

'A land of extremes!' I exclaimed. 'Typified by you and Miss Hertzigová.'

'Oh, there's people and people all the world over.' Mrs Panská waved an expansive hand.

There was no mistaking Mrs Panská's whereabouts. The floor shook and the glass and porcelain ornaments danced on their shelves as she walked. A series of grunts and squeaks brought me rushing into the room to find her standing on a chair dusting the book-case, looking like a circus elephant balanced on a wall.

If she topples off, she'll go clean through the floor, or two floors, I thought. 'Mrs Panská, don't do anything you can't reach safely,' I pleaded. 'Karel can finish off.'

'Now, you get back to your tapping and don't go upsetting yourself on my account. In your state, my precious, you must stay as cool as a dog's nose. I haven't had a fall in my life.'

Unconvinced, I obeyed and held my breath as I followed her progress along the bookshelves: Ugh, ugh, as she hoisted herself up, whoomph as she descended. Even when fairly statically employed, it was impossible to lose track of her for here Mrs Panská's exuberant nature burst into song, or would have done, had the supply of wind sufficed. As it was, she was reduced to whistling which she did very tunefully. Her repertoire consisted mostly of arias from Czech operas, so it was a not unpleasing background to my activity.

Mrs Panská left me her address. 'If you should come over queer, or need anything special, just send your husband for me and I'll be round as quick as I can stir my lazy bones.'

That evening I sighed to Pavel: 'What a pity pregnancy doesn't last two years. I'm sure I'll never receive such consideration again.'

Things were happening on the national scene, too. One was a currency reform to combat inflation. Every citizen had to hand in his cash and savings books, in exchange for 500 new crowns (about £2.10s); the rest was credited in frozen assets with no guarantee when the thaw would set in. My hard-earned remuneration from my English lessons became worthless overnight. The only consolation was that speculators were handing over much more for the same amount: one occasion when the have-nots had the laugh over the haves.

The next event was Labour Day. I wasn't feeling well enough to join the procession but I watched for hours from the pavement. The whole of Prague seemed to be on the move, cheering, singing and waving banners that endorsed nationalization and pledged millions of hours of voluntary labour. It was a spontaneous demonstration of unity and enthusiasm. The parade, in fact, epitomised the cheerful goodwill and optimism of the post-war period. Carried away, I too shouted: 'Ať žije mír!' (Long live peace) and 'Ať žije socialismus!'

The first post-war general elections followed soon after. Pavel, Karel and Eva were active in the advance campaign. On polling day I was violently sick but managed to get up towards evening. I cast my vote for Number One at five minutes before closing time, thereby assuming one 2,695,915th part of the responsibility for everything that was to come. We stayed up all night totting up the results as they were announced over the radio. The communists polled the largest vote, thirty-eight per cent. The combined communist and social democratic vote amounted to a majority.

Eva cried with heartfelt relief: 'Now we are really safe from the fascists!' Like many Czechs, she saw the communist victory, together with the Czechoslovak–Soviet treaty of alliance, as a guarantee of no further betrayal of Czechoslovakia by its allies. We toasted this victory and the Party leader's pledge that Czechoslovakia would follow her own road to socialism.

The summer months of that year were the happiest in my marriage. I felt fit. The long days were sunny. Harmony reigned in the home. All three of us looked forward to the baby. We spent hours discussing names. In the end we chose the internationally pronounceable Marie for a girl and Jan for a boy.

In October 1946 Czechoslovakia's first economic plan and our first son saw the light of day. I did my best to fit in with the spirit of the times by producing Jan five weeks sooner than planned and cutting down delivery time to two hours. True to Eva's prophecy, he was born in 'great style' — but in London. The Party had decided to post Pavel to the Court of St James on completion of his studies. I left earlier.

Four months later Pavel gained his doctorate, ironically in the law that was to victimize him so cruelly. But that is looking ahead. The present was rosy. His appointment as Press Attaché at the Czechoslovak Embassy and our rapturous reunion after five months' separation promised to be fruitful.

Our second son, Zdeněk, was born at home, a month premature. After washing Jan's nappies and giving him his tea, I barely had time to struggle upstairs before Zdeněk entered the world, unaided. He has shown an independent spirit ever since.

Chapter 5

Our three diplomatic years — from 1947 to 1950 — proved to be a period of fading promise and deterioration in relationships, both political and personal.

The Cold War was damaging East–West relations. Wartime unity was disintegrating. The two camps, socialist and capitalist, were becoming implacably hostile; my two countries were on opposite sides. Our Czech alignment could be assessed from our engagements diary. Most of our invitations were issued by the countries of the Soviet bloc, some by the Scandinavian countries and a few by the Indian High Commission. Our English contacts were journalists, left-wing MPs and members of the British Communist Party.

Events inside Czechoslovakia in 1948 heightened tension between my two countries. Not being on the spot, Pavel and I could not form our own opinion. We had only the official version to go by. According to this, twelve right-wing ministers had provoked a government crisis in order to forestall further socialist legislation. Spontaneous mass meetings throughout the country urged Beneš[15] to form a government without the ministers who had tendered their resignations, then to complete nationalization and enact a land reform. The discovery of extensive sabotage and preparations for an armed plot was reported. The ugly words 'civil war' were uttered at the Embassy.

15. Eduard Beneš (1884–1948) was the Foreign Minister of Czechoslovakia 1918–35. He was President 1935–48 except for a short period after the Munich Agreement in 1938. He resigned again in June 1948 and died in September of that year.

I thought anxiously of Karel who would be involved and Pavel who would chaff at being out of it.

To our great relief the opposition crumpled at the sight of the Workers' Militia, formed and armed to meet the emergency. Not a single shot was fired. Beneš formed a new government of communists and progressive non-communists under the communist leader Klement Gottwald.[16]

The crisis caused an epidemic of resignations at Czechoslovak embassies and consulates. In London eight non-communist diplomats asked for asylum. Their motives varied and were not always crystal clear. One of them had collaborated with the Germans; another had accumulated money abroad and went to Chile to spend it. (Jan Masaryk[17], the Czechoslovak Foreign Minister, said of him: 'He is an ardent numismatist, especially of new coins.') The Military Attaché appropriated official funds as 'compensation for the property he had left in Czechoslovakia'.

The resignations cast a shadow over the Embassy; nevertheless, the rest of us threw a party to celebrate the victory of the left and sang old revolutionary favourites and new militant songs with inspiring words like 'Now we've got what we wanted!' and 'Hey rup! Hole hey! Roll up your sleeves and get down to work!' We predicted that the wheels of progress would revolve at double speed, now that the lost capitalist spokes had been removed.

It was only in 1968, when press censorship was lifted, that the public learned of communist manipulations behind the scenes. At the time Pavel and I suspected nothing. We refuted Thoreau's confession: 'If I could not doubt, I would not believe.' For us the opposite was true: 'If I doubted, I could not believe.'

We had hardly recovered from the shock of the diplomatic defections when the shattering news of Jan Masaryk's death came. He was reported to have committed suicide by jumping out of the bathroom window of his Foreign Ministry flat.

16. Klement Gottwald (1896–1953) was a member of the CP Politburo from 1925 and was the leader of the 'Bolshevik line' which finally prevailed in 1929. From 1928 to '43 he was a member of the Comintern EC. He was leader of the CP in its Moscow exile during the war. He became Prime Minister after the 1946 elections, and then President after February 1948 until his death in 1953.

17. Jan Masaryk (1886–1948) was Ambassador to the Court of St James in the thirties, and then Foreign Minister in Beneš's London government-in-exile and in the first post-war coalition until his death in 1948. Whether he committed suicide or was murdered is still a matter of controversy. His father was T. G. Masaryk, the first President of Czechoslovakia.

Jan Masaryk, the son of the President of the First Republic, was a universally popular man. Pavel had known him well during the war, as Foreign Minister in the exiled Czechoslovak government and as the best-loved broadcaster to Czechoslovakia. Pavel used to say Masaryk chatted to his audience as though they were not separated from him by nearly a thousand miles and a death sentence if caught listening. Pavel had described to me with affection Masaryk's breezy manner and pithy humour, and had related numerous anecdotes of which Masaryk was either the narrator or the subject. Masaryk lugubriously defined himself as more of a clown than a statesman, a view that reflected his modesty rather than his ability, for he was highly esteemed by Allies and compatriots alike. I had seen him only once, at a small party. He appeared very much at ease with everyone and entertained us effortlessly with his sparkling wit and renderings of Czech and Slovak folk songs.

Pavel was one of the last people to speak to Masaryk. A Czech emigré went so far as to assert that Kavan had been summoned to Prague for the express purpose of defenestrating his chief. In fact, Pavel had gone to Prague for a briefing. He flew back immediately after the tragedy to report to the Embassy. When he arrived home, he dropped into an armchair, saying: 'I was talking to him at seven in the evening and the next morning he was dead.'

I asked if Pavel had suspected that anything was wrong. He replied that at six in the evening Masaryk was already in bed, flushed and in low spirits. He complained of insomnia and failing concentration. His mother had suffered from a mental illness. He was known to be subject to extreme moods and he was haunted by the fear of insanity. He told Pavel that he was depressed at international developments and the growing tension between the U.S.A. and the Soviet Union.

'His dream of a world fraternity was severely shaken,' Pavel concluded.

I observed that some British papers had described Masaryk's death as a protest against Gottwald's government.

'Masaryk was a man of the people not of political parties,' Pavel retorted. 'He said himself: "How can my friends abroad think I could go against the will of the people?"'

According to Pavel, Masaryk recognized that the new government was the people's choice, and therefore he had unhesitatingly accepted a ministerial post and publicly declared his support for

Gottwald. Pavel emphatically rejected the idea of *premeditated* suicide. For one thing, Masaryk had asked him to return in the morning to pick up a letter for the Ambassador in London. The heap of cigarette ends in the ashtrays in the morning suggested yet another sleepless night.

'Masaryk took his life in a moment of temporary derangement,' Pavel declared.

This categoric conclusion was one of Pavel's simplifications. He took no account of inner conflicts, psychological pressures or subtleties of motivation. He was interested only in political ambiguities: for or against. Secrecy surrounded Masaryk's death. Rumours that he had been murdered by the communist state security police persisted for many years. An enquiry initiated in 1968 was abandoned after the Russian invasion.

Czechoslovakia's *volte face* over Marshall Aid confirmed British fears that the Czechs were trapped in the Soviet net. Czechoslovakia could certainly have made good use of American dollars. Large capital investments would have speeded up the reconstruction of the economy. Jan Masaryk was to have represented the Czechs in Paris. Pavel was jubilant. 'We'll accept their money and avoid their political strings,' he declared.

But Stalin saw the Marshall Plan as a means to bind the recipients to the United States and isolate the Soviet Union. He framed an ultimatum: either an American loan or friendship with the Soviet Union. Gottwald chose the latter. Pavel accepted Stalin's — and Gottwald's — judgement unquestioningly. We still had unshakeable faith in the Soviet Union. We had been invited to private film showings and a recital of protest and battle songs by Paul Robeson at the Soviet Embassy. Songs of the partisans and films such as *Stalingrad* and *Meeting on the Elbe* had reminded us again of the Soviet Union's decisive role in the war, and of the heroism of the Red Army and the Russian people. Pavel believed that Czechoslovakia would be better protected by the Soviet Union than by the West.

Before the February 1948 crisis relations between Czechoslovakia and Britain had been smooth. An agreement to promote friendship, cultural exchange and understanding had been signed. Now that a 'disguised dictatorship of a single party' — in the words of the British government — had been established, the agreement was terminated.

When I returned to Prague two years later I found the British Council had been closed down, the only British paper available was the *Daily Worker*; Western books, films and plays were boycotted. In short, Czechoslovakia was completely cut off from the West.

While political relations got bogged down, trade went ahead. In the summer of 1949 Rudolf Margolius[18], a Vice Minister of Foreign Trade, came to London to negotiate a trade agreement with Britain. I mention Rudolf because he was one of the nicest Czechs I've ever met and his wife was to become my lifelong friend. The trade agreement was to have tragic consequences for Rudolf.

Coming events do not necessarily cast their shadows before them. While the Embassy celebrated the signing of the treaty, Rudolf had no presentiment of disaster. When Yugoslavia was expelled from the Cominform for 'betrayal of international communism', Pavel and I had no premonition of the impact it would have on our own lives. Would I have returned to Prague with Pavel if I had known what to expect?

As it was, our marriage was near collapse. Pavel was under considerable strain. The Cold War aggravated the difficulties of his job. Like Masaryk, he was worried about the international situation: world peace was menaced; the division of Germany was a threat to Czechoslovakia. The Embassy had divided into factions. He had incurred enemies among the staff, he told me, but would divulge no details.

He was smoking and drinking heavily. He began to suffer from high blood pressure. His Czech doctor detected signs of cardiac strain. After this diagnosis Pavel went about for days veiled in gloom and doom. Any suggestion on my part that he should sort out the piles of newspapers that were gracing, or rather disgracing, the living room, write some long-owed letters to friends in Prague or throw a little water over the Minx (we had bought a new car in London, Matilda had remained with Karel) met with the lugubrious prognosis: 'I shan't be here much longer. Do you have to bother me with trivialities?'

Alarmed at the prospect of imminent widowhood, I went to see his doctor who assured me: 'Provided your husband leads a normal, quiet life there is no reason why he should not live as long as you or I.' But Pavel refused to be reassured. His father had

18. Rudolf Margolius (1913–1952) spent the war in Nazi concentration camps. He joined the CP in 1945 and by 1949 had become Deputy Minister of Foreign Trade. He was imprisoned, sentenced and executed along with Slánský.

died of heart failure at the age of fifty. Pavel was convinced he was marked for the same fate. Fear of an early death, anger at what his family had already suffered and rage at his own disability erupted in fits of uncontrollable fury. A trifle would act as a trigger. A missing shirt button, mislaid car keys, a suit delayed at the cleaners', or a message forgotten would cause him to rant and roar like one possessed. I met these outbursts with a pained silence that invariably goaded him to further frenzy. Doubtless I should have shouted back and thrown things, but it was not in my nature: I was miscast in the great Slav drama of which Pavel was the centre. My English upbringing defined shows of temper as selfish and in bad taste. Whereas in Pavel's education self-control had not ranked high. He had bossed his younger brother, unopposed. His mother and uncle had indulged him. No one had gainsaid him.

Such explosions left me physically and mentally immobilized. I felt less of a person, less myself. I was affected not so much by the actual, as by the potential violence. In the aftermath Pavel would sulk and send me to Coventry. I found these long, heavy silences hard to bear. After a few days, I would swallow my pride and beg Pavel to end it. As a sign of forgiveness for my being in the right, Pavel would start talking to me again. He never *admitted* blame.

Perhaps if I had been less tired I would have coped better. But, even with domestic help, two babies took a toll of my energy. (Curse the baby books of that time, which forbade feeding at night and assured mothers that crying was good for baby's lungs.) I couldn't catch up my lost sleep during the day, for one or another of the boys was always awake. Pavel allowed himself no respite; I was allowed none either. In addition to my diplomatic duties, I was expected to attend trade union meetings and lectures in political theory at the Embassy, teach some of the staff English and occasionally help out with the clerical work. In short, my life was governed by musts. You must attend this function, invite these guests, join the Embassy's ladies' tea-party, visit the Soviet Ambassador's wife, go to that opening, or fashion show. I was told what to wear, what to discuss, what priorities to observe.

At the same time, I was largely in the dark about Embassy affairs: matters of real policy were discussed at meetings of communists, and these Pavel did not disclose to me.

I was too busy and too fatigued to study the news thoroughly.

In any case no world developments seemed as important as my babies. Even Pavel preferred a recital of his sons' achievements to a political discussion with me in the evenings. Consequently, in conversation with our colleagues, I sometimes confused names and events. This infuriated Pavel, and increased my disorientation.

I began to feel stupid and inadequate. I allowed myself to be swayed even when I knew I was right. For example, over the question of language, I suggested that we speak English at home and Czech elsewhere, so that the boys would be bilingual. Pavel was violently opposed, asserting that they would speak neither language properly. They would develop split personalities, not knowing where they belonged. Emphatically no English was to be spoken. I was to learn perfect Czech. We were to be a hundred-per-cent Czech, not an Anglo–Czech, family.

I yielded, against my better judgement. As a result, the boys knew little English when forced into exile later. I did eventually learn almost perfect Czech. For that I am grateful. But had I eliminated the last trace of a foreign accent, my shape would still have betrayed my origin; even my uptilted nose distinguished me as non-Czech. Moreover, not even a mastery of Czech enabled me to fathom Pavel. He remained an enigma.

We decided to take a holiday in Scotland without the children. I looked forward to the break. I fondly hoped that being alone together in new surroundings with no responsibilities would do much to restore our relationship. I could not have been wider from the mark. We got as far as Stirling without mishap. There Pavel suddenly stopped the car outside a clothier's and instructed me to go in and buy a length of Scotland's famous suiting for our Ambassador. Unacquainted with the Ambassador's preference, I asked Pavel to go with me.

He shook his head irritably. 'Use your own discretion.'

'It's too big a responsibility, please help me choose,' I begged, almost in tears.

This harmless plea sparked an incredible reaction. Pavel seized me round the throat and shook me like an old coat, screaming: 'Will you do as I say?'

His eyes were bulging with rage, mine with fear. We must have looked like a couple of gargoyles at close range. I was convinced I'd be stiff before Pavel realized what he was doing. Desperately I gasped: 'CD.' Reminded that a corpse in his diplomatic car might cause awkward comment, Pavel came to his senses. He released me and drove on, the matter of the Ambassador's suit forgotten.

Histrionics was one thing, assault was another. No one had ever laid a finger on me before. My whole nervous system quivered with outrage. When the agitation ceased, it was succeeded by total numbness. I looked at Pavel and felt nothing. Nothing at all. Appalled, I tried to digest this discovery.

'What's the matter now?' Pavel's impatient voice broke the silence.

'Nothing.'

He pressed me.

'Well,' I gulped, ' this was supposed to be our second honeymoon and you've spoilt it.'

'I've spoilt it! You started it by refusing a simple request.'

'It wasn't simple,' I kept saying.

'If you're going to rake this up every few minutes, we'd better call the holiday off,' Pavel growled.

He threw open the door, pushed me out into the pouring rain and drove off. Wet and shivering, I made my way back to the village we had just passed through. I saw with chilling clarity that my marriage had been a terrible mistake. We were totally incompatible. The British under-statement and the Czech over-statement just would not jell. Divorce was the only answer; I'd start proceedings immediately. The court would be on my side. Of course the papers would make political capital out of it. I could see the headlines: English wife throttled by barbarous Bohemian; wife seeks divorce rather than return to Iron Curtain country. I couldn't condone that. That would be playing into the hands of the reactionaries. And the publicity would ruin Pavel's career. He may have been nuts, but he didn't deserve that. I'd wait until we were back in Prague.

At the time I couldn't account for Pavel's behaviour. Now, with the perspective of decades, I understand him better. He was a man with a vision. He couldn't afford self-doubt: it would have diminished his drive. He wanted an easy, smooth relationship that would leave all his energy free for work and politics. He demanded unqualified love and devotion under all circumstances. Reservations unhinged him because he needed to be right and to be recognized as right.

I found out the time of the next train to London, then adjourned to the village café to while away the next three hours. A hot drink would have been welcome, but I was refused coffee because it was after lunch and tea because it was not yet tea-time. I made do with some bilious-looking lemonade. When I returned to the station, Pavel was waiting outside. He took my arm as though nothing had happened. He did not apologize, of course, but his lovemaking that night was particularly passionate. Perhaps he sensed how near he'd been to losing me.

I resolved to say nothing about divorce until the time was right.

In the meanwhile I made the best of things. I was supremely happy with my two delightful toddlers. Jan and Zdeněk were beautiful to look at — sturdy, curly-haired with small, neat features and large, bright eyes — and fun to be with: sunny, alert, responsive to imaginative games and always ready to laugh. I regretted that I could not spend all my time with them and had often to leave them with our Czech maid, a carefully screened working-class cadre who had little aptitude for childcare.

I appreciated the advantages of diplomatic life. After Czech shortages, diplomatic rations were a luxury, and a chauffeur-driven limousine was infinitely more spacious than a Prague tram. I got a kick out of being presented to their Majesties King George and Queen Elizabeth, and enjoyed the irony that only marriage to a Czech communist had opened the gates of Buckingham Palace to me.

Receptions with their groaning tables of caviar and smoked salmon were not exactly a chore, though Pavel took the edge off my pleasure by censoring my behaviour. Don't ask the wrong questions. Don't joke about serious matters. Don't wave your arms about when you talk. Don't laugh loudly. Don't treat a diplomat you've just been introduced to as though he were an old friend.

After the usual series of vodka toasts to peace and solidarity, Stalin, Gottwald and all the other socialist leaders, I would forget my censor. I might be relating a funny story to the Polish Ambassador with non-protocol verve and gesticulation. Pavel, lurking behind an aspidistra, would emit a loud, warning ahem. I'd fall silent in mid-word and mid-gesture. The Ambassador would beg me to continue. I'd scramble through to the punch line in a subdued monotone — much to the puzzlement of my listener.

Pavel need not have worried. My informality made us popular. At our dinner parties diplomats relaxed and loosened their ties while I disappeared to feed a baby or change a nappy. Often the evening ended in an international singsong on cushions on the floor.

I must confess my only contribution to diplomatic history was on the lighter side. After I'd introduced some English party games at a private gathering for our Embassy children, the Ambassador's wife asked me if I would arrange a St Nicholas party for our East European and Soviet colleagues. Rashly I agreed. Just before the guests were due, Pavel began to moan: 'It'll be a flop; you'll be a laughing stock!' I panicked. Why had I let myself in for this ordeal? Why did I never say No? It was too late to call the party off. I downed a double whisky and made Pavel do the same.

The guests began to arrive. The sight of formal black evening wear and solemn People's Democratic expressions sent my spirits down again.

The initial game of guess-the-name-pinned-on-your-back-and-find-his/her-partner got everyone off the political situation and away from wife or husband. So far so good. But that might have been classed as an intellectual exercise. The next item couldn't, by a long chalk. Each man was given a sheet of newspaper, five pins and three minutes in which to make his partner a hat. I anticipated a mass getaway. But no, the men applied themselves diligently to the task. The results had to be seen to be believed. The millinery talent of the Eastern Corps outdid Ascot! But the next item was the trickiest. If they went for that, they'd go for anything. It was musical chairs. As I reduced the number of chairs, protocol was flung to the winds and rugged individualism came to the fore. Counsellors created sprint records, dragging their long-skirted partners behind them. Ambassadors and cypher clerks fought spiritedly over seats. Pavel, ever apprehensive, predicted an exchange of diplomatic notes on the morrow.

My final test was the animal game. Remember, these diplomats had been starched stiff before leaving their countries. The majority of them were communists, to whom unconventional conduct was as alien as non-conformist beliefs. I explained the rules of the game to this dignified assembly. 'You've each got a card bearing the name of an animal. At the word go, each makes the noise appropriate to that animal and by this means locates the nine others in his team. The team that gets together first is the winner.' I gave the signal, expecting dead silence and embarrassed glances. But no! A collective roar of sound arose from about one hundred and fifty throats that shook the foundations. It also brought the police to the front door to ascertain whether the Embassy staff were being murdered by incensed emigrés.

Dedication is dedication, whatever the cause. Once my guests were committed to letting themselves go, they abandoned themselves wholeheartedly. More and more crazy games and dances were called for. I dare say that I did more for inner-bloc détente than a dozen political meetings. By three in the morning people were falling on each other's necks from mirth and exhaustion, irrespective of protocol.

For days afterwards the Czech St Nicholas party was the number one topic in the Eastern bloc. Pavel basked in reflected glory. Europeans laugh at the English and their childish love of games. But the party proved to me that all adults need play for release and the re-discovery of their childlike selves. An uncompromising representative of the socialist bloc is no exception.

As a result of that evening, some of our diplomatic acquaintances became personal friends. I recall, in particular, the Bulgarian Cultural Attaché and his wife, with whom we spent a delightful weekend at Stratford-on-Avon and a number of evenings at London theatres, and a cultivated Soviet Counsellor with whom we enjoyed stimulating discussions on a wide range of subjects.

Altogether, my pleasantest memories of that period are of informal evenings, mostly with Embassy colleagues — Eda Goldstücker, who was Counsellor, then Chargé d'Affaires and later Envoy to Israel, Alois Skoumal, our witty and erudite Cultural Attaché, and Evžen Zeman of our commercial office — but often with English friends like Harry and Marjorie Pollitt, fine communists and entertaining company; John Gollan, who was to succeed Harry as Secretary of the British Communist Party, and his lively wife Elsie; Konni Zilliacus, a left-wing MP and John Platts-Mills, a leading socialist barrister.

Our three years were drawing to an end. I was not sorry. My task had been easier than I had anticipated. Pavel's crash course in history had stood me in good stead. I had been able to identify with the Czechs and therefore to represent them. (I had even given some informal talks on developments in post-war Czecho-slovakia.) But on the whole I had not enjoyed the role of diplomatic wife who, after all, is a mere appendage, entirely subservient to her husband's career. I looked forward to a real job in Prague and a greater degree of independence.

It had been an eventful period. The Cold War had been launched; NATO had been formed; the Cominform had been created and Yugoslavia expelled from it; Germany had begun a miraculous economic recovery; the People's Republic of China and the State of Israel had been inaugurated; India and Pakistan had achieved self-government; the Soviet Union had exploded an atom bomb and American troops had entered South Korea.

Pavel had steered his way skilfully among the eddies. He had proved to be a successful diplomat. His war years had given him an insight into Western affairs and political thinking, and a genuine liking for the English. He had been trusted and liked by his associates in both East and West. He had spared neither time, energy nor money for his job. He had not sought to profit from it: he had bought no jewellery, pictures or furs to flog in Prague on our return as other diplomats had done. From Press Attaché he had risen to Chargé d'Affaires before his recall. He looked forward to a high appointment — a minor ambassadorial post, perhaps — on his next term abroad.

We were given a VIP send-off. Farewell parties were held for us every night for a fortnight. As we took our final leave on Victoria Station, the Soviet Counsellor gave Pavel a gold watch in memory of their friendship and cooperation. It became Pavel's most treasured possession.

Chapter 6

Our homecoming, at the end of 1950, was a rude shock. We were not prepared for the changed atmosphere. Gone was the exuberance of the liberation year. People were tight-faced, grim, tired of perpetual shortages. There was tension in the air. Political differences had sharpened; society was once more divided. Arrests had been made of foreign agents, but also of Czech communists. Among them were Evžen Klinger and Otto Šling whom we had known in London during the war. The Party was probing for further enemies within its ranks. Pavel found the Foreign Ministry veiled in unease.

Karel had inherited our previous flat and we were offered a partly furnished flat in a villa in the best residential part of the Smíchov district, called Na Hřebenkách. It was the epitome of Austro–Hungarian magnificence. (Actually, our flat represented only half of the original apartment, which had extended over the whole of the ground floor.) The rooms were huge and high, light and airy. The floors, made of large squares of highly-polished mahogany, glowed redly. Into the panelled walls were laid glass cabinets for the display of precious porcelain. From the ceilings hung enormous chandeliers, comprising hundreds of droplets, glistening like tears in sunshine. The whole of one wall of the central room was windowed and looked out on a garden of trees, grass and shrubs. In front of the window extended a vast oak desk, intricately carved and matching the imposing fireplace in the adjacent room, which was separated by tall, oak doors.

My legs buckled under me and I had a premonition as I sank into a velvet seat attached to the wall panelling. Give this no more than eighteen months, I told myself.

A few days later the first blow fell. Pavel was eating his dinner in silence. It was not his usual animated silence, in which problems were propelled back and forth, unripe ideas were shunted into sidings and fruitful solutions were sent up the main track into the morrow. It was a void, oppressive silence.

'Is there anything—' I was about to say 'wrong', but that might have provoked merely an irritated denial, so I substituted 'new'?

'Mm, yes. A regulation has been brought out. Employees with Western wives have to leave the Ministry.'

'Do you mean you are getting the sack because of the geographical accident of my birth?'

'Yep. It isn't a question of loyalty — you had a very good report from the Embassy — but of security,' Pavel soothed me. 'Actually, in my case, notice is not to take effect immediately. I am to complete some major projects before I go.'

Pavel's indefinite notice dragged on and he continued working with the sword of Damocles hanging over his head, a state of insecurity that was not exactly what his London doctor had recommended.

Having unexpectedly been converted into a liability, I was eager to prove that a bourgeois background was no obstacle to honest toil. Without telling Pavel, I went to the headquarters of the Women's Union and told them I wanted to work in heavy industry, the heavier the better. The clerk arranged a six-month temporary job at the Tatravagonka engineering works, which produced trams and train wagons. Pavel's reaction was as dispiriting as I had anticipated. 'Don't be absurd! You can't operate a machine, you're notoriously cackhanded. Even the egg-whisk falls apart in your hand. You'll probably maim yourself for life, and where will that leave your family?'

I declined to consider that possibility.

At four thirty in the morning the screech of the alarm woke me. I arrived at the factory gate at ten minutes to six and was directed to the cadre department; there I was told to report to comrade Králík in shop 620. Comrade Králík was standing hands behind his back, surveying his domain. His figure bulged under the faded blue coat. His name by an oversight was Rabbit; it should clearly have been Pig. (I had in mind, of course, a clean, socialist porker.) Small, darting eyes and a snub nose clustered in the centre of a wide expanse of pink flesh, flanked by large red ears standing out at right angles.

'Ha, another of you come to expiate your sins!' was his discouraging greeting. I flinched. In a sense he was right, but not entirely. I explained that all I wanted was to do some useful work at grassroots level. Králík shrugged. 'We'll put you on Technical Control. They need another hand and you can't do much harm there. Follow me.'

He led me through the shop, a cheerless building. The air was warm, and heavy with dust and metal particles. The dingy, biscuit-coloured walls were like the tear-smudged face of a grubby infant. The high, mottled windows streaked the concrete floor with dirty light; puddles of yellowy-brown liquid lay around. The machines from which the liquid trickled were a dark greenish-brown.

Striding ahead, Králík threw remarks over his shoulder. 'You'll find life here a bit different from what you're used to. I'm a disciplinarian. Six o'clock sharp the operatives are at their machines and you'll be in your pen. If you clock in late that means a day off your holiday. You've a quarter-of-an-hour for lunch in the canteen any time between eleven and two. That's generous. At other factories lunch is taken after the shift.'

We reached a small pen presided over by a school-marmish woman assisted by a dark and lively girl.

Králík introduced me. 'Show her the ropes, Comrade Horská, and keep a sharp look out for sabotage. You can't trust these foreign elements.' He left chuckling.

Comrade Horská spoke slowly and loudly as though all foreigners were congenital idiots: 'Every worker brings the first piece of every batch to us for checking. If we pass an incorrect measurement, all the parts in the batch will be inaccurate. If they cannot be adjusted, they go for scrap and the batch has to be machined again. You must be careful when counting the batches. If a batch is short, assembly is held up until the missing pieces are machined. All these precious hours can never be retrieved, and may mean the failure of the factory plan.' Luba, the younger woman, laughed good-naturedly: 'Anka thinks socialism begins and ends at this counter.'

A worker brought me a pin to inspect.

'This pin is three millimetres short,' I pointed out diffidently.

'Christ, that's nothing to do with me!' was the polite

rejoinder. 'I get 'em like that, see, I'm a driller. I only want to know is the distance from head to hole correct and is the ruddy hole the right size? The tapering pin goes in here, see. And holds the pin in place. It doesn't matter if it sticks out half-a-metre beyond.' He went off muttering: 'Don't know a pin from a knitting needle.'

Luba remarked dryly: 'Železný's soon forgotten that not so long ago he knew as much about drilling as he did about bear-keeping.'

After a substantial lunch in the canteen, Železný fell into step beside me.

'Where'd they direct you from?'

'I beg your pardon?'

'Who gave you the push?'

'No one, I wasn't employed before.'

'Oh, I thought you were a formerly.'

'A formerly?'

'A former teacher, lawyer, researcher and so on.'

'No, this is my first job.'

'Got the wrong pedigree, eh? Father had his own business?'

'Good heavens, no!'

'Is he German? You've got a bit of an accent.'

'No, English.'

'Ah, that explains it. Your husband fought in the West and this is the only kind of work you can get. Don't let it worry you; there's thousands of us. General sort of swop over. The highly qualified professional people are laying roads, building bridges and operating machines, and the dumb clots — whose fathers used to dig, sweep or brick-lay — are on top, telling the others where to lay the roads, what to produce and how to spend the country's money. The consequence is the roads look like ploughed fields, we make things we can't sell and the bridges can't be used for traffic. There's one called the Bridge of the Intellectuals over the Vltava at Bráník built by doctors of law. The bridge is all right, but the dolts in the top drawer forgot to plan a road leading to and from it! Then they wonder why the economy is going downhill like a ten-ton lorry with the brakes off.'

There was an India rubber quality about Mr Železný. He was round; he bounced as he walked; his face slipped into a variety of cheerful grimaces. He looked as though he would rebound to safety if he were dropped off the top of a cliff.

Having found an audience, albeit an incredulous one, Mr Železný continued: 'I'm here under the Desk-to-Bench campaign. "Too many fat backsides warming too many office stools. We need more hands at the bench, the seam and the furnace," they said. Seventy-seven thousand of us were re-directed.

'I'm not complaining about the job: I don't earn less. It's the principle I object to. First, I don't take kindly to being directed; second, this is a waste of good will and good people. What industry needs to increase productivity is more qualified technicians and engineers, not clerks, artisans and judges.

'The joke is, a Party member gets to be foreman, supervisor or such and goes bonkers over a lot of papers he can't get the hang of, and the works gets flooded with half-a-million screws and not a nut in the place, except the one behind the desk. Am I boring you?'

'No, no. It's very interesting.'

'Well, you see that tall lanky miller with specs. Looks standoffish? That's Dr Brugel. He was de-actionized.'

'Paralysed?'

'Not exactly. Put out of action by an Action Committee in 1948. They were set up to purge the reactionaries, or that was the general idea; but hit a Czech, particularly a communist Czech with an idea, and he'll swallow it hook, line and sinker, plus the bloke at the other end, if you get me. They sorted out everyone who they decided was a potential menace: Catholics, Sokolites, ex-Scouts. Brugel was a lawyer. The legal profession caught it good and proper. The lawyer's job is to protect the individual, so where the individual hasn't got any rights, it's a waste of good money paying lawyers, isn't it? They said: "Sign or get out!" and stuck an application to join the CP under his nose. But Brugel had principles. "I'm a Catholic; you're atheists," he said. "I support your social policy but I cannot join a party that denies God." So he was declared politically unreliable and flung out on his ear.'

I was disturbed by Železný's revelations. I had envisaged a socialism that would eliminate, not generate, injustice. But when I voiced my doubts to Pavel he dismissed them with the axiom: 'When you cut down a forest, chips fly.'

Rising so early in the morning simply to count other people's products was a disproportionate effort. Despite Pavel's gloomy prognostications, I was determined to get on to a machine. I badgered Králík. One day he came up to the pen, just before the end of the shift and shouted: 'Hey, you, Comrade English-woman, there's a batch here wants doing quickly. If you care to stay on, you can have a go.'

I followed him with alacrity. Králík gabbled instructions: 'The bolt fits here onto this jig; adjust the ends so that the drill passes through the aperture, press the starting button, apply the self-act lever, halfway through raise the drill slightly to release the swarf, switch on again but before the drill penetrates to the outside and scorches, take it through slowly by hand. See that the holes are perfectly perpendicular; this batch is for a job that's going to the Soviet Union. And — er — take care. You know the Czech saying: "Clumsy flesh has to go!"'

With my courage like a lump of cheese in my throat, I gingerly set the machine going. I had reckoned without the jet of suds. Suddenly, it became afflicted with a nervous twitch and poured its obnoxious liquid into my boot. What did I do first: stop the machine or quell the jet? Mistakenly I grabbed the jet. There was a noise like sizzling bacon and blue smoke rose from the drill hole. I stopped the machine and tried to lift the lever. The drill was stuck faster than Carver Doone in the bog.

'Well, how's it going?' Králík's gentle bass boomed in my ear.

Humbly I explained about the jet.

'Let's have a look at it,' he grunted. 'Ježíšmarjá, it only needs the stop-cock tightening at the joint. H'mm it won't grip, worn smooth. Well, tie it up with rag. Use your imagination, girl!'

That was the last piece of advice I had expected to be given on the shop floor. Králík separated the drill from the machine. 'Take the jig over to the locksmiths. They'll get the drill out for you. They've got the right tools.'

I staggered off to the locksmiths under the crushing weight of the jig. Ten minutes later I was back at work with a newly-ground drill and the conviction that this would be my first and last set of holes for the construction of communism.

The rest of the batch went without mishap. There were only three pieces left. My confidence rose above the plimsoll line, then the machine let out an ear-jarring shriek. The lever was free. I set the drill twirling again. A second screech. I put the bolt aside and finished the remaining two.

'That was a pip in the steel,' Králík explained. 'Very bad for the drills.'

And for the nerves, I added silently. I braced myself. 'May I carry on tomorrow?'

Králík hesitated, then said: 'All right, you can stay on while Mlýnek is off sick.'

'For Chrissake, what are you doing, Bek, you clumsy ox?' Our supervisor's angry voice sounded above the din early the following morning. 'This pile's millimetres out.'

Bek, a tubby turner, retorted: 'The first piece was okay — Technical Control passed it. Something must have come loose in this old bag of tricks.'

'It was in perfect order until you took it over,' Králík roared. 'If there's anything wrong with it, it's your own damn carelessness, or more likely wilful damage. What can one expect from a former hotel-keeper? You've lost your own business, now you're ruining ours. From now on, you're off machining and on sweeping.'

After the shift I went to look for Táborský, an elderly, taciturn fitter.

'Would you do me a favour, comrade.'

'Ugh, what?'

'Would you look at the machine Bek's been using?'

The fitter gazed at me through shaggy eyebrows that grew over his eyes like a Sealyham terrier's, concealing his thoughts more thoroughly than his clamped lips. He slowly raised an eyebrow and revealed one brown eye, in which there was a glint of something — could it be understanding? He nodded. Then he went over to the machine, examined it and tried it out.

'Inaccurate,' he pronounced.

'Could the defect have been caused by careless treatment?'

'Could've — over many years.'

'But that little chap, Bek, had only been on it three months.'

'Mm, machine's got to wear out some time. This one's pretty old. Needs a thorough overhaul.'

'Then why isn't that done?'

'I'm only the fitter for two shops. The supervisors won't allot sufficient time for machine maintenance, especially when they're running two or three shifts. It's pretty general. It'll catch up on them in the long run, though. Then, instead of expanding capital goods production, they'll be replacing what's got worn out through neglect.'

This was an unusually long speech for Táborský. I pressed my point: 'So it can't be proved that Bek was to blame?'

'Nope.'

'Couldn't you get him reinstated?'

He looked at me suspiciously.

'I'm not interested in him as a man or a class symbol. I just don't like injustice.'

Táborský waved his hand, gesturing at his many years in a patently unjust world. 'I'm not risking a head-on clash with Králík after all these years,' he replied.

'But?'

'You're young, you're new, you take everything a sight too seriously. I don't know why I should bother but I'll do this: I'll speak to the supervisor in 420. That's my other shop and that's where Bek is sweeping now. The supervisor is reasonable; he can put Bek onto a machine there.'

'Thanks.'

'Ugh.'

Just before lunch Táborský passed my machine. He nodded; he had kept his promise.

At 2.15 p.m. the morning shift crowded into Králík's office for the monthly trade union meeting. Králík opened with a critical attack on 620's standards. Quality was being sacrificed to quantity. 'Comrades, we are not going to build socialism on rejects,' he cried. 'Last year rejects cost our works two million crowns. This year there has been an improvement but it's still not good enough. The youngsters are the worst offenders. You've had it easy,' he thundered. 'You've given up nothing to achieve power, working-class power. We old communists had to risk our lives and liberties for what is yours by right under the Constitution. Bullets, baton charges and the inside of a prison cell were the answers we got to demands for work and a living wage.'

Luba muttered: 'Here we go again. Bloody Wednesday and all that. We can't help not having been born and shot at during the First Republic.'

Pulkrábek, another turner, spoke up: 'The Party can't live on its past. We've got to solve present problems. We're a long way from communism and reward according to need. In the meanwhile we've got families to feed. Instead of speechifying, why don't you come up with some useful ideas for avoiding rejects? It's not only the prestige of 620 and your bonus that are at stake, but our takings too. We don't exactly jump for joy when we have to machine a second batch for nothing.'

Železný put in: 'All it wants is for every worker to be issued with a Vernier gauge.'

'Where the hell will the money come from?' Králík growled.

'So he can check on his work periodically,' Železný went on, unperturbed. 'Or for you to go the rounds two or three times a shift.'

'Are you telling me how to run my shop, you ink-blotter?' Králík blustered.

'It's reasonable what Železný says,' broke in fifteen-stone Tonda who operated four centre lathes. If there was one man whom Králík respected, it was Tonda. Other voices murmured approval.

'Okay, okay, I'll do my best.' Králík could shift weight swiftly when the majority closed ranks against him. 'Comrade Mastná, put down in the minutes: Comrade Králík: socialist pledge: to make several extra rounds of inspection per shift with a view to reducing rejects. Send a copy to the Works Committee.'

Having adroitly turned the situation to his own advantage, Králík brought up the next item — delays in deliveries of material. The ball was kicked from Bartoň to Jarmila, the delivery girl, to Králík, from workshop to workshop, from factory to steel works and from there to the raw material suppliers and finally ended up at Ostrava waiting for vacant goods wagons.

'We've been through all this umpteen times,' a weary borer grumbled. Then someone else complained that workers were not paid for time lost through inefficient planning. This brought forth a tirade from Králík on production cost and lack of political consciousness. The situation was obviously aggravated by Králík's inability to foresee and forestall hitches. No one accused him outright for, I gathered, he tended to revenge himself on his critics by allotting them the least profitable batches. The argument died down among angry shrugs.

Králík announced a new check by the rate fixers. As this would inevitably lead to some hardening of norms, it met with resistance.

'We'll never increase productivity otherwise,' said Králík. 'Figures here show that the works as a whole wastes fifteen per cent of its working time. Workers don't start promptly; they extend snack and lunch breaks and many are at the clocking machines, washed and ready to leave, at two p.m. Full utilization of your eight hours will counter-balance speeded-up operations.'

This was a very different picture from the propaganda in the official Czech press, which presented soaring productivity, exceeded targets and cosy concord between floor and management. The factory seemed to be divided into those who were driving themselves to the limits of endurance for what they believed in, and those who took advantage of the shortage of labour to do as little as possible for as much as possible.

However, when Králík appealed for a Sunday shift to complete an order for the Soviet Union, which was behind schedule, there was no lack of volunteers. During the shift carping and discontent were forgotten.

When Mlýnek retired on a disability pension I was transferred to the permanent payroll. At the end of my second week as a full-blown driller, Pulkrábek came up to me with the words: 'Bartoň says would you mind dashing this job off; it's part of a batch that's already gone forward. This box got forgotten.'

The box was the standard type, with a green job card tucked down one side. But my early warning system was functioning. I glanced warily inside. A dark mass met my eye. An old trick! Fortunately, though a large spider will send me into hysterics, the genus *rattus* has never caused me to flutter. I pulled the dead rat out by its tail, and handed it and the job card back to Pulkrábek, saying: 'Please return this to Comrade Bartoň and tell him the size of the hole hasn't been specified.'

The young man grinned. Stifled laughter echoed round the shop. I had passed my ordeal. Thereafter the shop addressed me by the familiar 'thou'.

Friday was pay day. On this particular Friday I unfolded my slip and read 1500 crowns. Impossible! I went to Bartoň and asked to see the job books.

'Why?' he growled suspiciously.

'I think there's been a mistake.'

'If you've got too little, you'll have to put more effort into it next week. I've been on this job twenty years and I've never forgotten to book a job.'

I said gently: 'Comrade Bartoň, I've been over-paid not under-paid.'

His mouth dropped open as though his jaw had become dislocated.

'Then what are you complaining about?'

'I want to put the accounts right.'

'You must be joking! Well, if you insist, it's 102's business.'

The clerk there told me that no discrepancy had been discovered. He winked. 'Have a drink on me and forget it.'

I protested: 'I don't want to take socialist money I haven't earned. If everyone took home a few hundred crowns that weren't covered by goods produced, what would happen to the economy?'

He burst out laughing. 'My dear innocent, you shouldn't worry your little head about a paltry couple of hundred, if you knew how much material people smuggle home every week. There's hardly a man of them hasn't put together a washing machine out of snaffled parts.'

I couldn't believe my ears. Workers stealing under socialism!

I spotted a book labelled 620 and went through the items. Here was an error — a small batch of pins: 480 instead of 48, and farther down 25 plates for 300 instead of 30. 'There you are!' I crossed off the offending noughts.

'What are you doing to my books, young woman?' he wailed. 'I'll have to recast my figures and it's ten minutes to two.' He was outraged at having to put in a few moments' overtime on account of my eccentric integrity.

I asked Tonda, who was a communist, whether it was true that parts were taken out of the factory, hoping he would deny it. But he confirmed that this was so.

'But that's stealing!'

Tonda scratched his head. 'I doubt if the men see it like that. We own the means of production, don't we? So we can't steal what belongs to us?'

'As far as appropriating parts is concerned, the factory belongs to the workers,' I persisted, 'But when it comes to decisions of management, they don't feel it's theirs?'

Tonda was too honest to wriggle out of the question. 'No, maybe they don't — consciously. But they'd defend it with their lives if the capitalists tried to take it back.' He changed the subject. 'By the way, a party of us are going for a beer; we usually do on Fridays. Care to come along?'

Never in my life had I managed to get through a whole pint of beer, but if he'd asked me to share a cup of hemlock, I wouldn't have refused.

It was a poky little pub with smoke-blackened walls and ceiling. The beer was served in litre tankards. And it wasn't even gravity English bitter but a full-bodied ten. The waitress, of welterweight dimensions, wielded five full tankards in each hand. I needed two hands to lift one. 'Do or die,' I muttered and sent down half at one lift of the elbow.

Tonda produced an accordion and we all burst into song. Czech folk songs are so delightfully tuneful that not even hectolitres of flowing hops and malt can drown their inherent musicality. The repertoire is inexhaustible: if you were to ride round the world on a penny-farthing bicycle, singing non-stop, you would still have some over for an encore.

Further tankards appeared before me; my new status as a member of the labouring fraternity precluded refusal. Summoning the remnants of my willpower, which were floating in Pilsen's famous liquid, I downed several more.

'That's my girl!' Tonda rumbled.

'I dunno so much about that,' Železný grinned, looking me up and down in my usual slacks and sloppy sweater. 'Looks like they ran short of material when they assembled Ros: if it weren't for her nose, you couldn't tell whether she was coming or going.'

This raised a general laugh. In another land at another time, I might have made a fortune as a predecessor of Twiggy; as it was, I had to stand up to some good-natured teasing, for the average Czech man likes his pound of flesh.

When I stood up to go home, the pub tilted like a boat on the Mácha lake in a squall.

'I'll see you home, nipper,' Tonda offered.

He delivered me to my doorstep and rang the bell. Pavel appeared.

'Your wife, Comrade Doctor,' Tonda announced. 'She'll be all right after a good sleep.'

I endeavoured to draw myself up to a dignified height and step over my threshold. Instead, deprived of my support, I collapsed into Pavel's arms and blissful slumber.

Besides our regular pay-day celebrations, there were periodical ones to honour fulfilment of the monthly and quarterly plans.

I rejoiced at my own contribution. The woman at the drill behind me left and Králík let me take over her machine in addition to my own. By dint of drilling slow heavy pieces on one machine and small quick pieces on the other, I kept them both operating without loss of time. I had become a Stakhanovite of a very modest order.

My sons, too, were proud of my prowess. Whenever we entered a tram, they would enquire loudly: 'Did you make this one, Mama?'

Remote from higher politics, the factory gave me peace of mind. While I was there, engrossed in its problems, I forgot the phantoms that were stalking the land.

Since the rat business Jarmila had attached herself to me. She was an ardent communist and a functionary of the Youth League. She had left school at fifteen, become pregnant at sixteen, married at seventeen, divorced at eighteen and married for the second time at nineteen. She had three children, exuberant energy and boundless optimism. She had been born during the great depression, which had hit industrial Czechoslovakia severely. Jarmila desperately wanted the socialists to win the race. Aware that information on Britain and the West was slanted in the Czech media, she questioned me closely on conditions in England. She was disconsolate to learn that the British were ahead in some respects, for instance, that they worked only a forty-two-hour week.

'Many do overtime to make ends meet, and women's wages are only two-thirds or half of men's,' I consoled her. 'Czechoslovakia wins hands down on full employment, length of paid holidays and maternity leave. Why, you get marriage and confinement grants besides children's allowances, and you already have a graduated pension scheme.'

As a result of our chats I found myself a regular contributor to the *desetiminutovky* — ten-minute talks on current affairs held twice a week at the end of the morning shift.

Jarmila dropped a box of pieces beside my machine. 'Hey, Ros, seen the notice board?'

'No.'

'Well, take a look.'

Intrigued, I slipped round to view it. The retiring Shop Committee had pinned up a list of proposed candidates for the shop election. Most of them were the retiring committee, but four new names had been added, the last being Rosemary Kavanová. I felt absurdly elated. It was a mark of trust.

I was duly elected and appointed safety officer.

I, too, had succumbed to the theory, subscribed to by the

dedicated proportion of the population, that you were only half
alive if you were not working yourself to death. I, too, had been
persuaded that I was not justifying my existence unless I was
doing my utmost to drive myself out of it. Apart from joining
the Youth League and trade union (inescapable) and the Czechoslovak–Soviet Friendship Society (escapable but advisable), I
also attended meetings of the Women's Union, and was a part-
time translator. Now, at last, I had a function! This, of course,
involved yet more meetings — of the works' safety officers.

Socialist zeal had produced an epidemic of meetingitis affect-
ing most of the population. Apart from Party and trade union
meetings, and meetings of all the other unions, there were
Fighters against Fascism meetings, Defenders of Peace meetings, auxiliary Fire Brigade meetings, tenants' meetings, street
and local affairs meetings, parent–teacher and Friends of the
School meetings — all taking place once a week or once a
month.

No meetings out of working hours began on time — either
because people were coming from a previous meeting that had
ended late or were coming from home and knew that half of the
members would arrive late anyway. It was considered bad form
to end a meeting on time or be the first to leave. The subjects of
many meetings coincided, but presence at one did not excuse
absence from another, identical meeting. In any case, we kept
scores as a scale of our political enthusiasm. Sometimes people
turned up to the wrong meeting, or lecturers brought the wrong
notes, or made their appearance on the wrong day, or at the
wrong place. But they always found an audience of some sort
hanging around, so no harm was done.

At one evening meeting — the umpteenth on the Korean
War — held by our local Women's Union, I tried my socialist
best to concentrate on our leader's passionate address. I had
already sacrificed two Saturday afternoons to 'agitating'
(urging) our local inhabitants to join a protest march against
American barbarism — apart from contributing the earnings of
one shift to the Korean cause. This evening, therefore, I found
my attention wandering off the subject and on to the earnest
but exhausted faces round the table.

Having answered the call, women were struggling heroically
against heavy odds. A 48-hour week, plus two hours' commut-
ing, two hours' shopping and five hours' housework per day,
was not resulting in the picture of fulfilled womanhood that

might have been expected under a system that offered freedom from exploitation by man (except husbands), emancipation (from everything except child-bearing, home-running and the need to take up gainful employment because a man's salary could not support a family), and victory in the fight for equal rights and equal pay (by taking the less lucrative jobs the men were only too happy to leave).

True, the standard of living had risen since 1945 but it was partly concealed in low rents, free social welfare and health schemes. The women's standard was maintained at a low level by erratic distribution, and a labour shortage in the retail trade and public services. The new family and divorce laws had improved women's status in society, but it was still a man's world, and the women were a long way from full freedom.

We'd built up the capital goods sector. But when, I wondered, were we going to start thinking of the consumer? When would we have a broader selection of labour-saving devices? When were we going to improve quality so that a cotton dress wouldn't shrink from mother to daughter dimensions after two washings? So that handles would not fly off implements, and housewives off the handle? So that the male population wouldn't look like rogues on account of the razors not razing? So that the 'constant hot water' would not be constantly off because of constantly bursting mains? When were we going to manufacture fewer shoes for giants and pygmies and more for average-sized adults and children? Why wasn't the money that went into bunting invested in a detergent that would wash dirt out rather than in? I was fascinated to learn that we were producing our own ball-bearings instead of importing them from the Swedes (served them right for pinching our art treasures during the Thirty Years' War), but who was going to help the women bear their double/triple burden?

Proud of my affiliation with the toiling masses, I had discarded make-up, wore only my oldest clothes and preferred to freeze in 20 degrees Celsius below zero in an old-fashioned cloth coat rather than admit the possession of a fur. I gloated over my broken nails and scarred fingers and I did not regret having read no book and visited no art gallery since we left London. I wanted humbly to belong, not splendidly to stand apart.

Now, seeing thirty colourless women, dedicated but joyless, indispensable but uncherished, I suddenly rebelled. This was not what we had fought for. No wonder the pubs and the divorce courts were full. My next demonstration was going to be against the oppression of Czech women.

The voice droned on . . . casualties . . . hunger . . . disease . . . mutilation . . . There were tears in these good women's eyes. In mine too, for the evil, senseless destruction on one side of the world and the well-intentioned, slow self-destruction on the other side. My eyes were leaden. Only three hours' sleep last night, translating the *Trial of the Vatican Agents*. My head was lolling; I longed to get up and leave, but I could not confess to mere sleepiness in the face of suffering humanity. I stuck it out. The meeting ended with an appeal for volunteers to help at the local nursery school during the summer vacation. I stumbled home and dropped dreamless into bed.

I performed my duties as 620's safety officer assiduously, too assiduously for Králík with whom it was 'everything for the worker', bar anything that cost time, trouble or money. Our first clash was over duckboards. Why the hell was I ordering twenty new ones? Because the slats of the old ones were either broken or rotten. If an operative caught his foot, it could cause a serious accident.

'D'you think a man with any sense can't see a damn great hole under his nose?' Králík exploded.

'Of course he can,' I soothed him. 'But he's supposed to be watching his machine, isn't he?'

'Where's the dough to come from?' was the next question. 'If I take it out of 620's wages fund and the bonuses are that much smaller, you'd better hire yourself a bodyguard.'

'Then take it out of the shop's social fund. I'll get the Works Safety Commission to investigate, and if they think my demands would seriously deplete it, they can contribute from the works resources.'

'All right,' gritted Králík. 'You'll get your blasted duck-boards.' He added with heavy sarcasm: 'I suppose you'll be wanting bloody tiles on the floor next.'

'No,' I answered sweetly. 'We'd skid on those, but I'd like the hollows filled in. Suds collect in them and there is never enough sawdust, so we'll have to do the job properly with concrete.'

'This isn't a nursery school,' roared Králík, leaping to his feet. 'You're a machinist, not a bloody nurse maid!'

I retreated and sought Jarmila. Jarmila persuaded the Youth

League to put in a Saturday afternoon shift. We bought sand and cement from the extra earnings and transformed 620 from a map of the south Bohemian lake district into a smooth expanse you could have run a ballroom dance on.

My next tour of inspection brought me to the grinders.

'How are the suction pipes working?' I asked conversationally.

'Look, woman, these pipes haven't been sucking for a f——ing long time,' one of them replied. 'All they do is get in the bloody way.'

'I shall report it immediately.'

'You can put it down in six reports, nothing'll come of it,' said another. 'It never does.'

'It will now.'

'What'll you bet?' asked the first.

'A bottle of brandy,' I replied recklessly, adding: 'Russian.' One had to have the right affiliation even with booze.

A power press operator pointed out to me that his brake pin was wearing loose and likely to release the press at an unexpected moment. Táborský was off sick. I waylaid Králík just before two o'clock. He followed me reluctantly, gave the machine a cursory glance and roared that the damn part would last months yet, and that if things went on like this I'd bring production to a standstill.

Two days later the man was rushed to hospital with two fingers crushed. After that, the new suction pipes and one or two other improvements were plain sailing. We saved the brandy until the injured man returned to work and consumed it amicably together. He was put onto a brand new press.

Králík had not adjusted to the new era: in his mind the floor, whose battles he had previously fought, was naturally against the management, which he now represented. The whole shop grumbled — mostly off the record.

'Grumbling,' Luba snorted. 'It's a national pastime!'

'Perhaps you don't grumble in the right places,' I suggested.

'Where can we?' she asked. 'The trade union deals with complaints, but them top union functionaries are members of the Party. We'll never shift Králík.'

Jarmila was not averse to a little subversion. Together we organised a *secret* ballot in 620 — an unheard-of move. The result was overwhelmingly for Králík's ouster. Králík refused to recognise such 'unconstitutional, capitalistic proceedings' and swore he knew who was behind it. Then, to our surprise, he called an extraordinary union meeting to announce that he had been offered the position of deputy director in view of his service to the Party and industry.

Luba whispered caustically: 'When a Party functionary is kicked out, he always gets kicked up!'

Jarmila had been doing some detective work. She confided to me that Králík had designed a jig that had turned out to be inaccurate. He'd taken the innovation money before it had been properly tested.

'"Upstairs" didn't want him to face the music here if it leaked out: that's why they've removed him.'

The new supervisor was a technician who knew his job. In consultation with the Shop Committee he achieved a balance between the floor's demands and the needs of production. Productivity rose accordingly.

All factories were expected to make a special splash in honour of the October Revolution. Tatravagonka pledged to fulfil the year's plan by that date. The whole factory went mad keeping its promise. The management, too, played a part in this production orgy: planning methods were re-evaluated and electric trolleys were purchased to keep material moving. We cut breaks to a minimum and absenteeism dropped.

We made it. On 7 November the main yard was decorated with flags, the works band played socialist pop songs and the employees assembled to watch the last product of the planned year leave the gates — a beautiful yellow and red new-type tram with sprung seats, rubber tyres and four powerful engines. Our director informed us that if this pace was maintained, Tatravagonka would exceed its annual plan by twenty-five per cent. Two-hundred-and-thirty other plants had taken up our challenge and would fulfil their plans before the end of the year too. He ended on a triumphal note, unfurling a banner for the 'Best Prague Factory', and the meeting concluded with the Red Flag.

My doubts were set to rest. There might be shortcomings but it was only a matter of time before they would be eliminated. When it came to the nitty-gritty, the workers were solidly behind the system. Jarmila, it seemed was solidly behind me. She informed me that I had been proposed as a candidate to the

Party by 620's young communists (which meant mainly Jarmila).

'Me, a foreigner! They must be mad.'

I had intended to apply for membership when we returned to Prague from London. But after the influx of members in 1948, some at pistol point, as it were, the Party had closed its ranks. Now only the most trustworthy working-class cadres were considered, and they had to be nominated and serve a year's candidature.

'You're not a foreigner, you're one of us,' Jarmila protested warmly.

Did I still wish to join the Party? I still supported its aims, but I could not now condone all its methods. As a member, though, I would have the chance to voice an opinion from within; this would carry more weight than criticism from without, which tended to be construed as 'hostility toward the regime'. I was summoned for an interview by the works Party committee of the Youth league.

The chairman began: 'Comrades Jarmila Fantlová and Jan Šmíd of 620 have proposed Comrade Kavanová as a Party candidate. They base their proposal on her work in her shop.' He read out: 'Shockworker, member of the shop committee, attendance at political school, work pledges in honour of 1 May, 28 October, 7 November, shift for Korea, ten voluntary brigade hours a month, current affairs talks. A commendable record. Does anyone wish to question Comrade Kavanová?'

I looked round. The serious young faces registered approval. Pryl, a draughtsman, cleared his throat. All eyes turned from me to him. He spoke slowly, letting the words sink in. 'Yes, I do.' He eyed me coldly across the table. 'You have attended an institute of higher learning?'

'Yes.'

'You are British by birth and yet your husband was sent to the Czechoslovak Embassy in London in 1947.' He looked round the table, fixing each face with a gimlet stare. No one knew what he was driving at, but his voice was censorious. Easily swayed, the others tucked away their friendly smiles and donned neutral expressions. 'By the pre-February government, in which, no doubt, he had many friends, having spent six war years in England.'

'In the army, fighting in France twice and decorated for bravery,' I intervened.

'Comrades, does it not strike you as strange that Comrade

Kavan should have been sent to represent our Republic in his wife's country where she would, of course, have contacts in imperialist circles?'

'My contacts, as you put it, were on the British Left.' My own tone had grown hostile in reciprocity. What was this, a People's Court?

'Nevertheless, you welcomed your husband's appointment?'

'I certainly did not. I should have preferred somewhere else. We were originally to have gone to Belgrade.' I bit my lip. Tito was now the arch-enemy of the Cominform.

'You would have preferred that?' asked my opponent in the suave tones of a practised Public Prosecutor.

'Were you a member of an Action Committee?' I asked.

'Yes.' Surprised by my question, he had answered spontaneously. He recovered himself. 'I believe I am putting the questions.'

'Well, what has all this got to do with Ros — with Comrade Kavanová's candidature?' asked Jarmila bluntly.

'Yes, would you come to the point.' The chairman tried to assert his authority.

'This committee is here to judge Comrade Kavanová's suitability as a candidate to the Communist Party, the vanguard of the working class,' Pryl reiterated.

'If it interests you,' I broke in, ' an anti-Tito book by a Yugoslav diplomat who recently sought asylum here was written in collaboration with my husband.'

This drew no comment. He is indifferent to the truth, I thought. He is using words as a preamble to a foregone conclusion.

'Comrades,' he went on relentlessly, 'is it not singular that Comrade Kavanová, a foreigner of higher education and bourgeois family, should have chosen to work in a factory, professing solidarity with the working class, while employing a working-class Czech girl to execute the household tasks that all our working women perform themselves.' (There would have been no point in explaining that Květa, our last nanny-housekeeper in London, a marvellous girl who had become our friend, had remained with us because she had not yet found a job or lodgings to her liking.) 'Why, I wonder, should Comrade Kavanová have taken such pains to worm her way into the confidence of the workers in her shop and then proceed to provoke disharmony between the floor and the supervisor? May I remind you that even before getting herself elected to the Shop Committee, she went out of her way to support a member of the reactionary forces striving to undermine our proletarian dictatorship in league with imperialism.'

'Rubbish!' Jarmila snorted.

The chairman and Šmíd looked unhappy. The rest were taking their cue from Pryl. Their faces were rigid with pride in their revolutionary vigilance. They had the makings of first-class professional functionaries: district and regional Party secretaries, permanent members of youth secretariats. Equating reason with individualism, conscience with sentimentality, they would become nameless echoes of a nameless dictatorship. I felt immeasurably sorry for them.

The vote was taken; only Jarmila and Šmíd were for, the rest were against.

'May I say that my sincere desire to help your country build a just socialist society remains unaffected by your decision.' I looked at each one as I spoke, they avoided my eye. 'I regret not having gained this committee's confidence.'

So much for expiating the sin of my origin. Clearly, Pavel and I would never live down our years in the West. Thousands of Czechs and hundreds of English wives had emigrated after February 1948, yet we had returned. Wasn't that sufficient demonstration of loyalty? Naturally I was hurt at my rejection. But before long I ceased to regret it.

Chapter 7

Even high-ranking communists were now coming under fire. Rudolf Slánský[19], a deputy prime minister and, until recently, the Party Secretary-General, and Vlado Clementis, Foreign Minister and a member of the Central Committee, had been arrested.

Pavel came home one day looking very shaken. The state security police had been to his office. They had questioned him about instructions he had been given by Slánský and Clementis when he was in London. They had also interrogated him on his report on the Anglo–Czechoslovak Trade Agreement, his press conference after Masaryk's death and his activities in England during the war.

'It's old stuff. The police have access to all the archives. Why do they want this information from me all over again?'

'It's probably purely routine,' I soothed him. 'With all these spy scares they must be checking on everyone who has been in the West.' (No wonder the young communists had made short shrift of me.)

Pavel was subjected to several more interrogations. These brought back symptoms of nervous strain. He was sleeping badly and smoking heavily. The house was rent with unpredictable storms. In the absence of tranquillisers, I swallowed aspirins and kept the boys out of Pavel's way. He complained:

19. Rudolf Slánský (1901–1952) was a member of the CC and Politburo of the CP from 1929. He was in Moscow during the war and the Secretary-General of the CP until 1951. He was demoted to Deputy Minister until his arrest later that year. He was the main defendant at the show trial of 1952, after which he was executed.

'The situation is getting me down. Colleagues pass me in the corridor and pretend not to see me. I keep wondering if there was anything I overlooked in London or let slip through negligence.'

'You neglect things all the time,' I said lightly, 'like bills and birthdays, but not things that might interest the secret police. You have a clear conscience: there is nothing to be afraid of.'

I spoke with a conviction I did not feel. I, too, was gripped by fear. Pavel had long since ceased to take an independent stand. But he did not suffer fools gladly. Had he incensed some of the new ministerial cadres of limited vision and intellect? What of the enemies he had incurred at the Embassy? Had they cast suspicions on him?

I kissed him. 'You're working too hard. You need something to take your mind off the Ministry and the secret police.'

He soon found a distraction. With his usual lack of prior intimation, Pavel burst in on a Thursday with the news that he had acquired a *chata* and that we were going to see it on the coming Saturday.

A *chata* was a holiday shack, and the latest craze. It might be anything from an inverted hat-box to a converted cowshed. A family might decide to build one with material bought over long periods from the government, or pilfered from building sites, or might purchase a ruin from the local National Committee and inject new life into its bones. Pavel had elected the latter course.

We left the boys with Karel, and Pavel collected me from the factory at two o'clock. He was in high spirits as always when new vistas loomed ahead. We drove north-west from Prague. The countryside was neat and orderly. The scattered holdings had been combined to form extensive collective farms (not, we discovered later, without some coercion). The result was a patchwork quilt of large symmetrical pieces and almost invisible seams, for there were no hedges, and the old dividing strips of grass had been ploughed up. We passed through the Mělník wine-growing district with its platoons of vine sticks scaling the terraces. The undulating plain gave way to rounded hills. The valley opened and closed. Bohemian cottages, red-roofed and with white, pink, blue or green walls clustered in groups near the roadway.

We reached the former Sudetenland, and then the scenery changed. Volcanic pine-clad cones perched on the plateaux. Here and there red bulged from splits in the green like stuffing from a cushion. The brown-and-white striped German houses looked as sober and virtuous as Puritan maids.

The road twisted and turned, climbing steadily. We reached Nový Bor, a grey, unostentatious little town, and swept through the vast, deserted square. The serrated skyline grew higher and blacker, clouds began to roll down the mountain sides and encircle us. Pavel suddenly turned right along a path that cut through the heart of a forest and mist swirled around us. The Minx stumbled along the path for nearly a mile, then emerged, plunged down a short incline and came to a halt beside a grim, desolate edifice — the *chata* of Pavel's dreams. Not a diminutive nestling cottage, as I had pictured, but a barn-like two-storey house, built of timber and concrete; half of the roof and most of the windows were missing. It was one of the many buildings in the district that had fallen into disrepair since the German minority was expelled from Czechoslovakia.

Pavel was saying: 'We own an acre and a half of virgin soil to make fruitful with nothing but our bare hands! That's real life: a battle with nature and the elements! We'll enjoy transforming this heap of rubble into a dignified country residence.'

It was certainly going to require enough effort to take Pavel's mind off political shadows. I opened the front door, which hung askew on one hinge, and looked aghast at the sagging floorboards, peeling paint, seatless chairs and a couch with its upholstery ripped out.

With wilting spirits I was about to peck at the edge of the disorder when Messrs Nový, Šimák and Procházka arrived from the village with sacks of sand, lime and cement. Pavel had either performed some economic miracle, or made some fantastic promises. He immediately commanded me to make tea. After about an hour, during which I trudged fifteen times to the well for water for cleaning and mixing purposes, the water on the sullen stove was hot enough to make the tea which I poured into an assortment of chipped mugs.

Work progressed: rotten timber was carried out onto the field; new floorboards were sawn; cardboard was put into empty frames. Pavel rushed about revelling in the pioneering spirit and deferring to his collaborators. 'What do you suggest here, Mr Procházka?' 'Oh, certainly, Mr Nový.' 'Whatever you think, Mr Šimák.' He whispered to me: 'You have to be careful with these country folk. They are naturally suspicious of the city nobs. If they think you're taking their services for granted, they'll down tools and quit.' Their requirements were then transmitted downwards: 'Darling, mix some cement! Take some planks up to Mr Procházka! Find the nails! Bring the step ladder over here!' Then: 'Make a note that Mr Nový would like half-a-kilo of coffee beans from Prague next time we come, and Mr Procházka an alarm clock.'

If Pavel had been haunted by the secret police, he was now obsessed by the view and the old crock of a house that he had bought with 2,000 crowns in ready cash and 20,000 crowns' worth of frozen assets. He frequented secondhand shops and was for ever bringing home cupboards minus knobs, crippled stools, cracked bowls and collapsible tables, folding beds, straw mattresses and the enthusiastic declaration: 'Just what we need for Kytlice. It only requires a coat of paint (or minor repair) and it'll be as good as new. It was very cheap. They nearly gave it away.'

'I don't wonder,' I would murmur.

When the fourth table and tenth bed put in their appearance, I took a firm stand. 'If another article moves into this flat pending transport to Kytlice, I move out!'

Pavel sighed: 'The practical English! They have no feeling for romance!'

The boys, of course, revelled in the freedom of our Kytlice weekends. They built themselves a bunker and a tree house, gathered brushwood and pine cones for firewood, brought water and generally made themselves far more useful than at home. Pavel's favourite position was to stand, feet astride, on the threshold of his house, gazing with a faraway expression at his 'land'. I learned to dread that glassy, ecstatic trance: it always signalled the birth of some tremendous NEW PROJECT.

First, there was the cultivating mania. In soil that you could have scratched off the mountainside with a pin, in an open position, exposed to a searing north-east gale in all seasons, Pavel was convinced that, with the proper treatment and the application of a sort of Marxist Christian Science, we could produce succulent fruit and vegetables that would keep us in vitamins all the year round. I was allotted a slope facing due north, which supported thistles and nettles in exclusive abundance and told to turn it into good arable land. I had long since learnt that no logical argument of mine would move Pavel. He would be convinced only by trial and error: the trials were mine, the errors were his. Several weekends of slave labour by me despatched the thistles and stones, and the seeds were sown. On the following visit the patch was speckled with promising little green heads. Pavel was wild with enthusiasm.

'You see how quickly everything grows here!'

The next weekend this became abundantly clear: we had a sturdy crop of knee-high weeds. On principle Pavel never admitted defeat, and I saw only one way of securing my release. I bought a tin of weed-killer and emptied it over the patch.

'What have you done?' shrieked the proud landowner. 'The soil will sustain no life at all for three years!'

'Never mind, the boys can play football on it in the meanwhile,' I declared impenitently.

Then there was the bottling optimism. Pavel planted twenty spindly plum and pear trees.

'It rains here 355 days of the year and the mean annual temperature is the lowest in the Republic. It's unlikely that the fruit will ever ripen,' I observed.

'I have thought of that,' replied my indomitable husband. 'These are a specially hardy species. I've had them sent from the Giant Mountains. They will blossom and bear fruit a month later than in other districts, which is an advantage, for you will be able to finish bottling in Prague before you start bottling here.'

Actually, our first harvest was two pears and three plums per tree. My bottles soon showed a disinclination to remain inactive on the shelves, and we had to eat them up before they fermented, while there was still fresh fruit available in the shops.

At Kytlice Pavel threw off his demons. During the week he lapsed, alternating between despondency and rage. His step dragged; grey hairs appeared. Since the arrest of Rudolf Slánský's brother Richard[20], with whom Pavel had been

---

20. Richard Slánský was a diplomat before his arrest and a university professor in Prague after his release.

working closely at the Ministry, he had been even more strictly isolated by his colleagues. Moreover, he was sure our phone was tapped.

'If only I knew what was behind it!' he would cry. 'And what is yet to come.'

One freezing December evening I came home at eleven after the second shift. Pavel was sitting ashen and immobile, his meal untouched. He stared at me strickenly.

'What is it?' I gasped. 'Are you ill?'

'Eda's been arrested,' he croaked.

My mind reeled. The cold, unsentimental Slánský might have violated some ethical or legal norm, but not Eda. Eda could be guilty of nothing. The security police must be on the track of some major conspiracy; but communists like Eda Goldstücker and Vlado Clementis couldn't possibly be part of it: nothing would have induced them to betray their principles: neither wealth nor power. Was it that a group of post-1948 communists, fascists at heart, wanted to discredit old Party members in order to seize power? Who were the mysterious operators who had jurisdiction over life and liberty, against whom there was no appeal? I had a terrifying thought. Eda and Pavel had studied together and cooperated during and after the war. Pavel had worked with Richard Slánský, Deputy Foreign Minister Artur London[21], and Bedřich Geminder[22], head of the Party secretariat's international department. All four were in jail. The trail led to Pavel. Pavel would be next.

Pavel must have pursued the same thread. He said suddenly: 'We could get a divorce.'

We hadn't slept together for a year; the marriage was virtually at a standstill. But I had shelved the idea of divorce when Pavel's troubles with the police had commenced. The time had not been right. Now Pavel himself was offering me my freedom.

I thought, He's giving me the chance to bow out before the

21. Artur London (1915–86) fought in Spain as a communist. From 1940 he worked with the French resistance, but was deported to Mathausen in 1942. From 1949 he was Deputy Foreign Minister until his arrest in 1951. He was sentenced to life imprisonment in 1952, but was released in 1956. Since 1963 he has been living in France. His book about the trial, *On Trial*, was made into a film by Costa Gavras.

22. Bedřich Geminder (1901–1952) joined the CP in 1921 and worked for the Comintern for many years. From 1946 he led the International Department of the International Secretariat. He was arrested and executed with Slánský in 1952.

ship sinks. I could say: yes, give me a divorce; let me go back to England where people are not afraid of the concierge-turned-informer, of the ear in the wall, of enemies incurred unknowingly. I could say: I should have given you up during those initial weeks of our marriage when I saw that politics would always be your first love. I should have walked out after you nearly throttled me. I could say: I'm tired of making light of difficulties. I've had enough of moods and directives. I want to be understood, considered and cherished. But did you ever promise me that? Have you not fulfilled the one vow you made — that I should never be bored? In that case what cause have I for discontent? Is it your fault that I'm not equipped to handle time-bombs?

No, no, the fault was mine. I should have recognised my limitations in time. Pavel had not changed. I had changed. I had ceased to love him. I was to blame.

Aloud I said: 'You've got the jitters because of the political situation, and your verbal fireworks make me frigid. If we were in England we'd go to a shrink and get ourselves sorted out for a few hundred quid. As it is, what we all have to do is to wait patiently for things to improve, and then we'll live happily ever after.'

Pavel's fine, I told myself drowsily. He's honourable in a system that lends itself to corruption, a slogger under conditions where crossing t's and dotting i's passes for work, honest where deception is part of collective security. He continues to have faith under circumstances which others have fled. He has all the virtues in fact. He's just exhausting to live with, that's all.

For the boys' sake we tried not to let the gathering clouds darken the Christmas celebrations. Christmas is an extremely thorough affair in Czechoslovakia. The energy of the women-folk and the least resistant of the menfolk is harnessed to the baking of a thousand and one varieties of biscuit for weeks beforehand. Nearer to the event, there are two-foot bun loaves to be plaited and vats of potato salad to be prepared.

Květa had taken a fortnight's holiday to be with her mother in Moravia, and I had to cope with this outsize eating festival alone. Three days before Christmas, Pavel came in with a string bag in his hand — an unusual sight. Not that Pavel was unwilling. His standard reply to any request for assistance was: 'Yes, yes, in a minute,' but he was too busy saving the world and humanity to find just that minute. The bag, or Pavel, was behaving in a strange manner, jerking and twitching as though afflicted with St Vitus dance.

'Fill the bath with cold water,' he ordered.

'Is that the prescribed treatment?'

'It's a carp,' he explained. 'Been here since the sixteenth century.'

'I thought only tortoises enjoyed such an exaggerated span of existence.'

'I mean the species. It was introduced here in the sixteenth century when the Třeboň lake was constructed.'

The carp was accommodated in the bath. The boys spent many happy hours with their boats in its company. They christened it Kája after a Czech fairy story about a carp, and became very fond of it.

'I hope it isn't another custom to keep the goose on the balcony and fatten it?' I asked anxiously.

'No, indeed, I shall bring it killed from the market.'

He did. He placed a huge mound on the kitchen table and removed the Party newspaper that was adhering to it. It was a Pomeranian-style goose. Tufts adorned its head, neck, wings and legs. Accustomed to a clean-shaven, de-entrailed pyramid of fowl with the more indiscreet organs neatly parcelled and appended, I presumed this was another aspect of socialist realism.

After about an hour, I had reduced our Christmas lunch to stark nudity and gingerly set about dissection. I removed the head and feet and was about to throw them away, when Pavel pounced on them.

'What are you doing? You strip off only the scaly skin and then make soup.'

Pavel then explained in the tone he reserved for the young, the old, and the obtuse: 'The neck you will stuff and bake, the liver you will boil in fat to have delicately on bread. The stomach you will chop with rice. The rest that is not suitable for roasting you will throw in the soup.'

The next point was the assassination of Kája, for which neither of us was morally armed. We had to call in the concierge. Kája became a streak of speed on sensing his approaching end. The boys shrieked with laughter as the concierge wheezed over the bath, lunging unavailingly at the jet-propelled Kája. Finally, I suggested pulling out the plug. Poor Kája had no defence against this stratagem and was soon writhing on the bread board. At the first blow with the meat beater, he leapt into the air. His imbricated coat of mail flashed pure gold and his eye gleamed tawnily. Suddenly, he succumbed and lay helplessly on his side. Another blow and he was still, and immediately looked as though he had never been anything but dead. But only after the concierge had deprived him of head and tail, and he lay there bereft of personality, could I regard him with detachment.

At Christmas Eve supper Zdeněk asked timidly: 'Is it Kája?'

'Well, yes, it is.'

They sighed and even Jan, who normally had the appetite of a roadmender, pushed his plate away and said dispiritedly: 'I'm not hungry this evening.'

'Why didn't you leave him in the bath?' asked Zdeněk tearfully.

'You can have your boats tomorrow, anyway,' I promised.

'It won't be the same without him,' Jan sniffed.

'Would you like me to buy you some goldfish after Christmas?'

'Oh yes,' they chorused, brightening.

'Well, eat up your fi — your supper and I'll get you an aquarium next week.'

'Goldfish cost 250 crowns a pair,' Pavel muttered.

After our supper of fish soup, Kája, potato salad and biscuits we adjourned to the next room for the tree ceremony. The boys stood at the door and gasped with wonder. One candle was already alight: the star at the apex shone in the darkness like a real Star of Bethlehem. Pavel's lighted taper crept from wick to wick and touched the tips of the sparklers. Little creamy fingers trembled; tiny stars leaped and waned. The tree grew bigger and bigger. It towered and filled the room with its magic. The coloured glass balls, fish, birds and mushrooms flung the flickering light back and forth in sharp jabs of silver, gold, blue, crimson and yellow. The tinsel chains intercepted the flashes and flipped them to the silver-clad sweets and chocolates. Fantastic shadows capered on the walls. Round the bole of the tree heterogeneous shapes were vaguely outlined: satisfaction, surprise, disappointment, smiles and perhaps a few stifled tears — all reduced to anonymity by the uniform Christmas wrapping paper.

We stood motionless until the candles had shrunk to amorphous blobs of wax. Pavel pinched the last tottering wick; the snap of the electric light switch brought us back to the present. The boys moved bemusedly toward the pile of gifts. Each held his first parcel for a long time, loath to break the spell of conjecture. The emergence of the first mechanical toy — a Russian dancing bear — transformed the atmosphere to one of predatory curiosity: and eager fingers tore at the wrappings.

At length, shiny-eyed and surfeited, they allowed themselves to be coaxed into bed, together with toy tractors, pecking hens and goods trains.

Eva and a boy-friend, Karel and a girl-friend (he had contrived to get himself married and divorced in our absence) called in. Stoked with Hungarian white wine, the savoury varieties of the thousand and one biscuits, and Turkish coffee, we let ourselves go, Czech-style. That is to say, we told political anecdotes and literary and linguistic jokes. Having no hearth to gather at, urban Czechs are forced to assemble at round tables in their rare moments of relaxation. This in itself lends a conference atmosphere and imposes a certain standard of enjoyment. Indulgence in nonsense is out of the question. You will never find a Czech Edward Lear.

The rest of Christmas was passed in compulsory consumption of the food laid in: plaited bun loaf for Christmas Day breakfast; goose soup and roast goose, bread dumplings and sauerkraut for Christmas lunch, plus biscuits; cold goose, potato salad, and biscuits for supper. The goose turned up in various guises for a week, while the dripping cheered many a lean supper table in the frugal period between Christmas and pay day.

When the festive season was over the secret police claimed another victim — Rudolf Margolius. I went to see his wife, Heda, immediately after his arrest.

Heda's face was drawn, and she was chain-smoking. I had only ever seen her bubbling with high spirits. Her charm, original mind and quick wit had always made her the centre of attraction, whether among writers and artists, ministerial dignitaries or personal friends. The change moved me deeply. I searched for comfort — for her and myself.

'The police can't detain people indefinitely,' I said. 'And no court would convict Rudolf.' Rudolf, against whom, in a city that thrived on gossip, I had never heard a word of censure.

Heda sighed. 'Then perhaps he will leave the Ministry. I have begged him again and again to resign and take a less exposed position, but he always replies that as long as the Party needs him he will remain.'

Heda had had more than her share of tragedy. She and Rudolf and her parents had been sent on one of the first transports to the notorious Lódź camp in Poland. Later Rudolf was moved to another camp. By her presence of mind she saved her parents from the gas chamber several times, but when the end came she could only look on helplessly while they were dragged away. She herself had escaped. She had crossed the border into Czechoslovakia and walked to Prague, thinly clad in the depths of winter. After the revolution she and Rudolf had found each other. They thought their troubles were over. Now, it seemed, they might only be beginning. I left Heda full of foreboding. Rudolf was one more link with Pavel. Pavel had been questioned on the trade agreement Rudolf had negotiated with Britain, and on his 'contacts with Margolius'.

Chapter 8

Pavel's indefinite notice at the Ministry came to an abrupt end. He was assigned to the legal department of the Barbers' and Hairdressers' Corporation, dealing with complaints of burnt scalps, singed hair and cut throats, filed by dissatisfied customers. I had resigned from the factory because of a strained back and was now combining translating with housework, Květa having finally left us. Several months had gone by with no further arrests. So the five a.m. ring at the door bell on July came as a paralysing shock. We looked at each other dumbly. It could only be the security police. Somehow I found my dressing gown and went to open the door. Five impassive, broad-shouldered young men in standard leather coats stepped into the hall.

'Your husband is wanted for questioning,' one of them explained, not discourteously. 'A routine procedure.'

Of course, entirely routine, even the early hour.

'I'll make a cup of tea.'

One of them followed me into the kitchen. Pavel, too, kept up appearances, chatting to one of them while he washed and shaved. It would have been impolite to interrupt the conversation, therefore it had to be continued in the bathroom. He left the toilet door ajar. We both acted as normally as possible, as though we could ward off the abnormality of what had already come to pass that way; as though the right frame of mind could contain a situation in which we were so palpably helpless.

Pavel left with three of them. I slipped some lumps of sugar into his pocket, having heard of their reviving properties during long interrogations. We exchanged a brisk, leaving-for-the-office kiss. No significant utterances, no whispered protestations of innocence or declarations of faith. Just the quick dry brush of trembling lips on a cold cheek, the pressure of a hand that conveyed: 'Whatever happens, I am with you,' while aloud I said: 'Goodbye, darling, see you this afternoon.'

He was gone. For how long?

I went into the bathroom for an aspirin to clear my aching head. There was a splotch of shaving soap on the side of the basin. It was shaped like an octopus with one tentacle transfixed in the action of grasping, like Pavel reaching out for the thread of everyday life and finding it severed.

One of the remaining two security men said in the professional tone of a doctor about to examine a patient: 'We are obliged to search your flat.'

'If you can do so without causing too much disturbance, I shall be grateful. I can hear my two little boys getting up; I would prefer them not to be alarmed,' I said.

The young man nodded. But then Jan entered the room and asked directly: 'What are you doing here?'

'These gentlemen are from Tati's office,' I put in quickly. 'Tati has mislaid some papers and they are looking for them.' As hardly a day passed without their father searching for some item of major or minor importance, the boys accepted this excuse without comment.

The morning wore on. I answered questions, read stories to the boys, made fresh tea.

The older security man, stern and humourless, came over to me. 'What is this?'

A packet of white capsules among Pavel's papers. Poison? The last resort of the arch-spy? I explained that they were tablets for the relief of, of — a technical hitch: I could not remember the Czech word for indigestion — an upset stomach.

'And these?'

They were pills that Pavel had been taking for his heart, the others were for blood pressure.

'Your husband has a lot of pills,' he stated accusingly.

'He has a lot of illnesses,' I replied calmly.

'And what are these for?' he demanded with irritation.

'Hydrophobia,' I murmured.

He noted it down. Then he started to comb the bookshelves, selecting some books and putting them in his briefcase. Probably the authors were now proscribed. Pavel would never descend to book burning to suit the censor's whims. I translated the titles of the English books. Although mostly by communists, they were suspect. He had not heard of Harry Pollitt or Willie Gallacher, or Palme Dutt.

'Ha, what have we here?' He thrust a slim volume under my nose. It was a book of lewd jokes accompanied by suggestive drawings. 'You husband is an expert in pornography?'

Pavel? What a laugh! Pavel who was uncomfortable listening to dirty stories, whose thoughts were a hundred per cent bowdlerized, who never swore nor used terms of abuse even in his most abandoned rages.

'He borrowed it as an example of a degenerate Western publication and then forgot about it. He hasn't even read it.'

'A likely story,' the plainclothes man snorted.

I asked angrily: 'Has my husband been arrested for his taste in literature?'

'You will be informed in due course of the reason for your husband's arrest,' replied the other coldly. His eyes were pale and ruthless, blank windows on an empty mind; no education, no sense of proportion; he did not require either. He needed only one guideline — 'enemy of the people'.

He slipped the book into his case.

I said: 'I hope you will take good care of it; I shouldn't like it to corrupt the morals of the force.'

My irony was lost upon him.

They were leaving. The younger one thanked me for the tea. The older one threw him a contemptuous glance and stalked out, taking with him Pavel's gold-tipped fountain pen and the watch from the Soviet Counsellor.

I got lunch, sent the boys out to play in the garden, tidied up, translated a page or two, made supper, played with the boys, read them their bedtime story. But it was someone else performing these simple tasks. I was an onlooker. It brought back the time when I had been bombed out. I had seen the visual image of the burning house as a reflection in a mirror, heard the roar of planes remotely, muffled behind a thick, concrete wall. My mind had entrenched itself in a reinforced, reality-proof dugout. I am not really there when something unbearable happens to me. But for years afterwards I suffered the experience acutely in nightmares.

It was late in the evening. The day that had changed our whole lives had passed quietly. Pavel had not returned home.

People disappeared from public life and were spoken of in whispers as though they were dead. Now Pavel had joined these unnamed ghosts.

By the next evening my numbness had worn off. I began to notice the strange void around me. Nagging suspense and Pavel's oppressive presence had been removed. Pavel was behind bars. The horror of it flooded over me. What must he be thinking? 'Why me? What does it all mean? When shall I see my family again?' When, indeed? How long would he be gone, leaving me alone, solely responsible?

In our marriage, Pavel had made all the decisions; my life had rotated round his axis. Now I felt like a satellite flung off into space, required to revolve round its own axis, ignorant of its orbit and the forces against which it would have to contend. I heard Pavel's voice, saying: 'You'll never manage on your own.' My old sense of inadequacy returned and overwhelmed me. I didn't have the wisdom to guide the boys in a hostile environment, or the resources to withstand repression. I felt afraid of the future, afraid of the police and what they had yet in store.

I thought of Heda who had borne up bravely all these months. I was not alone. I stood up. The very action of straightening to my full height gave me resolution. I wouldn't allow 'them' to crush me. Intimidation was their trade mark. I would fight back with the only available weapon — courage. If I lacked it, I would fake it.

I phoned Karel. He came round.

'Why didn't you call me straightaway?' he asked.

'Yesterday there was still hope. What can we do?'

We started writing the first of many letters: to the Ministry of National Security, the Ministry of Justice, the Party Central Committee, protesting at Pavel's detention, demanding an explanation. These institutions either ignored our complaints or informed us at their leisure that 'the case is under consideration'.

Their father's absence passed unnoticed by the boys for a few days. He had often come home after they were in bed and left before they got up. But on Sunday they asked: 'Where's Tati?'

Should I tell them the truth or make up some feasible story like a trip abroad? The truth would be a shock; a lie would be difficult to sustain. But they might learn the truth from a thoughtless neighbour, and then I would lose their trust. So I said slowly; 'Some bad men are plotting to overthrow the government. The police have been wrongly informed that Tati knows something about it. They have taken him away to question him. When he has proved to them that he was not involved, they will let him come home again.'

They looked at me gravely, trying to assimilate this staggering indication of chaos in the grown-up world that until then had appeared to them stable and well ordered.

'Will it take long?' Jan asked.

'It may.'

Tears came to their eyes. I put an arm round each. 'You must be brave the way Tati is being brave. He is lonely and longing to see us, whereas we have each other.'

The boys grew up suddenly. They were no longer cuddly toddlers but solemn, wise youngsters, prematurely awakened to injustice and a sense of responsibility. They started attending nursery school so that I had more time for translating, and they did simple shopping on the way home. Outwardly they were calm, but one day I overheard Zdeněk saying to a recalcitrant member of his animal family: 'You be good, or they'll take you away, like they took Tati.'

Translating at home enabled me to fit in with the boys' timetable but the work was sporadic and so were the payments. I would have to get a regular job. Presumably I knew enough of my own language to teach it. The head of the English department of the Language Institute explained sadly that he had had to cut down his staff of full-time teachers but that he might be able to find me a few evening hours in two months' time. Studying English was discouraged, but we were still selling a third of our produce to the capitalist and developing countries. I looked up the addresses of foreign trade corporations where an English typist might come in useful. The first two were already stocked. At the third, a dapper little man almost embraced me with rapture.

'Do we need an English secretary? Very badly. You have Czech citizenship?'

'Yes, my husband is Czech.'

'Excellent. And you speak good Czech. I was afraid I'd have to send off this correspondence in my own inadequate English.' He whipped round his desk on small, light feet and picked up a pile of papers in pale, podgy fingers. 'You wouldn't glance at them, would you?'

I took the drafts, and covered them with red improvements while he exclaimed: 'Yes, yes, how stupid of me! Sequence of tenses! How time has wrought havoc with it! Ah, the English syntax! The years have snatched it from me, but it returns, it returns! Quite, quite, present tense in a conditional clause. I am as rusty as an old nail, I see that.'

'Oh no, a little brushing up will put everything right,' I murmured hypocritically.

He handed me an application form to fill in.

'Born in London, original nationality British,' he frowned. 'That is a certain disadvantage.'

I pointed out that I owed my perfect knowledge of English to this simple fact.

'True, true. Well, it cannot be helped,' he sighed. 'Parents born in England, resident in England. We cannot do anything about your parents,' he admitted in deep gloom.

My pen hovered over the set of rubrics reserved for my husband.

'What is the difficulty?'

'Shall I put my husband's last occupation?'

'Why, is he an invalid?'

'No, he is in custody waiting for some misunderstanding to be sorted out.'

The cherubic face drew back from mine, deathly pale. My would-be, and now would-not be, employer jumped up, pushed my handbag into my hand and showed me unceremoniously to the door.

'Good gracious, madam, why didn't you say so in the first place? Wasting my time! In jail — and she asks for a job here! My work is highly responsible.' He looked around frantically for signs of my having stolen orders of bottling machines for Zanzibar.

'Goodbye, comrade, I hope you find a suitable typist before your foreign customers cancel their orders.' I departed, blinking back tears of disappointment.

The *coup de grâce* was delivered the next day — a note summoning me to the Foreign Ministry's cadre department. The officer was a competent woman of about thirty-five. She spoke briskly: 'It is not a personal matter. We have nothing against you. But you must understand, under the circumstances — until your husband's — er position is cleared up' (she didn't believe it would be!) 'the Ministry — for security reasons — cannot maintain contact with you. You see that, of course, comrade?'

I did not. I did not see at all how my translations of articles that were checked before distribution could in any way affect the security of the state. I asked: 'Is it in the interest of the state that my children should starve to death?'

'Indeed not,' she replied in a shocked voice. 'You will be able to find work elsewhere, but the Ministry has certain regulations.'

'So has everyone else,' I remarked, not without bitterness.

To find myself unemployable in a state of full employment was an irony that I was in no mood to appreciate, especially as there was no unemployment benefit. The Labour Exchange only offered jobs in industry that I could not accept: my back was still troubling me and the shifts would make it impossible for me to look after the boys. The matter of a month's rent due nagged like toothache.

As I came into the flat the phone was ringing. It was Karel. He told me to take down an address. 'Go there tomorrow, they need a tracer.'

'A bullet?'

'No designs, plans — for the electrification of the railways. You trace other people's drawings.'

'Sounds pointless, anyway I've got no experience.'

'Do you need a job, or don't you?' Karel's carefully modulated voice fairly crackled down the line.

'Like hell I do.'

'Well, what are you quibbling about? Go along and see. Convince them you can learn; it shouldn't be difficult.'

In the Kavans' estimation nothing was ever difficult! If they wouldn't let me type letters that were going abroad, they'd never entrust me with plans of the railways. Sheer desperation led me to adopt an air of bravado. I strode into the office of a nervous, middle-aged man and without preamble delivered myself of the following:

'Good morning, I hear you are looking for a tracer. I have never done anything like it in my life, but I used to paint flowers rather nicely at school. I have been turned down wherever I have applied for work because I made the grave political error of being born in England of English parents, and my husband is detained on some unspecified charge, of which I would stake my life he is innocent. You must give me a job, first because I have two children and it is surely not feasible under socialism that they should go in want; second, I am not involved in my husband's case and it is intolerable that a wife should suffer for the problematic sins of her husband; third, I can learn anything under the sun, which will enable me to support my sons. I have even learnt Czech!'

It was an inspired performance.

Sympathy and apprehension chased across Mr Němec's face. As a human being he was on the side of the young mother in distress. But, I learned afterwards, he was a Catholic and therefore his perch was precarious: could he endanger it further by such a politically doubtful acquisition? His colleague, a younger man, put in quickly: 'The political responsibility lies with the cadre officer.'

The chief opened a slim black box, asking: 'I suppose you know what these are?'

I answered: 'They look like dental instruments, but they are probably what you use for your drawings.'

In despair Mr Němec handed me a ruler and pencil. 'Draw me a line,' he said.

I executed it with a bold, optimistic stroke.

'H'm, a steady hand. Looks promising. We'll take you on a month's trial, if the cadre department agrees.'

The administrative offices were in the main building a few streets away. A motherly woman in the personnel department handed me the familiar form. I filled it in and she offered to take it in to the cadre officer and put in a good word for me. I waited, clenching my hands, willing him to sign it. She emerged smiling, and said, 'It's all settled.' (Later, that cadre officer lost his job for carrying out his function in conformity with his conscience rather than the regulations.)

I sped back to the technical offices.

'You may start tomorrow,' said my new boss. 'We are short-staffed.'

I didn't get a wink of sleep. My confidence dropped to zero again. Arithmetic and geometry had been my worst subjects at school, accuracy my weakest point. I'd never hold the job down. I'd be tramping the streets again at the end of the month.

My first drawing the next day was marked TOP SECRET. The very illogicality of that struck a hopeful note.

This was my first contact with apolitical technicians. There were no sons of the ex-rich or collaborators among them. Although they could not claim affiliation with the working class, they were not intellectuals and none were Jewish. They had never been outside the country, and they didn't have relations living abroad. They were unassailable. They lived under the regime with reservations but without fear.

Mirek Podchůzka, a young man with thinning hair and a thickening waistline, greeted his new assistant with a groan: 'A female! What luck! I'd as soon expect a nun to catch syphilis as a woman to do accurate work!' He asked abruptly: 'Have you heard the one about the priest and the Stakhanovite milkmaid?' and he related a lewd joke.

Fortunately, smut and vulgarity lose their impact in a foreign tongue. Words that would have died on my lips in English had become everyday fare at the factory. Mirek failed to bring a blush to my cheeks. I racked my brains for a suitably near-the-bone counterpoint. The only joke I could remember was the one about the two lords fishing off a pier. One caught a beautiful mermaid, looked her over and tossed her back into the sea. 'Why?' asked his friend in astonishment. 'How?' enquired the first laconically.

Mirek chuckled condescendingly. He pinned a crumpled plan of the Main Station (marked TOP SECRET) onto a drawing board and fixed a piece of tracing paper over it. 'That's the part we are concerned with at the moment. We have to work out where the suspension points require fitting with stitch wires to make them more flexible and where ordinary droppers will do. For Gawd's sake don't muck it up! We're dead short of tracing paper. Božka, who's in charge of the stores, is worn out sleeping with the paper storemen in order to get us extra rations.'

For the rest of the day I airily scattered 'crap' around and invited Mirek to 'kiss my fanny' whenever pen, ink, nib, compass or one or other of his instruments mysteriously disappeared. After three days of teasing, singing salacious songs and attempting to confuse me with instructions and counter-instructions, to which I retaliated in like vein, Mirek gave in and asked: 'Care for a drink on the way home?'

In the small wineshop a stone's throw from the office, he confided: 'I was afraid that having a female among us would spoil the fun. I can't stand females who snivel when you pull their legs and faint at unexpurgated expressions. You know what Hašek's secretary asked when he first dictated the word 'shit' in *Švejk*? 'Shall I dot it?' 'If you've ever seen dotted shit, you may,' he replied. A woman who can swear like a trooper and support two kids without moaning is all right by me. So here's to "tykání".'

We clinked glasses and emptied them bottoms up as a pledge to address each other by the familiar 'thou'.

'Tell you what,' Mirek added. 'I'll guarantee your job in exchange for stories of your life.'

From then on Mirek took me under his wing. If you took him with a pound of salt and remained unruffled under all circumstances, he was a staunch friend. He began every morning with: 'Have you heard this one?' His jokes fell into two categories: rude and radioactive. The latter were anti-party or anti-state jokes, for which one could be sent to the uranium mines. For instance: XY, a Party leader, returns from a visit to Moscow. His wife asks: 'Were you unfaithful to me, dear?' He replies: 'Only five times dear. You know how it is, the comrades think of everything; it's part of the room service. And what about you, miláčku?' She answers: 'Only twice.' The Party leader asks: 'Who with, miláčku?' She replies: 'Once with the Czech Philharmonic, and once with the Sparta eleven.'

I had already observed that the Czech regards eating as one of the more sacred pleasures of life. Early in our marriage Pavel had dropped the remark: 'My mother never gave us the same meal twice in a year.' I had not taken it up. Apart from his conspicuous silence when other husbands extolled their wives' culinary exploits, Pavel had submitted with good grace to his fate. My apologetic preamble: 'It hasn't turned out quite like the book,' was accepted with the reply: 'That's all right, I eat anything,' while his expression conveyed: 'And, my God, I have to!'

Mirek excelled at gastronomic description. In moments of boredom at work he would recite a eulogy on the previous evening's meal, which immediately commanded the attention and expert comments of his colleagues. Mirek provided incontrovertible proof of his own contention: 'The Czech is a true animal, built compactly round his alimentary canal.' Every two or three days a large vanilla cake, jam-filled bun loaf or fruit-laden slab of pastry would be housed in the bottom drawer of his desk, and slices would be hacked off every hour or two, in addition to his regular mid-morning snack of bread and cold pork and mid-afternoon snack of bread and salami.

Observing my lean and hungry look, Mirek would usually push a piece over to me with the polite prompting: 'Go on eat it up; I'm as full as a sheep's gut.'

Towards the end of the month I handed Mirek the tracings on which I had lavished the maximum care, if not talent.

He picked up the top one, exclaiming: 'What in the name of all the saints is this? The groundplan of a kitchen? *Himmelhergot*, this bit looks like a stove pipe with rheumatic knee joints!'

'It's the contact wire.'

'And these harpoons?'

'The dimension indicators.'

He clutched his hair. '*Krucinálfagot!* Your lettering looks as though a spider with dysentery had fallen into the inkpot and bolted across the page.' But seeing my face he said: 'Don't look so glum. It's not the end of the world.'

'But it may be of my term with this firm.'

'In a bull's arse! Quit worrying; it'll give you wrinkles. What did I promise? You shan't be thrown out on the cobblestones. A few of these tracings'll pass. I'll re-do this heap of crap myself and share out the rest. The boys'll have them done in no time.'

The result of my month's probation was a pile of professional tracings.

'I am amazed at your progress,' declared Mr Němec. 'I shall have no hesitation in recommending you for a permanent job.'

As far as anything is permanent in this time and place, I added silently.

A buff envelope awaited me at home. My heart missed a beat. For six weeks I had heard nothing of Pavel. This must be news at last. I tore it open. The Ministry of National Security informed me in two type-written lines that my husband was 'remanded in custody on suspicion of anti-state activity'. I read it several times, uncomprehendingly. It was not unexpected. Heda had received a similar communication. Yet now I stared at the words as though they were in a strange language. My head buzzed, my eyes blurred, I could not move. I tried to get a grip on myself. A drink would have helped, but my shoe-string budget cut out alcohol. My Russian teacher's universal panacea would have to do. I tottered to the window, threw it open and took ten slow deep breaths, emptying my mind. My nervous system returned to normal. I tried to view the situation calmly. Suspicion was a far cry from proven guilt. I must not dissipate my energy in needless pessimism; I needed every erg.

The next day I stayed on in the office to finish some work. Mr Němec's assistant, Sláva, dropped in. He glanced at my drawings.

'Ah, the Spišská Ves-Žilina line. I hear you're doing well. I had a hunch you would. When recruiting staff, we put a premium on enthusiasm rather than qualifications, as no one in the country has had any experience in electrification, except Němec. You said: 'I can learn anything' with such conviction I thought the time spent in training you would be a good investment. And', he added bashfully, 'I admired your spirit.'

Perched on the edge of my desk, he began to talk about the problems of our department. There was a lack of know-how, yet the ban on foreign travel precluded inspection of completed tracks abroad. No technical literature from the West was available. Consequently, calculations had to be made, tables compiled and problems solved from scratch, whereas reference to foreign experience would have saved time and effort. There were also difficulties with material. Under the present autarkic system all equipment had to be made in Czechoslovakia. Copper for the contact wire had to be imported from the Belgian Congo for hard currency, of which Czechoslovakia was short. We would soon be obliged to replace copper by steel aluminium conductors, which would bring fresh problems.

Once broached, Sláva flowed like a tapped barrel. His job was his life. He would have gone on happily for an hour or two, had I not reminded him of my obligation to purchase and cook supper for two hungry boys. But I performed these unimaginative tasks in a pleasant glow. I was learning a job that was new not only to me but to Czechoslovakia. The electrification of rail transport was in its infancy and I was one of its godmothers.

After the chat with Sláva, I was promoted from tracer to draughtswoman. I was still largely at sea because I was learning piecemeal. I gathered that we were using a 3kV d.c. overhead contact system; the current was supplied via main and auxiliary cables to the contact wire and collected by a pantograph attached to the roof of the locomotive. From sketches and photographs

I could visualize the situation on an open line. Complications set in in stations and junctions, and bends in the track were a jungle of catenaries running parallel to the lines and crossed by others at right angles.

I was impatient to learn the whole system. I persuaded Mirek to take me to the Main Station with a plan of the layout so that I could coordinate reality with its blueprint. Armed with our pass cards, we scrambled over lines that ordinary mortals might not cross. I recognized with joy the different kinds of contact wire anchorage, rigid or movable. Parts with unpronounceable names, like *boční držák*, acquired feasible functions when seen in the round and in context. Gradually the mystery sorted itself out. I began to follow with interest discussions about current collection in low tunnels, or in the vicinity of domestic power grids and other unorthodox situations.

Mirek gave me my first design to execute. His instructions were colourful, if not explicit: 'The bastards that laid this track for steam had no consideration for future electrification. They constructed a pig of a bend that is making me a bloody heap of trouble. Take these two parts and cook up something to hang them together.'

The finished design drew the comment: 'It doesn't exactly fit like a baby's bot in a chamber pot; but, as the degree of tolerance is large, I'll pass your puerile effort.'

I was as elated as if I had had a masterpiece accepted by the Royal Academy.

To mark the occasion, a long-awaited letter from Pavel arrived. It was short:

'Darling,

It is many years since I last wrote you a love letter. Today I should like to write one again. I see now that I am bound to you by closer ties than I had imagined during the past years when we were both often stubborn. My greatest concern is what you and the children are living on. Are you still getting articles to translate? Do not worry about me. I have everything I am entitled to.

Love and kisses to you and the boys.

Your

Pavel.'

I read and re-read it. Tears were running down my face, tears that washed away tempers and misunderstandings. Like an art restorer soaking away overlayers of paint to reach the original, they left only the passion and tenderness.

There was exciting news for me at the office too: Mirek and I were to be the first to try out a new method, using a contact wire with flexible fastening and no steady arm, which, it was hoped, would save thirty to forty per cent of wire. The line, running from Čerchov to Lipno, in southern Bohemia, had to be modernized for the transport of heavy freight now that a dam and reservoir were planned at Lipno. The technical bug had bitten me. My thoughts became entirely absorbed by the Čerchov–Lipno line. Original plans and designs accumulated under the abbreviation KAV.

No sooner had I reinforced my defence line of working enthusiasm, than I received a stab in the rear from the security police. Two plainclothes men came to the house to abduct the Minx. I objected that my husband had been neither charged nor sentenced and would certainly be released from custody.

'No one ever is,' was the ominous reply.

They drove off. But I had removed and sold the good tyres, and replaced them with old ones as bald as eggs. I hoped the police would discover to their cost that the brakes worked only by the grace of God.

The police had undermined my resolution not to indulge in fruitless conjectures about the future. The likelihood of Pavel's release seemed more and more remote. Suspicion was tantamount to indictment. How long would I be able to keep going? To augment my meagre earnings I had taken a part-time job at the Language Institute (screening for jobs on an ad hoc basis was less stiff than for full-time jobs). On three evenings a week I conversed in English for four hours, after nine hours at the drawing board, while the good-hearted women of our house fed, bathed and bedded my two poor sons by rota. This might go on for years.

I thought of Pavel, accustomed to dominate. How was he faring in prison, at the mercy of moronic warders, despised by his inferiors, misjudged by his peers? How was he employing his restless energy with nothing to occupy him? He had always had a tendency to hypochondria. At the first sign of a cold he would take to his bed with his favourite bottles of medicine. A sore throat or a headache sent him in search of the thermometer.

A coated tongue presaged the onset of some dire disease. How then was he enduring the privations of prison life? How was his heart standing the strain of uncertainty?

A weight of depression settled upon me.

My colleagues made several abortive attempts to cheer me up. One morning, after an hour's subdued silence on my part, Mirek observed with his customary bluntness: 'Rozmarýnka, you look as though you had sour cucumbers for breakfast. What's up?'

I told him.

'A dose of *Švejk* is what you need,' he declared.

Our two bosses being away on a tour of inspection the mice felt free to play. Mirek took a tattered volume from his desk, announcing: 'Comrades, a few words from our inimitable morale officer, Jaroslav Hašek, for Comrade Kavanová's benefit. In view of her present situation, Švejk's interrogation on suspicion of high treason may prove edificatory.'

My colleagues brightened. Mirek read aloud:

'Mounting the staircase to the Third Department for interrogation, Švejk carried his cross to Golgotha, blissfully unconscious of his martyrdom . . .

As he came into the office, he said: "A very good evening to you all gentlemen."

Instead of a reply, he got a poke in the ribs and was told to stand in front of a table, behind which there sat a gentleman with a cold official face and features of such bestial brutality that he might have fallen out of Lombroso's book, *Criminal Types*.

Giving Švejk a bloodthirsty look, he said: "Take that idiotic look off your face."

"I can't help it,' replied Švejk seriously. "I was discharged from the army for idiocy and officially pronounced an idiot by a special commission. I am an official idiot!"

The gentleman of the criminal mien ground his teeth:

"What you are accused of and what you have committed proves that you are all there."

And he proceeded to enumerate a whole series of different crimes, beginning with high treason and ending with abuse of his Majesty and members of the Imperial Family . . .

"What have you to say to that?" the gentleman with features

of bestial brutality asked triumphantly.

"There's a lot of it," Švejk replied innocently. "You can have too much of a good thing."

"So you admit it's true."

"I admit everything. You've got to be strict. Without strictness we wouldn't get anywhere. Like when I was serving in the army . . ."

"Shut up!" the police officer shouted, "and speak only when you're questioned! Do you understand?"

"You bet I do," said Švejk. "I humbly report that I understand and that everything you are pleased to say is crystal clear to me."

At his second interrogation Švejk was asked: "Do you confess to everything?"

Švejk fixed his kindly blue eyes on the pitiless man and said softly: "If you want me to confess, Your Honour, I shall. It can't do me any harm. But if you say: 'Švejk, don't confess anything!' I'll deny it with the last breath in my body."

The severe gentleman wrote something on the document and handed Švejk a pen, ordering him to sign it. And Švejk signed Bretsneider's deposition with the following addition:

All the above-named charges against me are founded on fact. Josef Švejk

. . . His fellow prisoners deluged him with questions, to which Švejk replied clearly: "I have just confessed that I probably killed the Archduke Ferdinand."'

Everyone in the office laughed. They all knew their *Švejk* by heart, but the book never ceased to strike a chord. Little did we dream that this bizarre passage would soon become a monstrous reality.

Chapter 9

The trial of the 'Anti-state Conspiratorial Centre' in fact outdid Hašek.

The different people who had been arrested at various times over the previous three years were now linked in one large-scale conspiracy, led by Rudolf Slánský. Thirteen other conspirators were named, including Rudolf Margolius, Otto Šling, Vladimír Clementis, Artur London and Bedřich Geminder. Scores of 'witnesses' for the prosecution were to be called. I presumed Pavel would be among them.

The trial started on 20 November 1952 and lasted a week. Parts of it were broadcast over the radio and reported in the press.

I do not know how I got through those days of suspense, waiting for Pavel to speak. I remember my mounting horror as the state prosecutor enumerated the charges. I had expected error, negligence, deviation from the Party line — all of which are open to loose interpretation — but not espionage, sabotage of the economy and undermining domestic and foreign policies, in short high treason. According to the prosecution, the conspiracy had been master-minded by Tito with the aim of moulding Czechoslovakia's future on Yugoslav lines and of weakening the Soviet Union's position in the communist sphere.

The star spy part was allotted to Konni Zilliacus who, masked as a left-wing Social Democrat, had travelled to the People's Democracies, meddled in their internal affairs and established contact with right-wing Social Democrats and hostile elements inside the communist parties. He had been 'directly responsible for Yugoslavia's defection to the war-mongering West', the prosecution claimed.

I could not believe my ears. Zilly, the *enfant terrible* of the Labour Party, a spy! I pictured his great bulk and round face, with its protruding teeth ever visible in an amiable grin, gracing receptions held by the Eastern bloc countries, liked and trusted by all. It occurred to me that if he were really the 'master of deceit and provocation' described by the prosecution, he must have been spying on the other socialist countries as well, yet he had not figured in the Hungarian and Bulgarian political trials.

I recalled the many pleasant evenings we had spent at the Zilliacuses in Maida Vale; in particular a candle-lit dinner party at which I had set my hair alight rocking with immoderate mirth at one of Zilly's jokes. Pavel and Zilliacus had frequently exchanged views on British and Czechoslovak policies. With a sinking heart, I wondered what fantastic accusations would be brought against Pavel.

I missed the excerpt from Slánský's testimony while I was putting the boys to bed. I switched on the radio in time to here the presiding judge, Dr Novák, ask witness for the prosecution Dr Eduard Goldstücker: 'When and how did Slánský gain your collaboration in his anti-state activity?'

A shiver went down my spine. The question was a presumption of guilt.

Eda replied: 'It was the beginning of 1946. Slánský told me he was aware of my past, of my Jewish bourgeois background . . .'

This was nonsense. Eda came from a poor family in a small Slovak village. His father had caught malaria at the front during the First World War and had died in 1924 when Eda was eleven years old. His mother had barely made ends meet, working as a cook.

Eda admitted sending correspondence between Zilliacus and Clementis, Geminder, Slánský and Frejka[23] (Head of the Economic Department of the President's Office) via Artur London. He gave no details, but his use of phrases such as 'accomplices', 'maintaining contacts' and 'infringement of state security' imparted a cloak-and-dagger colouring to what I believed to be a harmless exchange of letters. I remembered

---

23. Ludvík Frejka (1904–1952) joined the CP in 1923. He fled to England in 1939. In 1945 he became Chairman of the Economic Commission of the CC and economic adviser to the Prime Minister. He was executed with Slánský in 1952.

hearing about one of them. It contained an analysis of the Israeli situation by Bohuslav Kratochvíl, who had been our Ambassador during part of our stay in London. Together with articles by Zilliacus on the same subject, this had been despatched to Clementis for reference at the United Nations.

Questioned about his appointment as Envoy to Israel in August 1949, Eda replied that it was his reward for arranging espionage contacts with Zilliacus. Slánský asked him to establish similar contacts in Israel which, Eda admitted, was pursuing a policy 'in the interest of Western imperialism'.

This was confusing: a year ago the Soviet Union had been the first country to recognize the newly founded State of Israel; Czechoslovakia had supplied arms to Palestine from 1945 to 1948.

I was at a loss. Something was wrong. Eda had spoken calmly and slowly, as was his habit, and yet there was a difference. I couldn't nail it; but it was there.

'Dr Pavel Kavan.'

At the sound of his name all my senses were alert. The prosecutor addressed him as 'Zionist bourgeois nationalist and Titoist.' I gripped my chair. The appellations were in themselves an indictment. But they were completely untrue. Zionism had been of mere academic interest to Pavel; he had never advocated it as a solution for Czechoslovak Jews. In fact Pavel never referred to himself as a Jew. His parents had been assimilated by the non-Jewish community when he was still a boy and he regarded himself first and foremost as a Czech. Had it not been for Hitler, the racial criterion would not have been applied to his family. Since 1948 Pavel had been an anti-Titoist in accordance with the Party line. In 1951 he had accepted the diplomatic defector's account of Yugoslavia as a police state where capitalism was being restored against the wishes of the people. The term nationalist puzzled me. It could perhaps be applied to Pavel in the sense that he was proud of his country's traditions and achievements. But that could hardly be defined as a political crime. Later I learned that nationalists were people who put their country's interests before those of the Soviet Union.

The prosecutor asked Pavel whether he was a member of the anti-state conspiracy. Holding my breath, I waited for his denial. My heart was thumping so loudly I could hardly hear his voice.

'Yes,' Pavel replied. 'During my stay in London I acted as an intermediary between Konni Zilliacus, agent of the British Intelligence Service, and Rudolf Slánský, head of the anti-state conspiracy, and his accomplice Bedřich Geminder.'

Pavel was referring to a meeting he had arranged between Zilliacus and Slánský in Prague in August 1946. He could not give the substance of the conversation because it had been conducted in Russian. Asked for details about further espionage contacts, Pavel said:

'At the beginning of 1948, when I was working at the Czechoslovak Embassy in London, Zilliacus asked me to visit him in the House of Commons. He gave me a copy of a speech he had made in Parliament, and a letter, and asked me to convey them to Slánský. I sent them to Prague by courier with a brief covering letter. In July Zilliacus handed me a sealed envelope in his house and asked me to send it to Slánský.'

'But, you didn't know what was in it. Why don't you say so, you fool?' screamed a woman's voice. With a shock I realized it was my own. Involuntarily I had rushed across the room and shouted at the set. Unnerved by Pavel's inexplicable behaviour, I returned to my seat, scarcely able to concentrate on the rest of his testimony. Then — surely my dazed senses had played me false? — Pavel began his next reply before the prosecutor had properly formulated the question, like an actor skipping his cue. His cue! The thought hit me like a physical blow in the chest, causing me to gasp for breath. Pavel had known what question to expect. Did this mean that he had known all the questions beforehand and was drawing attention to this salient fact?

Stunned by the implications, I missed part of Pavel's testimony. When I had gathered my wits, he was saying: 'I sent several letters from British agent Konni Zilliacus to Geminder, the content of which I do not remember . . . I passed on two espionage reports from Margolius to Zilliacus, one in the spring of 1949, the second later in the year; in this Margolius informed Zilliacus of difficulties encountered during negotiations on the British–Czechoslovak trade agreement.'

In actual fact, I remembered, Rudolf had merely requested Zilly's assistance in ironing out differences.

Pavel was asked what he knew of Artur London. He replied:

'He was one of the leading members of the Trotskyist–Zionist faction at the Ministry of Foreign Affairs. He maintained espionage contacts with British agent Zilliacus for

Slánský and Geminder . . .'

I reflected: Pavel had a great admiration for Artur; if he had been answering freely, he would have told the court that Artur had fought in Spain and had been awarded the Croix d'Honneur for his services to the Maquis.

The witness was told to stand down. One question blotted out all others in my mind. On principle Pavel never admitted blame; how then had he been forced to confess to something of which he was innocent? I turned over Pavel's testimony. His voice had sounded normal, but something was unnatural. Then it came to me. His speech was in the style of written, not spoken, Czech — the written Czech of newspaper editorials. Pavel and Eda, whose natural modes of expression differed vastly, had employed exactly the same phraseology. This, too, suggested that they were reciting a script that had been written before the trial opened.

Rudolf Margolius's testimony, which followed soon after, confirmed my hypothesis. He spoke in a high-pitched monotone, as though in a trance. He confessed to 'widespread espionage and sabotage in foreign trade, aimed at disrupting the Czecho-slovak economy', motivated by hatred toward the working class and the Communist Party, which attitude he owed to his upbringing in a Jewish capitalist family. Most of his relatives were active Zionists, he said, who had emigrated to capitalist countries, mainly Israel, after the war.

Lies, lies, I cried inwardly. Both his parents and nearly all his relatives were gassed by the Nazis. He joined the Communist Party partly out of admiration for the courage shown by com-munists in the concentration camps.

Sadly I pictured Heda listening in. I had visited her in hospital on the first day of the trial. She was very ill: hollow cheeks, eyes glazed with morphia and sunken in huge black rings, lips yellowish-grey. She had been relieved to see me: a friend who believed as firmly as she did in Rudolf's innocence. The women in the ward were talking about 'those traitors' and their 'chances of the rope'.

After denouncing himself as an enemy of the people, who had tried to undermine socialism and Comecon, Rudolf ad-mitted: '. . . I sent espionage reports to Zilliacus through Pavel Kavan in London.'

There was a macabre irony in the situation: two friends were sending each other to the gallows while their wives were trying to comfort each other.

Rudolf was charged with 'agreeing to export television tubes under the trade pact with Britain,' knowing that they could be used for military purposes. He admitted that he had thereby 'strengthened Britain's war potential and weakened Czechoslovakia's defence capability'.

My mind flashed back to 1949. The Czechs at the Embassy had teased Rudolf for his extreme caution. He had conferred with Prague at every stage before proceeding with the negotiations. In no way could he be held solely responsible: the treaty could not have been signed without the approval of the Czechoslovak Economic Council; the government had ratified the signed agreement.

The voice that was Rudolf's and yet was not Rudolf's went on in the same vein: exports of this, imports of that; every item that had crossed the border had injured Czechoslovakia's interests, proving that Rudolf's aim was to orient Czechoslovak trade away from the Soviet Union and toward the West.

I was too exhausted to demolish all the arguments. The whole trial was a nightmare. The next day I went to see Heda. Ill as she was, she had been discharged from hospital on the ground that the current shortage of beds left no room for the wife of a traitor.

'You heard Rudolf's testimony?' she asked.

I nodded, declaring that I didn't believe a word of it. A man whose life was at stake did not incriminate himself without a stumble.

'He had to memorize it, I know he did,' she cried in anguish. 'He had a bad memory for facts, he always had to look them up.'

Assuming that the defendants were unwilling actors in a prepared scenario, the question still remained: how had they been induced to perform? Particularly someone like Rudolf who had no faculty for learning by rote?

Heda was convinced drugs had been administered.

Drugs that would destroy the will and leave the memory intact? No, no, I protested, not in civilized Czechoslovakia.

Heda gripped my hand. 'They won't hang Rudolf, will they? Tell me they won't let him die.'

Ah dear Heda, I would have given ten years of my life for that assurance. I stroked her hand wordlessly.

She vowed: 'I'll scrub floors for the rest of my life, if only they don't hang him. If they give him a life sentence, I'll be happy.

Just to visit him once a month, to know that he is alive and thinking of us is all I ask. How can I live without him? There will never be anyone like Rudolf.'

'At least you have known real love,' was all the comfort I could give. It was trite but so true. Few find true and lasting love, perfect companionship and understanding that deepens and ripens with the years, as they had done, so that to know them was to enrich one's own life.

Heda smiled wistfully: 'Yes, no one can take that away from me.'

I had found blatant loopholes in the testimonies given by Pavel, Eda and Rudolf. I was still unable to explain why the leading spy role had been assigned to Konni Zilliacus. Then Karel turned up with a book concealed among the office files and tins of fish in his brief-case. Karel had a remarkable talent for procuring proscribed literature. I read it long into the night, and Zilly's transgression became clear. He had written in praise of Tito after Tito had been outlawed by the Soviet Union. He had cast doubts on the authenticity of the political trials in Bulgaria and Hungary. He had described reforms carried out by Tito's government that might well have awakened a desire for emulation in the other socialist countries. Zilliacus had had to be discredited.

The trial wore on. Not one of the accused or a single prosecution witness attempted to defend himself. All pleaded guilty to every item in their indictment. Not a voice in the mass media questioned the speciousness of the prosecution's arguments or the lack of real evidence. On the contrary, public hysteria was whipped up. Hundreds of resolutions demanding the death sentence, purporting to come from factories, offices, trade unions and so on, were quoted daily in the press.

Everything hinged on the defence counsel. I waited tensely for the defence lawyers to speak. A little research would have armed them with arguments to demolish the prosecution's case. Alas, the defence was a mere formality. No witnesses were called. The defence put no case. Its role too had been precisely defined.

The prosecution demanded the death sentence for all fourteen defendants. The monstrous charade was almost played out. The presiding judge pronounced the verdict: Guilty! It was a foregone conclusion. That was the real conspiracy: a conspiracy by the security police, the judiciary — and who else? — to condemn fourteen men for crimes they had not committed.

Eleven defendants were sentenced to death; three — Artur London, Evžen Löbl[24] and Vavro Hajdú — to life imprisonment.

I spent a sleepless night. Every time I closed my eyes figures dangling on the end of a rope dragged me back to consciousness.

On the afternoon of 3 December the executions were carried out, just six days after sentence had been passed. The curtain had dropped on one of the most shameful episodes in Czecho-slovak history.

After an interminable day, staring at drawings that conveyed nothing to me, I took the tram to Letná. With infinitely sad eyes, Heda was alone in her still flat. Even the clock was silent. Rudolf's photograph was in its usual place on a small table, but the gentle smile which only yesterday had been full of peace and hope now seemed far away, dwelling on thoughts we would never read.

'Did you see him?' I asked. 'Or don't you want to talk about it?'

'Yes, I saw him,' she said quietly. 'But the guards would not let me take his hand and give him a last kiss. We were separated by two wire partitions.'

Facing each other like animals in a zoo. They weren't even allowed to spend their last moments together like human beings.

'I promised him that I would bring Ivan up to be proud of his father's memory, that I would fight to clear his name. Then they led him away. We had had only a few minutes together, but I think he went to his death knowing that he was not alone.'

She looked so frail, as though a puff of wind would blow her apart. She struggled for composure. 'Yesterday I thought I would die if they murdered Rudolf. But I must live, because of Ivan.'

Knowing Heda's extraordinary vitality, I was convinced she would rally. She would never recover from the inward wound but outwardly she would regain her zest for living. She was like

---

24. Evžen Löbl (1927–87) joined the CP in 1934 and spent the war years in En-gland. He was Jan Masaryk's economic adviser and worked in the Ministry of Foreign Trade after 1945. From 1948 he was a Deputy Minister until his arrest in 1951. He was sentenced to life imprisonment, but released in 1960. Until 1968 he served as the director of the State Bank in Bratislava. He emigrated in 1968 and now works as a lecturer in the USA.

the rose that thrived on a dunghill, and bloomed far into the bleak winter.

The trial left me plagued with questions. What purpose had it served? At a guess I would say it served as a cover-up for economic deficiencies. I knew from my factory experience that blame could not be attached to a handful of top-notchers; inefficiency and muddle existed at all levels. Nevertheless, the Jews had been offered as the time-honoured scapegoat. (The prosecution had stressed the Jewish origin of the majority of the defendants and witnesses.) The defendants had been accused of serving Western interests. This would justify discrimination against all those who had lived or fought in the West. The trial would also act as a warning to potential Czech Titoists, and to the Slovaks: the main crime of which the Slovaks, Clementis, Novomeský[25] and Gustáv Husák[26] (who ousted Dubček in 1969), were accused was 'bourgeois Slovak nationalism'.

Who, then, were the fabricators? I did not believe a trial of that dimension could have been staged without full discussion by Gottwald, the Party presidium and the Politburo. Heda and Karel, and surely other wives and relatives, had addressed letters to the Party leadership and the Ministries concerned, setting out the true facts and suggesting that the confessions had been obtained under duress. In any case, the leading politicians and economists must have recognised from their own knowledge and experience that the indictment was an invention. They could have saved the defendants, had they wished. If they had not chosen to do so, it was from fear of being incriminated or because they themselves were among the fabricators.

Why had there been no public outcry? I could not understand this. Then I remembered the *Trial of the Vatican Agents*. I had

25. Laco Novomeský (1904–76) joined the CP in 1926 and worked as an editor of Communist newspapers and established his reputation as a poet. Imprisoned in 1951 for bourgeois nationalism, he was released in 1955. From 1968 he was a member of the Presidium of the CC of the Slovak Communist Party.

26. Gustáv Husák (1913–) was a member of the illegal Slovak Communist Party in Bratislava during the war. In 1951 he was sentenced to life imprisonment but was released in1960. In 1968 he was a Deputy Prime Minister and was elected as First Secretary of the CP in April 1969. He became President in 1975.

taken it at its face value, having no counter-evidence. I found my copy of the transcript and re-read it. With growing consternation I recognized the same technique, the same mechanical responses to a prepared script, the same confessions of sabotage and foreign contacts. I was appalled. I, too, had condemned innocent men. These monstrous proceedings made monsters of us all. (In self-defence I could only say that reading a transcript in Slovak, with which I was less familiar than Czech, made a far weaker impact then hearing the drama enacted.)

In the light of my self-discovery, I tried to re-assess the effect of the Slánský trial on the public. Spies and saboteurs — real or invented — had been served up since 1948. The atmosphere existed for the unmasking of a gigantic conspiracy to end all conspiracies. People who had believed the previous trials must believe the latest one too. Many would not find the manner in which the trials were conducted strange: 'self-criticism' was a Party ritual; turgid anti-imperialist hysteria had long been the language of the media. On the other hand, the Slánský trial had exceeded all bounds; this must surely give rise to misgivings. Communists, of course, would be bound to smother any suspicions, pledged as they were to trust the Party implicitly. Noncommunists, if my colleagues at work were any guide, regarded it as one of a series of rigged trials.

'This one's a case of dog eats dog, that's the difference,' said one of them. 'Švermová[27] was jailed for preparing a coup against Slánský. Then she's accused of backing Slánský, Clementis and Šling against Gottwald. Taussigová[28] caused Šling's downfall and ends up testifying as Šling's accomplice! Not that I'd waste a night's sleep over a bunch of commies. No offence, Rozmarýnka, your husband may be a cut above the rest.'

Mirek burst out: 'Slánský, Reicin[29] and Šváb are the very ones

---

27. Marie Švermová (1902–   ) became a member of the CP in 1921 and of its CC in 1929. After her brother, Karel Šváb, was executed with Slánský in 1952, she was sentenced to life imprisonment in 1954. She was released in 1956, rehabilitated but not reinstated politically.

28. Jarmila Potůčková-Taussigová spent the war in the Ravensbruck concentration camp. After the war she worked for the Party Control Commission and was a member of the CC. She was imprisoned in 1951.

29. Bedřich Reicin (1911–1952) became a member of the CP Secretariat in 1936. He spent most of the war in Moscow and remained in the army after liberation. He was Chief of Military Intelligence, then Deputy Minister of Defence. He was executed with Slánský in 1952.

who built up the state security into a man-eating machine. Šváb was responsible for sending Milada Horáková[30] to the gallows — a mother and a woman of guts who'd spent five years in Gestapo prisons. She was executed on trumped-up charges of treason because she was a leader of the Socialist Party and a Catholic.'

'But surely this sort of madness is alien to communism,' I protested.

'You're nuts!' said Mirek. 'You're the only one of us here who's suffered politically, yet you still believe in Marx as the new Messiah. Poor Rozmarýnka,' he reached out and ruffled my hair. 'Your Mum must have dropped you on your head when you were in nappies.'

The trial of Dr Horáková, accused of organizing a conspiracy of former capitalists and members of the pre-February parties, had been held in the summer of 1950, while we were still in London. Officially, the Embassy had condemned her. I had known too little of the political background to form an opinion. Inwardly I deplored the sentence: to hang a woman for a political crime was diabolic. Yet I had kept silent. My happy life with my children in safe, sane England had pushed Dr Horáková out of my mind. Now I remembered her with horror and remorse.

I felt completely disorientated. But of one thing I was certain. Pavel was innocent. He was incapable of betraying his political ideals or of committing a dishonourable act in their defence. I was glad I had been rejected by the Party. I was not bound by Party discipline. I was free to believe implicitly in Pavel's innocence. Pavel was still alive. Pavel might yet be saved. There was no vehicle for public protest. The censored press would publish nothing. But what about a petition to the government with signatures? I was sure that if I spoke to people individually, I would convince them of Pavel's innocence. Hundreds would sign.

Karel dismissed the idea with scorn. 'Don't be so naive. This isn't England. You'd land the signatories and yourself in jail and the boys in a home. You've got to keep out of trouble: they need you.'

That was the one argument that carried weight. But I still

---

30. Milada Horáková (1901–1950) joined the Socialist Party in 1929. From 1945–48 she was a member of Parliament. She was executed in 1950.

protested that to remain silent was to condone the whole farce.

'Leave it to me,' Karel exhorted me sternly. 'I know who to speak to on the Central Committee.'

Alas, the Central Committee did not want to know the truth. No one would receive Karel. We continued to write letters to the relevant authorities. They went unanswered. Karel lost his executive job and was demoted to unskilled worker in a glue factory. From time to time he believed he had found a way to a communist in a high place, but his hopes were always dashed.

It was assumed among our friends that the prosecution witnesses would eventually be brought to trial. I could ascertain nothing from the authorities, not even where Pavel was held. I wrote to the central prison authority requesting a visit. This, too, met with silence.

Chapter 10

At last, some weeks after the trial, permission to visit Pavel arrived. It was for Karel as well as me. We were to report at the Bartolomějská Street police headquarters. Pavel was to be brought there from prison. Inside the building we were escorted by two armed guards. Suddenly I feared the meeting I had been looking forward to so much. Pavel had been in prison for six months. He had been subjected to interrogations. God knew what ghastly methods had been used to extort his confession. Would he not be a physical and mental wreck? I steeled myself as we were led into an office furnished with black leather chairs. Pavel was already seated. Unexpectedly he was in civilian clothes. He looked paler, thinner, older, lined and saddened, but his spirit was unbroken, as far as I could see.

'You may speak of family matters only,' the guard inside warned us, taking up a stand by the window.

I sat down and looked into Pavel's eyes. He gazed steadfastly into mine. They were not the eyes of a guilty man facing the family he had shamed. Nor were they the eyes of a coward who had abjectly confessed to imaginary crimes and incriminated others in order to save his own skin. A wave of tenderness enveloped me. I leaned toward him and kissed him quickly. His face lit up and looked less grey and drawn.

'How are the boys?' he asked.

'Oh, they're fine.' There was no point in telling him that Jan was at home again with one of his periodical inflammations of the middle ear.

How was Zdeněk getting on at school, wasn't it too great a strain on his constitution; shouldn't I have left him at nursery school another year? How was Jan's handwriting, had it improved?

'And how about you? Isn't your job too difficult for you? It sounded awfully technical in your letter.'

Proudly I launched into a description of my work.

'But how can you manage a demanding full-time job and the boys, now that you have no help in the home?' Pavel persisted.

His unchanged attitude brought home to me the fact that I had changed. I had grown accustomed to my dual role as breadwinner and housewife; it no longer seemed insupportable. I reassured him and went on to brighter things. I told him of the puppet shows and children's theatre I took the boys to on Sunday afternoons, a film I had seen. (It was the only one since he'd been arrested but I made it sound as though the cinema was a regular part of my life.) He enquired after Eva and Karel's new wife. It was all so inconsequential. There was so much I wanted to ask: Why? What have they done to you? What will happen to you now?

Karel offered a bag of sweets to Pavel, rustling the paper furiously and talking loudly. Pavel took the hint; he whispered to me out of the corner of his mouth: 'I am innocent.'

'I know,' I mouthed back.

'Speak up!' called the voice from the window. The young guard took up a position nearer to the table, which precluded further attempts at unobserved communication. The most important thing had been said; explanations would have to wait. The guard glanced at his watch.

'Time's up.'

Pavel's face, which had been flushed with animation, paled and set into grim lines. His eyes filled with the sadness of an animal that anticipates separation and cannot express its grief. I threw my arms round his neck, kissed him on the lips and whispered: 'Don't despair! We all believe in you. You'll get out,' before the guard seized my arm and pushed me roughly through the door.

I stumbled out of the building, fighting back tears. That night I couldn't sleep. Pavel's image formed in my mind's eye. Shaven, wearing a lounge suit, seated in an armchair. So nearly the picture of a free man, yet so far from freedom. Once again the tragic hero.

A few days after my visit two security men came to my office. It was about 4.30.

'Come along with us, Mrs Kavanová.'

The dreaded words. My heart sank. This was it. What about the boys? Who will tell them? Who will get the supper? I breathed deeply. Don't anticipate. Play it by ear, step-by-step. An ice-cold calm took hold of me.

'If you'll take a seat until we finish work,' I indicated a small empty office.

'Tell your boss we've come for you; he'll release you,' said one of them.

'I'm engaged in work of national importance,' I parried. 'Our deadline is approaching. It's essential I complete my task.'

'Mrs Kavanová, I'm losing my patience,' the security man snapped. 'Just explain the situation to your boss.'

Shrugging, I repaired to Mr Němec's office. He turned deathly pale and croaked: 'The security police, here! In this building!' I thought he was going to faint. 'Go, go, get them out of here. Never mind your desk. Someone will clear away for you.'

Our Hillman Minx was drawn up outside the building. One of the plainclothes men motioned me to get in the back with him. The other took the seat next to the driver. No one spoke.

'Well, gentlemen, how is my car behaving?' I asked sarcastically. 'I hope you've had the brakes fixed.'

One of them grunted in reply.

'Where are you taking me?' I asked.

'You'll find out,' the one next to me snarled.

We did not turn off toward Bartolomějská, but headed across town — perhaps towards the Pankrác prison. The silence was getting on my nerves.

'What do you want of me?' I asked, to break it.

'We want to ask you a few questions,' replied my neighbour ominously.

I resigned myself to the worst, closing my eyes to restore order to my mind. When I opened them, to my surprise the car was drawing up in front of our house. I was ordered to get out. I waited. We all waited.

'We're here,' one of them pointed out.

'Yes,' I said. 'You may open the gate.'

Surprised, the man did as he was bid. I stepped through first, head held high. It was a very minor triumph, but at least I'd forced them to treat me as a woman. Inside the flat I waited again. At length one of them demanded: 'Where is the radio you removed from your car after your husband's arrest?'

Was that all they wanted? Why couldn't they have said so in the first place, instead of leaving me in suspense? I protested once more that my husband had been neither convicted nor sentenced, therefore they had no right to his property. It was futile. They merely repeated their question and sat down, indicating they had all the time in the world.

I thought: If I deny I have the radio, they'll search the flat and make a hell of a mess. I said: 'It's here; it needs repairing.'

Untrue. I'd intended to flog it, but hadn't yet found a purchaser. After the confiscation of the Minx, I'd removed the tubes and put them in a separate drawer, just in case. I handed over the radio. It would be useless to the police: that make of tube was unobtainable in Czechoslovakia.

'That will be all — for today,' said one of them as they left.

I dropped into a chair. Now that they were gone, my calm deserted me. My heart was racing. They'd played a cat-and-mouse game with me. I shook with rage and hatred. They were omnipotent; they enjoyed their power to intimidate. I recalled Mr Němec, cowering, a picture of fear and apprehension, yet he had nothing to hide. The whole population was at the mercy of the secret police. I got up and found the tubes, wrapped them in newspaper and took them to the dustbin in the yard. Then I made myself the one cup of coffee I could afford each day, and pushed the matter from my mind. After all, what was a car radio?

It appeared that the local National Committee, too, had a stake in our property. I was requested to be at home on a particular date. At nine o'clock precisely two gentlemen presented themselves. A visual replica of Laurel and Hardy, apart from the headgear. They removed their caps and stood as silent as pall-bearers. However, they had come to praise Caesar not to bury him.

Once inside the door, Hardy whispered: 'We knew your husband well. He was a good communist. We don't believe this spy stuff, but,' he sighed heavily, 'we have our job to do.'

Laurel added: 'We'd prefer different work. But if we gave notice, we'd be branded as disloyal. We'd never get another job.'

They both looked on the verge of collapse. I made them some tea.

Hardy explained: 'We–er have instructions to draw up a list of the contents of your flat, pending confiscation.'

I repeated despairingly that my husband hadn't been sentenced.

'We know,' Laurel hung his head. 'And we sincerely hope he won't be. But after his testimony it seems unlikely.'

Hardy broke in: 'All we have to do for the present is file a list. Then Josef and me'll forget about it — as long as we safely can.'

Having completed the inventory, Laurel mumbled: 'I'm sorry, we'll have to seal up your husband's personal effects.'

The mournful pair carefully laid Pavel's suits and shirts and underwear in a large trunk. I slipped sheets of *Rudé Právo* in between, hoping it would discourage the moths as much as it did its readers. Pavel's black dinner jacket lay on top. I dropped in a packet of dry lavender. Like a bunch of flowers thrown onto a coffin before it is lowered into the grave. I shuddered. The lid was closed down and the trunk was sealed. It was to be left until called for. They had found Pavel's self-winding wristwatch and a fountain pen in a suit pocket. 'We'd better take these,' said the thin one. 'It'll look suspicious if we go back empty-handed. They'll stay in our safe until your husband returns. Goodbye, Mrs Kavanová, and good luck!' They shook hands sorrowfully.

Their visit had both cheered and chilled me. They represented officialdom at local government and Party levels, yet, acting on their impression of Pavel's character, they were prepared to stall for time. On the other hand, they had made plain that if convicted, Pavel's sentence, like those of the defendants in the Slánský trial, would include forfeiture of property.

The mixture of tragedy and comedy that was now my life brought a visit of another kind. Mirek and I were to inspect our track. Hanka, a young English pupil of mine, offered to look after the boys so that I could be away for two or three days.

We arrived at the depot in the evening and the assembly team allotted us a train wagon divided into cubicles as lodgings. Men were getting used to the women in dungarees, but I was apparently the first they had seen on the job. They looked upon me as an improbable joke but threw in a little respect when they discovered that some of the blueprints they had been working from were — incredibly — mine. I looked forward to the morning and the sight of the designs I had put together with more hope than skill in three-dimensional reality. I could hardly believe that the poles — like working mothers — would really bear the stresses and strains expected of them.

We set off with the assembly team to check the installation of the contact wire. The operation was conducted from the roof of a diesel-driven workshop train, which was covered with a thin coating of snow and ice. It was a miracle I wasn't swept off as I side-stepped to avoid the contortions of the wire, ducked to evade unattached ends of carrier cable, eyed the track for unexpected bends, all the while consulting my blueprints.

We returned to the depot for lunch, during which I remarked to Mirek: 'It's rewarding to work on something that'll be here after we're gone.'

'Sentimental crap,' Mirek replied elegantly. 'I don't give a lamb's fart what happens after I'm pushing up the daisies. The day the whole Czechoslovak railway network is electrified is as far as I look ahead, and I'll probably have to live to be an octogenarian to see that. But if it will make you happy, you may picture your great-grandchildren joyfully riding about on great-grandma's railway line.'

He smacked his lips over our goulash and dumplings. 'Not bad. Meat's kind of sweetish. Maybe it's horse.' He chuckled. 'Reminds me of our neighbour during the war. Mum used to leave our leftovers by the open kitchen window at night to keep them fresh. The old faggot from next door used to slip out onto the verandah and nick a portion. One day our cat Blackie got hit by a car. Mum wept buckets. Then she dried her eyes and made a pie with the choicest bits of Blackie and left it by the window. The next morning it had clean gone. Mum nipped in next door to borrow some salt and mentioned that a thief had bagged her cat pie in the night.

'"Cat!" gasps greedy guts, turning green. "Yes," says Mum. "The people of Stalingrad ate rats and dogs, so I thought I'd try Blackie. What's the matter, aren't you feeling well?" The old faggot made a beeline for the loo and threw up like a sick mule. She never touched a thing from our window sill after that.'

Satiated, we went back to the track. It had stopped snowing, visibility was good but our diesel engine was nowhere to be seen.

'Something in this smells,' pronounced Tomik, a borer, and he went off to investigate. After all, you can't mislay a thing like a diesel engine. He came back storming: 'Of all the blasted cheek! The demolition gang nabbed our diesel to remove the old wooden poles.'

What a magnificent theft! Although I was continually being warned by well-meaning strangers: 'Young missus, look to your handbag, it's half-open, you cannot be too careful', this was my first experience of real robbery.

The foreman declined to hang about workless, having pledges and plans on his mind. He set off to hire another engine. The small depot did not abound in extra, idle engines. Its only reserve was a black steam mammoth, dating back to the last century. The foreman persuaded an equally ancient driver to bring it up the line. The men hitched on the workshop and, squealing and snorting, the museum piece began pushing us slowly along. When it had wheezed to within sight of the spot where we had left off in the morning, it came to a halt. We scrambled along to the footplate. The driver scratched his head. 'She's got enough coal, engine's in order, maybe she's low in water.'

We scattered over the fields in search of a brook. I was accustomed to getting people out of bed, popping into pubs or lowering myself into river beds because Matilda or the Minx had boiled themselves dry, but a steam engine! Really, one could rely on the Czechs to introduce a novel note into any proceedings!

'Water, water!' yelled Mirek at length. We rushed to the spot, formed a chain and began passing a bucketful up to the foreman who was sitting astride the funnel and peering in from time to time with an electric torch.

'Strewth! It's like spitting into a gorge,' he groaned. 'At this rate we'll be stuck here all night.'

A rumble in the distance attracted our attention. Our diesel was returning on our track. With one accord we blocked its path, and when the diesel pulled up with a scream of brakes, we boarded it pirate fashion. A fierce argument ensued, which I expected at any moment to draw blood, but, as usual, it produced more noise than damage. When the commotion had died down, the 'demolishers' abandoned ship, we coupled our workshop onto the diesel and proceeded up the line.

When we returned, the penitent demolishers had stoked up the stoves and brewed us scalding tea with rum. The next day Mirek and I were taken farther up the line; we trudged ahead to examine the poles. Towards evening Mirek stated: 'We're approaching a tunnel. It's near the border. I'll be guarded by a dolt of a sentry. You, Rozmarýnka, keep your mouth shut. Leave the talking to me. With your accent and the present spy hysteria, he's sure to take you for an agent. The local police'll be as daft as they were in Švejk's day. We'll be detained for days answering idiotic questions, like Švejk was when he got lost in these parts.'

We could see the entrance to the tunnel. The sentry trained his rifle on us. The fact that he was stamping his feet to keep warm and his hands were shaking with the cold added a touch of piquancy, like lemon rind to sweet Vermouth. He lowered his rifle to demand our passes. Delighted at the unexpected encounter with human flesh and blood, he prolonged the interview as long as he could. He examined our documents with slow thoroughness, and stirred the contents of our rucksacks. His efforts to draw me into a discussion on the hazards of the track cost me several warning kicks on the ankle from Mirek's hefty snow boots. At last, with his mind on supper and our schedule, Mirek dragged me away, through the tunnel and along the track to a small station where we were to catch a train to České Budějovice. The station master welcomed us with the announcement that our train was three-quarters of an hour overdue. As our hot baths and hot supper receded further into the future, Mirek grumbled: 'We'll have to electrify the bloody timetables as well!'

He soon recovered his good humour and drew the tattered *Švejk* out of his rucksack. 'Here's the bit I was telling you about. Švejk has been apprehended by Flanderka, the local constable, who is convinced that he's a Russian spy. Here's an example of the cross-examination.

'"Flanderka, do you know how to take photographs?"

"Yes, I do,"

"Then why don't you carry a camera with you?"

"Because I haven't got one," came the clear and frank reply.

"And had you had one, would you have taken photographs?" asked the sergeant.

"If pigs had wings," replied Švejk, simply, and he unflinchingly bore the scrutiny of the sergeant whose head was aching so badly that he could think of no better question than "Is it difficult to photograph a station?"

"It's easier than anything else," answered Švejk, "Because it stays put in one place and you don't have to keep telling it to smile nicely. . . ."

The sergeant wrote down: "Among other things during my cross-examination he admitted that he knew how to take photographs and he liked stations best. It is true no camera was found on him but it can be presumed that he has hidden it somewhere and that he doesn't carry it on him so as to divert attention away from himself, which is supported by his confession that he would photograph if he had a camera . . . It is only thanks to the fact that he did not have a camera handy that no photographs were found on him."'

The more I knew the Czechs, the more I understood the attraction of *Švejk*. Švejk is a symbol of the moral victory of the underdog over the tyrant. His very acceptance of fate becomes a form of passive resistance. Though outwardly submissive, he retains the inner right to consign his superior to hell. His loquaciousness breaks his opponent's spirit; his imperturbability renders him impotent. In every encounter Švejk makes authority look ridiculous, which removes the sting from subordination.

Švejk holds out the hope that astuteness disguised as stupidity and evasiveness combined with mockery will eventually erode the edifice of power.

My next taste of track life took me to Slovakia, to a section of the Žilina-Spišská Nová Ves line, where work was still at the initial back-breaking stage. Armed with a pot of yellow paint and a brush, Mirek and Franta and I plodded along the track, measuring out the future poles, and painting them on the rails.

'As the youngest, in experience if not in years, it's your job to carry the rucksacks,' Mirek stated.

'But they're heavy,' I protested.

'Damn it! Are you in favour of equality, or aren't you?' he demanded. 'You are? Well, then, you can't complain. Crucifix, that's women all over; they want it all ways!'

I said no more and meekly loaded myself with our belongings. After the third stretch, Mirek relented. He took them from me, saying:

'We'll work by rota.' He offered me a lump of raw bacon fat

on the end of his pocket knife accompanied by a draught of hot grog from a bottle wrapped in asbestos. I choked and my eyes watered.

'Knocks the wind out of you, doesn't it?' Mirek laughed. 'In the words of the dissolute sailor: Grog should be so strong that if someone falls overboard he can swim the Channel. After weak grog, he'd drown like a kitten.'

Considering the distance we were from the sea, I thought Mirek could have followed a more moderate recipe. For a long time I felt as though I were carrying a lighted torch inside me.

The station master referred to his timetable. 'By regulation you can't leave here until ten minutes after a train has passed through and you must be back fifteen minutes before a train is due. To that, we must add the time you'll need in the tunnel. I haven't such a long interval. I shall be obliged to hold up the goods train for you.'

'Here, Rozmarýnka, take the plan and read out the distances, and Gawd help you if you make a mistake. It's a pig of a job to drive a fixture into a tunnel wall. If anything has to be done twice, you'll face lynching.'

With these cheering words, Mirek thrust the crumpled, paint-splotched plan into my hand. Our powerful lamp cut a chunk out of the darkness of the tunnel; the metallic twang of the steel tape against the rails sounded like off-stage thunder. The higher pitch of our voices reflected a slight doubt that the station master would indeed detain the goods train.

Without any warning a sheet of sound blasted our brains like the shelling of Portsmouth Harbour, Cup Final victory and Beethoven's Ninth rolled into one. Sparks rent the darkness and smoke filled our noses and throats like hot, sooty cotton wool, as a gargantuan combination of steel and power hurtled towards us. This violent onslaught on all the senses produced a moment of sheer terror. We pressed ourselves into an alcove, and emerged afterwards as black as the Kentucky Minstrels and as subdued as choirboys.

'The express was a little item that escaped the station master's notice,' remarked Franta with a shaky laugh.

'All in a day's work!' commented Mirek. He took a swig of the dissolute sailor's grog and passed the flask to us.

Never had life seemed sweeter.

Chapter 11

The sweetness soon evaporated back at the office. News had got around of an official *volte face* on the subject of diplomas.

'Changing their bloody minds again,' Mirek grumbled. 'When the universities were re-opened after the war, they crammed them to overflowing to catch up on six years of ignorance. By 1948 education was a handicap. If your father was a drunken navvy who couldn't sign his name and your mother a whore, and you just about knew which end of a broom sweeps the road, you stood the optimal chance of promotion. If you'd gone farther than the senior elementary, you were a bloody intellectual conspiring to upset the political applecart. Seventy per cent of our top Johnnies haven't even been to secondary school, though a few have got phoney degrees in Marxism–Leninism. Now it's dawned on them that we won't attain a state of abundance by digging faster with our bare hands: we gotta have scientific and technological progress. But if a Czech wants to scratch his left ear, he does it with his right hand behind the back of his neck; combine that with the present habit of aping the Russians on the swings and roundabouts, and you can see that this is going to take a heck of a long time. Now, on top of that, they've decided that without a bloody *bumashka** people can't go on doing the job they've been doing for years and know like their own boots. All us *projektants†* who've only been to the secondary tech have got to sign on for five years of extramural drudgery to get a degree if

* Russian for paper.
† Draughtsmen.

we want to hang on to our jobs.'

A thoughtful gloom settled on the office.

'Keeping the population busy could be one way of keeping them out of mischief,' Mirek mused. 'It'll be interesting to see the results. Either alcoholism, crime and adultery will decline for sheer lack of time or we shall all be driven to drink and fornication out of pure despair, and the suicide rate of those who can't stand the pace will rise.'

A works crash course in mathematics, mechanics, physics and chemistry was organized for those who lacked even basic qualifications. The degree of concentration required to follow yard-long equations at six a.m. proved beyond me. When the examination days were announced I judiciously went sick and applied for a postponement. This was repeated several times. Eventually, on the strength of a rubber stamp and a signed statement by Sláva that I attended the course and would undoubtedly have passed the examination had I not been prevented by illness from taking it, I stepped up onto the next rung. I was now a fully-fledged, if technically undernourished, designer. I had no compunction about this deceit. To my mind, the effort of remaining upright with both eyes open between six and seven in the morning three times a week for several months deserved some recompense. As regards material reward, my salary leapt by nearly a third.

My complacency was short-lived. One day the door burst open and a short, stringy apparition in a battered leather windcheater, bristling with at least three days' whiskers and bottled indignation, appeared before us, bawling: 'Which bloody stupid ox is Kav?'

'Crucifix,' whispered Mirek. 'Old Švabinský. He's the assembly foreman from the Kolín–Pardubice section we've been working on. What's up, mate?'

'Up? The ruddy arms are up, that's what! Up without a check, if you ask me, though what the hell you bloody boffins do all the time, Gawd only knows. Some straw-stuffed idiot in your circus can't count. Over a metre too long they are in one section. They oughta come down and go for salvage, except that my men can't hang about doing nothing while a new lot are provided. They've wasted enough time as it is. And would've wasted more, if I hadn't had a brainwave. Brilliant it was, but I ain't paid for fantasy; I'm not a stinking designer. I had one hell of a job shortening the carrier cable and mucking about with contact wire fixtures. So which of you gawping bastards is Kav?'

I emerged from behind my drawing-board: 'I — I am.'

"Ha, not an ox, a cow!'

He advanced, exhaling fire and brimstone. Mirek called out: 'Calm down, Cockroach, it's Rozmarýnka's first mistake; she probably counted in the rent.'

The Cockroach cast an appreciative eye over the cow. 'You must be that foreign bird the boys was talking about.' He lowered his voice. 'Actually there was only about five arms that was too long but we like to put these pen-pushers in their place once in a while.' He lowered his voice still further: "You doing anything this evening?'

I hesitated. The ethics of my position as a grass widow ruled out dates; but as insurance against future slips it seemed prudent to gain the Cockroach as an ally. I replied warily that I wasn't doing anything in particular.

'Meet you outside the Tatran at eight?'

I nodded. He strolled out, growling for effect: 'Well, don't let it happen again.'

The Cockroach had put a few under his belt before turning up for our date. It was an evening devoted to the art of fencing. I foiled the Cockroach's advances as tactfully as I could. Whenever his wandering hands under the table became too persistent, I jumped up and suggested dancing. When the crush on the dance floor led to too many liberties, I dragged him resolutely back to the table. He took my defence tactics in good part. I got home at one in the morning feeling I had more than atoned for five over-long arms.

Altruism is a short-term virtue. Now that the temporary exigency had become a permanent emergency, the ladies of our house withdrew their assistance. I was therefore obliged to give up my evening lessons. Without my extra earnings there was no way of paying the rent for our luxury flat. The only solution was to exchange it for a smaller one.

I went to the agency that mediated such exchanges (which then had to be approved by the respective National Committees). No sooner had I paid the fee than I was invited for coffee by Dr Gertruda Sekaninová-Čakrtová[31] who lived in the flat above us. She was a Jewess of great beauty and intellect who had survived the 1948 purges as a Deputy Minister of Foreign Affairs. Apart from her indisputable merits, her strongest card was her dead husband. To be the widow of a war hero was the soundest alibi in the early fifties.

Truda's friendliness towards me had not changed after Pavel's detention. In this respect she was more courageous than other Party friends whose lines had gone dead when Pavel was arrested. Truda announced that she had arranged for me to exchange my flat with a Foreign Ministry official. My request to see the flat before making a decision surprised her. However, she telephoned for an appointment.

The official's flat was in the Špejchar district. Even if climbing five flights of stairs had not rendered me speechless, I wouldn't have found words to express my disappointment. The flat faced north and overlooked a busy thoroughfare; it consisted of two tiny rooms and a bathroom, and a kitchen recess. I sidled towards the radiator. It was cold. As the sun never reached the rooms, the flat would never be warm. No wonder the official wanted to vacate it.

I felt confident I could do better through the agency. The official, however, informed me that his Ministry and our two National Committees had already sanctioned the exchange.

'So I have no choice! This is a *fait accompli!*' I cried.

The official said nothing, but I could read his thoughts: he was in a strong position; I was on weak ground.

On Monday morning I joined the queue outside the office of the chief housing manager for the City of Prague. After a three-and-a-half-hour wait, I was admitted.

'Yes,' barked the bulky individual behind the desk. 'What do you want?'

I glanced at my watch. Twelve o'clock. The man was hungry. He was also goaded to a high pitch of irritation by the futility of his job. The housing plan was behind schedule; every day he faced mobs of irate, unhoused citizens who would remain irate and unhoused for the next decade or so. He glared at me with

---

31. Gertruda Sekaninová-Čakrtová is a former Deputy Foreign Minister and one of the five members of the Federal Assembly who voted against the treaty legalizing the stationing of Soviet troops in October 1968. She is a Charter 77 signatory and a member of VONS.

bulging, bloodshot eyes. I was backing a 100:1 loser.

'I wish to register a protest,' I announced with as much firmness as I could muster.

'Oh, you do?' The weight of sarcasm would have crushed a dinosaur. Presumably no one ever went there with any other purpose.

'Yes, I'm being forced to exchange a large, luxurious, sunny, three-and-a-half roomed, centrally heated flat in a quiet villa for a small, miserable, sunless, two-roomed flatlet on a busy arterial road. As the local authorities have given their blessing to this unnatural bargain without my consent, I have been compelled to go over their heads and request you to abrogate the negotiations.'

The bulldog leaned across the table, bared its fangs and demanded icily: 'And who, may I ask, is forcing your hand in this peculiar manner?'

'Dr — an official at the Foreign Ministry.'

'How many persons occupy your large, luxurious, sunny flat, madam?'

'Temporarily, one adult and two children. That's why — '

'The word temporary intrigues me,' cut in the bulldog. 'Your name, madam?'

'Kavanová.'

'Not the wife of that traitor Pavel Kavan?'

'No, I mean yes. That is I am his wife, but he's not a traitor. He got into the trial by mistake.'

The ulcerated housing manager leapt to his feet. 'You have been offered a two-roomed flat in Prague, and yet you come to me to complain! You may consider yourself fortunate, madam. We are sending the likes of you out of the capital to the border regions.' His bulging eyes rolled menacingly. 'Now, get out of here before I accede to your request and intercede in your case. I have a plentiful stock of sunless, one-room shacks in the Šumava forests, from which you may take your choice and a list as long as Wenceslas Square of citizens who will be grateful to occupy your Dr What'shisname's two rooms.'

I withdrew. The hubbub of the Špejchar crossroads was preferable to the solitude of the Šumava forest.

As I had anticipated, the boys' health deteriorated in our new surroundings. The air in the centre of Prague was heavy with dust. There was no garden to play in. The flat was cold at its warmest. As the final stroke of misery, we had to endure six weeks without heating in the middle of a Siberian winter because the concierge had forgotten to order winter stocks of coal in the summer. Not a germ avoided us. On top of the complete set of children's diseases, the boys were afflicted with bouts of septic tonsilitis, running ear and bronchitis. They were suffering from vitamin and protein deficiency. Fruit, vegetables, butter, meat, fish, milk and eggs were in short supply. But even when these foods reached the market, most of them were beyond my means. After a pay rise and reduction in rent, my income still barely covered essentials. (The cost of living was geared to two incomes per family.) I walked past expensive oranges and lemons with tears in my eyes. Many of the cheaper wholesome foods eluded us too. These were usually delivered to the shops during the day when I was at work and unlike most employed women I had no babička (granny) to queue for us. My heart bled to see the boys paying with their health for the injustice perpetrated on their father. I gave them the best of what little I procured, while my own diet consisted of bread and dripping, potatoes and salami.

The boys accepted our penury stoically. They bore hours of loneliness on a sick bed uncomplainingly. I could not afford to take time off. When they were ill Mr Němec sometimes allowed me to go home at lunch time so that I could give them a quick meal. Otherwise, all I could do for them was to phone for short chats and to remind them to take their medicines.

They had been bright and beautiful youngsters when we left England. Now they were pale and listless. Deprived of their father and largely of their mother, the joy had gone out of their lives. School was dull and unimaginative. The education system had been re-modelled on Soviet lines with the emphasis on parrot learning. Conformity was the keyword. Self-expression, individual taste and judgement were discouraged. Sport was at a minimum. In short there was little outlet for boisterous spirits.

The boys attended school from 8.30 to 1.30, and spent the rest of their time at the day centre. The one near our villa had provided plenty of activities. When we moved, they were less lucky.

Zdeněk was suffering from an eye infection. After work I called at the day centre — a single room attached to the school — and asked the harassed woman in charge if she would administer the prescribed drops at midday. She refused point blank to lift a finger for 'the son of a traitor'.

'But children should not suffer for the sins of their fathers,' I protested.

'Mine did,' she burst out unexpectedly. Her children had been denied secondary education and her husband had lost his job in 1948 because he was a member of a right-wing party. 'My family suffered at the hands of the communists, people like your husband,' she cried.

'I'm sorry,' I said. 'Truly sorry. But don't you think we women should stand together against further injustice?'

The din in the room had grown to a crescendo. The woman shouted at the children to sit down and shut up. I said that they couldn't be expected to keep still for hours on end. Why didn't she arrange a programme? Why were there no creative materials? She told me that the local council didn't provide any.

'They would if you badgered them,' I insisted, remembering my experience with Králík.

'I'm not paid to do anything but mind the kids,' she said. She hated the job but she couldn't get anything else apart from factory work.

'I'm sorry for you,' I said as I left. 'So much hatred in your heart.'

The next day I asked Mr Němec if I could go to the day centre at lunch time. He looked unhappy. The Party boss had noted my absences. (He was referring to the hours I spent waiting with one or the other of the boys at the doctors' surgery.) Reluctantly he gave permission. When I reached the day centre, Zdeněk told me the minder had already given him his drops. I went over to her and took her hand: 'Thank you, I really appreciate what you have done.'

She smiled bleakly.

The following week Jan had a temperature. Mindful of Mr Němec's heartfelt prayer: 'I do hope your children will stay healthy for a while, Mrs Kavanová, our department is getting a bad name,' I dosed him myself and left him in bed. After several days his temperature soared alarmingly and he had developed a hacking cough. I worried all the evening. I was sure he ought to see a doctor, but that would mean more trouble at the office. If only we had a granny. A granny was an indispensable adjunct to the Czech welfare state. Jan coughed and burned with fever all night. In the morning I phoned the health centre and asked for a doctor to call, but was told to wrap Jan up and bring him along. I took a taxi, which made a considerable hole in my budget. The doctor diagnosed pneumonia. Pneumonia! And I had left him unattended because kindly Mr Němec was afraid of his superiors. I obtained a certificate of absence for the statutory three days and on the fourth day I went to the Party chief, slammed the certificate down in front of him and accused him of responsibility for my delicate child's illness.

'Women form forty-six per cent of the work force; without us the economy would collapse. The country is underpopulated; it needs children. What is the use of progressive legislation if the comrades don't support us?' I demanded.

I threatened that if he uttered any more complaints about 'absentee mothers' I'd protest to the President, the Minister of Health, the Minister of Education and the Union of Women. Without realizing it I had raised my voice at each institution until on the word 'Women' I reached a veritable crescendo of wrath. Conscious of the thinness of the partitions between his room and the surrounding offices, the political boss assured me loudly that the Party appreciated working mothers' difficulties and I was on no account to neglect my sick child.

'You won't object, then, if I take off a further three days, without pay?' I asked in a loud bellow for the benefit of the listening ears beyond the partitions.

Trapped, he acquiesced.

Unhappily, the boys suffered more than I knew. Young as they were, they did not worry me with their troubles. Years later Jan told me of discrimination by heartless, politically zealous teachers, and of ill-treatment by schoolmates. In one instance a gang of bigger boys had beaten him up as 'the son of a traitor', knowing that the staff would not intervene. They had called Jan a dirty Jew and stood on his stomach. How could any one stand on a child's stomach? Jan defended his father's honour, puzzled as to why being a Jew (he had not even been aware of the fact that he was Jewish) should make him dirty.

His teacher made him the scapegoat for every untoward happening in class. On one occasion he was unjustly accused of breaking a window. To his surprise another boy stood up and took the blame. Aleš[32] was not the true culprit and his action was a public demonstration of support for a victim of the Establishment. This launched a lasting friendship. Jan learned that Aleš, on principle, took an anti-Establishment stand on every issue in defiance of his father, a highly-placed Party official. Later the situation was reversed. Aleš' uncompromising attitude involved him in serious political trouble and Jan defended him.

On working days I left the house at 6.30 a.m. and returned at 6 p.m. (3 p.m. on Saturdays). Cooking on a broken-down stove, supervising the boys' homework and mending their clothes took up most of the evening. Cleaning, washing and ironing were crammed into the weekends. From time to time, Slava procured some extra work for me to do at home. Strange stratagems were employed to combat the manpower shortage. Firms farmed out work to each other and fiddled the accounts to pay outside labour. This practice contravened the law, but to have paid their own employees overtime would have incurred heavy penalties. I needed the extra money, but I still feel bitter when I recall the little time I had left — perhaps half-an-hour each evening — for reading to or playing with the boys. I can still hear my impatient voice urging them to hurry up and finish their homework, get to bed, get to sleep, or get out of the way so that I could get on with the next chore.

Come what may, Sunday afternoon at least was for them. We would go to the park or to the open country on the periphery, to the children's theatre or the cinema. Or, if the weather was bad, we would stay in and dress up and act fairy stories, or paint, model or play cards.

I tried to keep my spirits up for the boys' sake. For my own sake, too. I had learned the truth of the adage: 'Laugh, and the world laughs with you; weep, and you weep alone.' And I knew that I had a long haul ahead of me. If I weakened at the beginning, I'd never make the end. I was not expected to weaken. 'You have your British sense of humour,' Czechs pointed out. 'Ours is the humour of the gallows, of pessimism. Yours is the humour of optimism; it will pull you through hell unscorched.'

32. Aleš Macháček (1946–) worked as a drainage and irrigation expert in Southern Bohemia after graduating from agricultural college. He was arrested in 1977 and sentenced to three and a half years for distribution of literature from abroad and of Charter 77's founding Declaration. He emigrated to England in May 1985.

Not quite. There were times when I felt distinctly blackened round the edges; when despair and loneliness threatened to suffocate me. After Pavel's arrest old friends had severed connections. My colleagues were friendly during working hours; outside the office they went their separate ways. Karel was immersed in his own emotional problems after the failure of his second marriage. I saw little of him. Eva was working outside Prague. She, too, had been caught up in the wave of anti-Semitism that had swept Czechoslovakia. On being told by the director of the bank that he was forced to demote her, she had declared: 'I'll not sit in the typing pool on sufferance as a superfluous Jew. I'll go to the mines. There's such a shortage of labour there that no one will give a damn about my race.' She had walked straight out and gone to Ostrava, a mining town in northern Bohemia. My very dear friend and fellow Englishwoman, Yvonne, had been exiled with her Czech husband and family to an isolated place in the country. Heda and I were so busy we rarely saw each other. Worst of all, I had no family to turn to. My parents had been refused visas to visit Czechoslovakia.

Moments of weakness would creep upon me unawares, after the boys had gone to bed, usually when I was on the loo. Without warning I would burst into tears. The tears would flow and flow, as though from a leaking pipe. I didn't even try to plumb it. Then suddenly I'd see myself, pants round my ankles, bottom freezing, eyes puffing up. A pathetic and ludicrous sight. I'd laugh. Literally, I cried until I laughed. Then I'd get up, haul up my pants and choose one of two restoratives: Shakespeare or dance. I'd read Shakespeare aloud in the bathroom. The drama dwarfed my own. Everything faded except the poetry of the language. My constricted soul expanded. I read myself out of all consciousness of time and place.

Or I would put on a record and dance. My favourites were Tchaikovsky's *Italian Capriccio* and Janáček's *Symphonietta*. I'd pile the chairs and tables on the sofa and improvise ballets. I'd whirl and leap and pirouette until I dropped, physically exhausted, spiritually renewed and able to go on.

Perhaps what really exhausted me was the knowledge that Pavel was far worse off than me. I might be tired, worried and depressed, but at least I was at liberty. As long as I had my freedom, I would never succumb. Or so I thought.

It was ten o'clock at night. My leaden eyelids drooped and obscured the drawings I was working on. My worst enemy was sleep, or lack of it. Every night I was woken innumerable times by heavy lorries hurtling past the house and the screech of trams braking under our window. Worries that I suppressed in the daytime sprang to life and plagued me like gnats. After a few hours' interrupted sleep I often lay awake until morning. Consequently, by early evening I craved my bed. That night I struggled to concentrate through a thickening fog of fatigue. I shook my head to clear the haze. A stabbing pain in my side caused me to double up in agony. I waited, holding my breath. Another knifelike jab. I gritted my teeth and between increasingly frequent spasms finished the drawing before daybreak. By the morning I couldn't move without pain. A scared Jan phoned the doctor who actually came. He prodded me indifferently and pronounced his diagnosis: '*Žlučník.*' What the hell was that? I looked it up in the dictionary. Gall-bladder. That meant nothing to me. Insides had never been referred to in my healthy family.

I was outraged. How dared a portion of my anatomy behave so treacherously! I had believed in the ascendancy of mind over matter, convinced that my constitution could stand unlimited abuse. My assumption had been proved false. It was unfair. Protesting vehemently, I was packed off to hospital. Jan was despatched to Karel's and Zdeněk to a distant cousin in Moravia. The consultant appended acute anaemia, murmuring to his assistant: 'A bad case of malnutrition. Looks like an inmate of Belsen, poor thing.'

After the hospital, further treatment at a spa was recommended. The left hand of the state having reduced me to impotence, the right hand was sparing no expense to return me to circulation. My congenital resilience served me well. After three weeks of iron-flavoured water, mud packs and carbon dioxide baths at Karlovy Vary, I was eager to return to the fray.

First I re-visited old Prague. I went there alone. I always felt that Prague had a personal message for me which would be communicated only if I were alone. This communion unfailingly brought me peace. On that day the ancient stones assured me of the continuity of history. They reminded me that abiding values outlive historical disasters. They showed me the trials as a single contortion in the long human saga. I viewed our situation in the context of the whole, reminding myself that we were exceptional. Families, in which there were no Jews, Spanish war veterans, anti-fascist fighters, Catholics or ex-factory owners enjoyed a reasonably untroubled existence.

Charged with positive thinking, I called on Heda. I was appalled to find that she and Ivan had been moved into one dingy room with a handful of belongings; the rest had been confiscated. This brought home to me the fate that might yet befall us, and sent the negative scale plummeting again.

Weighing the pros and cons and baffling contradictions of life in Czechoslovakia was to remain the most permanent of my many occupations.

Chapter 12

As far as the eye could see there were stationary trams.

'All out and slog it!' called the conductress with odious cheer.

I ran most of the way and arrived at the office panting and well overdue. 'I'm sorry I'm late,' I gasped. 'There was no electric current on our line.'

'Yes er — quite so.' Mr Němec gave me a peculiar look. 'I think you'd better have a look at this.'

He handed me a newspaper. It was *Rudé Právo* of 27 May 1953. I scanned the page — the usual stuff: Soviet Red Cross delegation in Prague, young miners pledging 2,500 extra tons of coal in honour of the coming Youth Festival in Budapest, etcetera. Then my eye was caught by a short paragraph in the middle of the page.

Trial of Accomplices of the Anti-State Conspiratorial Centre from the Ministry of Foreign Affairs. Eduard Goldstücker, Pavel Kavan, Karel Dufek and Richard Slánský were tried before a Tribunal of the Supreme Court on 25 and 26 May. The charges were treason and, with the exception of Karel Dufek, espionage.

As accomplices of the anti-State conspiracy led by Rudolf Slánský, the defendants conducted large-scale subversion in the Ministry of Foreign Affairs on instructions issued by Geminder and Clementis.

Witnesses and documents testified against the defendants who confessed to the crimes in the indictment. They were found guilty and sentenced: Eduard Goldstücker and Richard Slánský to life imprisonment, Pavel Kavan and Karel Dufek[33] to twenty-five years. All four defendants were sentenced to forfeiture of property and loss of civil rights.

I slumped against the filing cupboard. Gripping its sides for support, I found myself whispering, 'But he hasn't done anything.' I clenched my teeth to hold back further words. With a supreme effort of will I straightened up and handed Mr Němec his paper. With a murmured thanks, I turned to leave the room. Mr Němec suggested I take the day off. I replied that I had a lot to get through before our deadline and that sitting at home alone would be worse than occupying myself with work. I was thinking: Twenty-five years for putting three sealed letters into the diplomatic bag. Did ever a postman's job cost a man so dear? Was this the end of our dream? For Pavel twenty-five years in prison, for me twenty-five years' loyalty to a dead love? Twenty-five years was only five years short of my whole life — an eternity. I could not conceive of eternity.

Concentrating hard on not breaking down, I went into my own office. An uneasy silence prevailed. For once there was no leg-pulling. I started the last job of the month. My brain functioned independently: it was still plugged into a power source; the rest of me was a tangle of disconnected wires.

At lunch in the canteen Mirek talked shop as the safest noise to make. We returned to the office. Again a hush descended, like a sudden fall of snow. My eye fell on my pile of finished drawings. I goggled: thick black tongues like an oil slick had spread over them. Franta started to splutter: 'I'm terribly sorry, Rosemary, I knocked over my bottle of India ink. The top wasn't screwed on properly.'

At that moment a thunderbolt exploded in my head, my whole body convulsed as though struck by lightning. A voice that I couldn't believe was my own screamed abuse: 'You flaming idiot! You lousy, blundering ox! All you're good for is boozing and screwing! When the hell did you turn in a decent job? Not content with doing bugger all yourself, you've gone and loused up my month's work.'

33. Karel Dufek was sentenced to 25 years with Kavan in 1953 and released in 1955. He was made Ambassador to Brazil in 1969.

Tears of rage and grief stung my eyes. I rushed out of the room, locked myself in the lavatory and sobbed hysterically. The tears were for Pavel, the grief was for his terrible fate. The control I had exercised all the morning had been shattered by a bottle of ink. The storm eventually spent itself. I wiped my face with my handkerchief. What now? The longer I stayed in this wretched lavatory, the worse fool I'd look when I emerged. I walked out and along the corridor and opened the office door. Tactfully, no one glanced up. I slipped into my place next to Franta, muttering:

'I'm sorry, I didn't mean all those things I said. You should have picked a better day.'

'That's all right,' he replied awkwardly. 'We've shared out the ruined drawings. We'll all stay behind and re-do them. You'll be able to hand them in tomorrow as scheduled.'

'Thanks.' I tried to sound grateful, but at that moment I didn't care whether I ever saw a drawing again. I felt unutterably weary. 'I think I'll go home after all,' I mumbled and tottered out of the room. A strong arm took mine outside the door. It was Mirek.

'Come on, I'll get you a taxi.'

'But — '

'Don't argue, here's the fare.' He stuffed some notes into my pocket.

I told the boys I had flu and went to bed, unable to focus on the future or the present. In the evening Heda phoned her sympathy and support. Eva, too, phoned condolence and comfort from Ostrava. She assured me the political sentences would be halved eventually; there could be a two-year remission for good conduct. Pavel might be out in ten years.

I clung to that. In ten years Pavel would be forty-eight. There would still be time to build a life together. But how were we going to maintain any meaningful contact for twenty-five, or even ten, years? Pavel was entitled to write a one-page letter every month but there were frequent unexplained gaps: his letters were censored. He could not describe the conditions under which he lived or his innermost thoughts. He usually referred to books he had read and the progress he was making in Russian, and requested Vitamin C tablets and further reading matter. He always pressed for details about our lives. I did my best to keep him abreast of the boys' development and make him feel part of our lives, but there were so many subjects to avoid, or at least gloss over. The constant effort on both sides to write cheerfully about blatantly cheerless times made natural communication impossible.

I took out his old love letters and re-read them. I searched his prison letters for the odd personal line. In one he had written: 'I have a lot of time to think here. I see now that I was not always good to you. You cannot imagine how sorry that makes me.'

How many times would we see each other in ten years? Nearly a year had passed since my last visit. I wrote yet another reminder to the authorities that I had received no reply to my last request for a visit.

In the meanwhile I set about lodging an appeal. With Karel's help, I discovered the identity of Pavel's 'defence' lawyer, and obtained an appointment to see him. I asked him why he had not contacted me before Pavel's trial. He replied that he had been appointed by the court a few days prior to the trial and had seen Pavel's dossier only a day before. He claimed to have done his best. The original sentence had been the rope. He had got it commuted to twenty-five years. His voice was cold and tired. If he doubted his client's guilt, his face betrayed nothing. He had his own skin and his family to protect. He avoided my eyes. I urged him to appeal. He replied flatly that in cases of treason there was no appeal.

Karel and I composed our own letter of appeal. To no avail.

Now that Pavel had been sentenced, the Kytlice National Committee announced that they had officially confiscated half of the house (the other half, fortunately, was in my name), and that they would let it as soon as they found a tenant. For months I lived in dread of confiscation of our belongings, but time went by and the Smíchov National Committee men did not appear. I assumed they had 'lost' Pavel's file, as promised.

Letters from Pavel had ceased. I worried that he was ill. Then I received a permit to visit prisoner No. 2645 at the Leopoldov prison in Slovakia.

I took the night train to Žilina. The compartment was freezing. I sat through the long night awake, but in a half dream. I had to wait a long time at Žilina for the local train. I was chilled to the bone with foreboding as well as the early morning freshness. I recalled the last time I had been here — the jovial company of the track workers, the deference with which the station master had treated the female 'engineer' from Prague. Now I was alone, the wife of prisoner No. 2645, allowed a second visit after nearly a year. The sun had warmed the air by the time the train came in. It had slatted wooden seats and was full of Slovak peasants carrying baskets with squawking ducks and other farm produce. Even on a warm day, the women wore scarves on their heads and long skirts with several petticoats. The men wore black hats and heavy black boots and clumped up and down the wooden floor like infantry recruits. A gypsy family ate and squabbled noisily in a corner.

The train coughed and chugged across the countryside. Leopoldov. The name had a formidable ring. I alighted and trudged in the direction indicated by the ticket collector. On the horizon, surrounded by a flat, lifeless plain rose a vast eighteenth-century fortress. The sun beat down and I was soon as hot as I had been cold in the night. The nearer I approached, the higher the wall grew. How hopelessly high it must have seemed to the men inside! The fortress was encircled by a moat. I crossed the bridge and rang the bell. The sentry glanced at my permit, told me to wait and closed the heavy door.

I waited for over an hour. I was beginning to feel faint: I had not eaten since the previous evening. At last the door opened again and I was admitted. The walls inside exuded a sinister chill.

'This way, you' The armed guard, a short man with a brutish face, walked beside me. He opened a door. My heart sank. We were in a large room divided down the middle by a wood and glass partition, sub-divided into small cubicles. The guard jerked his thumb and I entered a cubicle. On the other side of the partition Pavel was led in. His appearance shocked me. His hair was cropped short and his skin was pasty from lack of air and exercise. In grey, shapeless prison clothes he was a faded nonentity. Pavel, the irrepressible individualist, had become part of a uniform, dejected mass. The thought was unbearable. In the middle of the partition there was a grating. We stood to speak through this. A guard's head was a few inches from Pavel's; he was staring insolently into my face, conveying that I was the dregs of society, undeservedly on the free side of the partition. My guard stood close behind me, his weapon drawn.

We talked about the boys — the only safe subject — and their approaching vacation, three weeks of which would be spent with me in Kytlice and the rest at a pioneer camp. It was the strained, polite conversation of people who had been acquainted many years before and had met accidentally in an inconvenient place at an inconvenient time. Pavel had not been well but the pills I had sent had helped and he was working again. I showed him the latest photos of the boys through the glass.

'They are growing and changing.' He was thinking: How changed will they be by the time I see them again?

'Once you're transferred nearer Prague, I can bring them with me on a visit.'

'Yes.' He did not sound very hopeful. Suddenly he burst out: 'I know you are very busy, but couldn't you write at least a few lines?'

I was dumfounded. 'But I've written every fortnight over the past months. The boys and Karel have written too.'

'End of visit,' announced Pavel's guard, seizing his arm.

As he was dragged off, Pavel shouted: 'Write to the central detention office and complain that letters are not being delivered. Insist on an explanation.'

As I stumbled back to the station, the way was blurred. I let the tears fall unheeded. A ten-hour journey for a ten-minute visit! I had found nothing to say of comfort. I was haunted by the hurt look on Pavel's face when he reproached me for not writing. I imagined the gnawing doubts, the fears that he had been forgotten, that we no longer cared. To permit mail and then to withhold it was a monstrous kind of torture.

On the train back to Prague an old woman confided to her neighbour that her cousin and his wife had committed suicide after the recent currency reform (the second). They had lost virtually everything. 'That's something else Slánský and his gang have on their conscience,' she concluded.

I felt too dispirited to argue that Slánský had been dead for several years and some of his 'gang' had been in prison for several years before the reform had been carried out. New, and presumably more reliable, cadres had had ample time to put the economy to rights. Strangely enough, no improvement had been noted after the 'saboteurs' had been disposed of.

Every now and then a new, unfailing remedy for the sick economy was announced. For example, centralization of small enterprises into large, more efficient units and, when that failed, decentralization into small, more efficient units. In one of the bouts of ministerial expansion, the Ministry of Transport's lustful eye alighted on our little office, and we had to move into the vast Ministerial building overlooking the Vltava.

The Ministry, of course, filtered its takeover. Every new employee was always screened, even if he had already been screened and passed as an A1 citizen by six preceding enterprises. Dossiers were passed from one cadre officer to another; the subjects never learned their contents, never ascertained the source of libellous statements, of undemonstrable doubts or damaging suppositions.

'They' — the secretariat wallahs on the fifth floor — sent for Kavanová. Five of them were seated in a semi-circle wearing the incredulous expression of owls that have suffered a slight stroke. My dossier was open in front of them.

The chief cadre officer strained a thin squeak through his temporarily paralysed vocal cords: 'How is it possible, Mrs Kavanová, that you, an Englishwoman with foreign relations and, moreover, a husband in jail, have been operating in a key enterprise?' He fixed an accusing eye upon me as though I had seeped up between the floorboards.

'I was signed on in the usual way, as you can see by my file,' I answered

'This serious oversight must be rectified without delay.' The other owls nodded as vigorously as their state of shock would permit. 'Your employment at this Ministry will be terminated immediately. In lieu of notice, you will receive one month's salary.'

I had taken a hell of a lot of trouble to learn my job; now that I had got the hang of it, no one was going to throw me out. If they did, it would have to be bodily, from the fifth floor! I drew a deep breath and rattled off:

'I have been working on the electrification of your railways for three years. I have had access to all your secret plans and blueprints. I have photographed every design and every inch of your railway network, all your stations, tunnels and installations in the vicinity of the tracks. I have sold these photos to the Americans for vast sums which I have stashed away in Swiss banks. You can sack me but the harm has already been done.

You will have to re-lay and re-route your entire network!'

Not an eyelid batted, not a lip twitched, but the barb had gone home.

'Hmm.' To fill the embarrassed silence, the chief owl turned over the papers in my file. 'Engineer Němec evaluates your services highly. Under the circumstances and with regard to the importance of the work you are engaged in, I think my colleagues will agree to waive our original decision and retain you on the staff; but,' he added sternly, 'you will not be permitted to work on the tracks. Your activity will be confined to the Ministry. You will kindly hand in your railway pass card.'

This was a blow for it meant no more cheap travel. On the way home I dozed; the jogging tram took the form of a train compartment; the passengers dissolved into Slovak peasants. Superimposed upon them was the figure of Pavel in his prison rags.

Our mail box contained a single slip of paper — a money order for ten crowns from Pavel. The equivalent of a few shillings, it nevertheless represented many hours of labour. At least it meant that Pavel was working. I bought the boys a slice of ham each to celebrate, and wrote to Pavel to spend any money he earned on extras in the prison shop. Heaven knew he needed them. The infrequent parcels I was allowed to send were limited in scope and weight, and there was no guarantee of delivery.

The money order was the last news of Pavel for some time. Again I was concerned for his health. When at last a letter came, it was from a different prison. It confirmed my fears: he had suffered a heart attack. I was stunned. He had served only two years of his sentence, and already he was seriously ill. He would not survive ten years.

In desperation I wrote to President Zápotocký[34] appealing to him to save Pavel's life by granting clemency. It was hard to plead for pardon for uncommitted crimes, but, I thought, once Pavel is out he can fight to clear his name.

I took the letter to the Castle, intending to deliver it to the President in person. I slipped past the first sentry and tiptoed

34. Antonin Zápotocký (1884–1957) became a member of the Politburo in 1929. He was in Oranienburg concentration camp throughout the war. From 1948 to 1953 he was Prime Minister of Czechoslovakia and then from 1953 to 1957, President of the Republic.

up the stairs but was caught at the next floor and bundled unceremoniously downstairs to a small office where I was instructed to leave the letter. Like all my previous communications, it was ignored.

Pavel's new prison was nearer to Prague. At the next visit Karel took Zdeněk to see his father. Jan, as usual, was ill in bed. Father and son had not seen each other for three years. Zdeněk reported wonderingly: 'Tati cried.' He had been immeasurably shocked by his father's tears.

Nevertheless, as Pavel's next letter showed, he had been immensely cheered by Zdeněk's visit. He now felt much better and was working out of doors.

Chapter 13

'You must have some relaxation. Nothing but the office, household chores and preserving the lives and limbs of two boys for the next umpteen years will drive you up the pole,' said Hanka, the girl friend of one of my colleagues.

So, to postpone the onset of insanity, I accepted her invitation to go to a dance with the two of them. Several young people joined our table and the wine bottles emptied rapidly. The talk was cheerful and inconsequential. Politics faded. Hanka, pink from the dance floor, led a young man to our table. 'Look who's here,' she cried. 'Milan!' Hanka introduced us. He said he was delighted to meet me in a low, musical voice. I studied the owner. He was at least six years younger than me. His fresh complexion spoke of winds and forests. The clear, golden-brown eyes held the deep calm of solitude. It was a sensitive face, overlaid with a charming simplicity. He asked me to dance. Only dimly aware of the music and the other couples, I responded effortlessly to my young partner.

'You are so light, it's like dancing with a flower,' he said. 'Hanka's spoken about you,' he added, smiling into my eyes with affection as though we were old friends. I knew nothing of his background — family, education, status, politics — but I knew everything of the intrinsic man: good, gentle, incapable of an unkind thought or deed, with an innocence that sprang not from ignorance of the world but from purity of spirit. There was pleasure in our physical contact, but his embrace was protective rather than sensual. His light brown hair smelt of pine needles and his hands were strong and firm.

He was a biologist, concerned with optimal conditions for

tree cultivation. Czechoslovakia's chronic wood and paper shortage made this priority research, but Milan himself was interested in natural, not industrial growth. Besides his work, music was his great love. His family illustrated the adage 'every Czech a musician'.

'We all play an instrument,' he said. 'I play the piano, my father plays the violin, my elder brother the oboe and my younger brother the French horn, while my mother sings. The whole family meets at home at weekends for musical evenings. I should like to take you to our village some time. Perhaps when we hold the next fête. Someone kills a pig. The villagers turn out in national costume and perform south Bohemian folk songs and dances.'

I mused: The people of a small nation, insecure in their boundaries and sovereignty, lacking material comforts, cling to what is permanent: the soil, tradition, folklore. Folk songs and dances live on naturally; they do not have to be fostered by enthusiastic cranks.

Milan was saying: 'The scenery's just wind-blown peat moors, mists and silence; not the picture postcard kind, but I love it. It may be dank and desolate, but a man comes to grips with his soul there.'

I wanted the night to last for ever, but three o'clock drew on relentlessly. Milan would say goodnight. Tomorrow morning he would be a glowing memory of a few hours' brightness. He took possession of me and called a cab. The driver, revelling in the empty roads, sped round the curves and corners so that we were pressed close together. I exerted all my strength to control my long dormant need as it was stirred into acute awareness. Dignity had to be preserved if the evening were not to turn to bitter ashes in my mouth. Milan shook hands at the street door, then he turned my hand and gently kissed the palm. I trembled at the unexpected tenderness. He was immediately concerned.

'You're cold. You must go in. It's late and you're tired. You could easily catch a chill. Drink some hot milk before you go to bed. Promise?'

I nodded dumbly, whispered goodnight and turned abruptly. My eyelids were pricking. Somebody cared whether I was tired.

'I'll phone you at your office at two tomorrow,' he called as he left.

I fumbled for my keys with shaking hands. I staggered up our five flights. I pulled off my dress and dropped into bed in my slip, too exhausted by my turbulent feelings to undress.

At two o'clock in the afternoon the phone rang. My heart thumped so loudly I could hardly gasp out: 'Hullo, Kavanová.'

'Milan here. How are you? Have you thrown off your cold?'

Even over the phone I felt the comfort of his presence.

'Yes, thanks, I'm fine.'

'Good, so when can you be free this evening?'

This evening! My eyelids had been drooping all morning. I had anticipated crawling into bed as soon as I had got the boys under the covers. But without hesitation my voice was saying: 'Eight o'clock.'

'All right, see you at the Three Bears at 8.30.'

I had to buy coffee on the way home and make myself three cups. But by the time I had bathed and changed, my fatigue had fled. In the tram going back to town I hugged myself to still the excitement bubbling under my skin. Then a chill struck me, like a thick cloud passing over a blazing sun. Wine and oaks might improve with age, but not me. I was thirty-one and careworn; delicate crowsfeet fanned out from the corners of my eyes. The dance hall had been discreetly lit; I had been flushed with wine and the thrill of my first evening out. Now I had pale blue shadows under my eyes. Milan would spell out the years. He would make polite conversation and then, showing the utmost tact, would suggest that we leave early so that I might get some rest. The next day, he would return to his tests and I would lick my injured pride. I stood up to leave the tram and return home with my vanity intact. At the exit I told myself that would be cowardly. I would see it through. I would be nonchalant and cheerful, and bring the evening to an end with calm finality.

Milan was already there. He hurried eagerly towards me.

'Have you been waiting long?'

'No, only about five minutes, but it seemed an age. I was worried that you'd changed your mind.'

He had been worried! I began to feel a little less like an ancient, water-logged barge, abandoned to its fate. We sat down at a corner table for two. Milan took my hand.

'I'm so thankful to see you again. I've been thinking about you all day.'

Again the vibrant sweetness of his voice plucked at strings I thought had long since snapped. We drank wine and talked, and I forgot the years that lay between us.

Milan called himself a religious man, but he was a philosopher rather than a practising Christian. Love, not politics, was his solution to the world's heartache. He believed that humankind had a greater potentiality for good than evil. Left to ourselves we would live and let live, but extraneous factors goaded us to seek domination over others as a safeguard against subjugation.

'Nevertheless, people are happiest when doing good. And leading simple lives,' he added. 'Exaggerated concentration of power or wealth is alien to the Czech nature. Since the time of Hus we've been seeking a better way of life.'

I reflected: whatever the starting point, any intellectual discussion with a Czech ends up with Hus.

All too soon it was nearly midnight and we ran for the tram before the hourly intervals set in. As I jumped aboard, Milan called 'Phone you tomorrow, same time.'

Milan taught me to be, not only to do; to feel as well as think. And he loved me for what I was; not for what I accomplished. He knew the colour of my eyes; he noticed that I had tiny ears and dainty hands and feet. In fact, by highlighting the parts where Nature had dealt kindly with me and ignoring the deficiencies, he made me feel more confident.

I re-learned what I had long forgotten: to switch off activity without pangs of guilt; to live intensely when only sitting in the stillness of the pine woods. Life with Milan was a dream suspended in time and space, and contained by both. Yet, its very limitations made it eternal, and placed it beyond right and wrong. I lived on two planes of unreality: hell and heaven: a husband jailed in a twentieth-century witch-hunt; a perfect lover loaned on an indefinite contract. Hell was for twenty-five years; heaven was here and now.

Milan was heaven-sent in many practical ways too. He brought home hares and venison that he had shot. He mended gadgets that continually fell apart in my hands. He constructed kites and devised other entertainments for the boys on Sundays. He looked after them two evenings a week, which enabled me to resume my teaching at the Language Institute. Above all, his caring gave me the strength to survive. I was sure Pavel would not grudge me that. If I had been jailed for twenty-five years I would have expected Pavel neither to forget me nor to live alone.

Milan decided I needed a complete break, even from the boys.
He suggested a canoeing holiday. I would take only one week
off without the boys. Hanka offered to stay at our flat, then
promptly caught an infectious disease. That left only Fate. Fate
was a shapeless, universal aunt who manipulated the scales of
fortune — occasionally in my favour — and always for a price.
This time she exerted herself on my behalf. Our doctor at the
children's hospital prescribed a month at a rest home in the
country for the boys who were still underweight after their
winter pneumonia.

Milan proposed we 'do' the Lužnice, starting at Veselí. We
pushed off in gentle country; the river meandered among lush
meadows; willows inclined over us, dipping green finger tips
into the water. We paddled for miles, taking a short rest at
midday. After eleven hours in a C-shape, I would have disem-
barked at the first patch of moorable bank, but Milan had
specific requirements: flatness of pitch, shelter from wind,
accessibility of twigs, position for viewing the sunrise. By the
time he had found a spot to his liking, it was dark. Before I had
finished unloading the canoe, he had coaxed a few damp twigs
into a blaze. He pitched the tent, then sat strumming lazily on
his guitar while I cooked the meal in a blackened cauldron.
Everything tasted of spice and smoke, but squatting on the
ground with Milan, eating straight out of the pot, even
paprikaed charcoal would have been a feast.

Sky and stars. What more did you need?

Milan stamped out the embers and we crawled into our tiny
tent. We snuggled together. Love and warmth inside; cool
silence outside. I dozed fitfully, my consciousness as a verte-
brate heightened by unfamiliar contact with the ground.

'How did you sleep?' Milan asked, crouched over the
breakfast fire.

I wavered between honesty and hardiness. In the end I
admitted that I lacked both practice and natural upholstery for
slumber with nothing but a piece of canvas between me and the
earth's crust.

'We'll make you a mattress. Bracken stuffed into a sack will
serve well,' said Milan instantly.

We had to ourselves the river, the scents — and the mos-
quitoes. I have never had illusions about my sex appeal, but I
have an irresistible attraction for all airborne creatures that bite.
Large, inflamed lumps do not add glamour to uneven sunburn.

My knees, the back of my neck and the tip of my nose were a fiery red, the rest was pale pink. Add to this the unaesthetic symptoms of hay fever and you may easily have the end of a beautiful romance. The mornings were the worst. I emerged into warm sunshine and miles of pollen-bearing countryside. Reveille usually comprised ten or fifteen sneezes. Eyes puffed and streaming, voice muffled, nostrils red, I stumbled about getting breakfast with a huge handkerchief in constant use. A glance in the mirror annihilated the last shreds of my ego.

'What do I look like?' I groaned.

'Marvellously funny,' Milan grinned.

Milan named trees and bushes as we passed, and flowers and mosses when we stopped. He recognized birds by their call and animals by their spoor. He talked about the nurture of trees and the habits of woodland creatures, about soil composition and the nitrogen cycle. It was all about life. My thoughts had been for so long occupied with the denial of life, that I listened enthralled.

Just below Týn the Lužnice flowed into the Vltava. We entered a canyon.

'When the Orlík dam is completed this section of the river will disappear. This is the last time we'll be shooting these rapids. Keep a look out for boulders but leave the main steering to me,' Milan called out.

We were soon hurtling along at exhilarating speed on what, I was relieved to find, were more or less beginners' rapids.

'Oh look, Milan, a carp!' I pointed to the reeds on my right. Suddenly instead of racing past us, the world began to revolve around us. We were stuck on the top of a concealed boulder and the current was pulling us round in circles. The harder Milan tried to dislodge us the faster we were spinning. It looked as if we would be making the most of the rapids until the dam was completed and the rising waters floated us off. The resourceful Milan spotted a submerged rock nearby. 'I think I can just about get both feet on it. I'm going to push the canoe clear from there. Now, be a good girl, wedge your paddle against the boulder and try to hold the canoe steady.'

He leapt out, balanced on the rock, heaved the canoe toward him, jumped in and gave a strong thrust against the side of the boulder. We rocked madly, the current seized us and swept us downstream.

'That wasn't a carp, you know,' Milan observed good-humouredly. 'Carp don't live in fast-flowing water. And now would you mind watching out for rocks and not fish.'

The cliffs rose higher and closed in upon us. From the cool depths the sky looked far away. Gnarled roots and trees began to burst through the rocks, and soon the granite was covered with a wild tangle of growth. We were in Hell's Gorge. Milan announced: 'We can take the next weir.'

'Take?' Removal was clearly not what he had in mind. 'You mean — shoot the sluice?'

'Yes, it looks dicey but there's nothing to it really. The essential thing is to keep the prow pointing straight ahead; if we hit the waves at an angle, it's touch and go.'

'We'll capsize?'

'We might. And that can be unpleasant. A battering against underwater rocks can break a leg. People have even been known to drown.'

I could well imagine that: I found swimming difficult enough with two sound legs. We paddled hard to keep the canoe straight against the currents that were pulling strongly towards the millstream on either side. As we approached the sluice, Milan called to me to lay my paddle in the canoe and sit perfectly still.

Over the top we went. I held my breath. We swept down the smooth tongue of water at lightning speed. At the bottom the waters, lashed in all directions, crashed together and spumed up fountains of spray. We hit the first wave fair and square. The prow and I rose out of the water at an angle of forty-five degrees, then headed downward in a nosedive calculated to take us straight through to the river bed. But no, the wave parted and we smacked on to the next crest and from there bounced from foaming crest to foaming crest, on and on downstream until the waves had spent their fury. Then we paddled to the bank and moored the canoe.

'Jolly good for a first attempt,' cried Milan, leaping ashore. 'You were as cool as a cucumber — or an Englishwoman!'

As a precaution we had removed our belongings and left them on the bank. It was a long trek back to collect them. After that we 'took' several weirs successfully. It was an exciting sport, but Milan's constant refrain: 'We haven't capsized yet. Amazing! Everyone capsizes at least once on their first trip,' made me uneasy. Being religious, he was not superstitious. I was.

As I crawled into the stable comfort of my sleeping bag, he said: 'Tomorrow is the last sluice. It's a really tricky one. After that there are only locks with gates.'

I should have quit with my laurels dry. The day did not begin auspiciously. A chill, damp wind was blowing, the grey skies hung low over the treetops and the pit of my stomach was a long way down. The nearer we got to the sluice, the more nervous I became. We were in the grip of the current; it was dragging us to one side. We crossed the top almost diagonally. I thrust against the demonic rush of water with all my strength, then sat tight. Milan almost succeeded in straightening us but the sluice was too short and too steep. We reached the churning inferno at the bottom, aslant. A powerful wave struck the side of the canoe, tilting it high into the air. Instinctively, I ducked and the next second I was staring at the inside of the canoe as it reared above me. My last thought was: Who will look after the boys? I was sucked down and down; I fought to rise to the surface, but I was rolled over and over among the stones and mud at the bottom of the whirlpool. My lungs were being crushed, my head was bursting and there was a drumming in my ears. A strong arm caught hold of me. I surfaced and drew in a deep gulp of air. Milan supported me as we tossed like corks downstream. Eventually we kicked ourselves free of the current and swam to the bank.

'Go back and change out of your wet clothes while I retrieve the canoe and paddles,' Milan ordered me.

I walked back to where we had deposited our things. I transferred everything further downstream, lit a fire, rigged up a line and hung my wet clothes on it. Over an hour later Milan was in sight, clinging close to the bank where the current was weaker. We moored the boat and sat down on the grass, breathing heavily. I handed him his bag of dry clothes.

'Whatever made you behave so illogically?' he demanded. 'If you had thrown your weight to the right instead of the left, you could have counterbalanced the force of the wave and I could have set the canoe on a straight course.'

For the first time there was a note of asperity in Milan's voice. I had failed him. But I had been badly scared. I needed comforting not scolding. For five days we had been as close as two human beings can be; now we were separated by one false move and a line of wet clothes.

'Are we to proceed?' I asked distantly.

'No, wait, I bought some rum in a pub. You must drink hot tea with it. Have you put any water on to boil?'

I had not. Wordlessly, Milan delved into the bag for the drinking water bottle, poured some into the cooking pot and added a sprinkling of tea leaves.

'I don't want any,' I protested childishly, swallowing a hiccough. The coldness in my bones would not be dispelled by hot rum. I gazed over the now hostile Vltava and the dreary, sodden meadows; the forlorn scene was nothing to the desolation in my heart.

In a flash Milan was at my side. 'What's wrong?'

With a sob I flung myself into his arms.

He murmured endearments, rocking me like a child. 'I spoke sharply. Forgive me. I thought I'd lost you.'

That night was the sweetest of all.

The morning sun on our last day was hot. The scenery was less wild and romantic; no more proud castles perched on stern promontories. The Vltava valley had widened. The slopes were gentler and covered with mixed forests. We had views of bays, tents, occasional chalets and tranquil reflections on smooth expanses. The even current bore us steadily toward Prague. We negotiated locks and the Slapy and Štěchovice dams the conventional way. Towards evening Milan moored the canoe at the foot of Vyšehrad and we completed the journey by tram. As we parted, I told him that it was the most wonderful holiday I had ever had.

'Next year we'll do the Váh or the Dunajec in Slovakia.'

I smiled acquiescence, but I knew there would be no next time.

Basking in the warmth of fresh memories, I reached home. There were three letters, one from each of the boys. They were all right. The food was good and the teacher-nurses were nice. That was a relief. The third letter was from Pavel.

'. . . I am desperate. Again I have no letters. If you have found someone else, I do not wish to stand in your way. I have no right to ask you to wait indefinitely, but do not cut me out of your life. Give me at least news of my children. Whatever my failings as a husband I do not feel that I have failed as a father . . .'

I sat motionless. The joy, the physical well-being of the past week fell away like autumn leaves. Why had my letters been withheld again? 'I do not wish to stand in your way.' Dear Pavel, it was nobly expressed, but the very hopelessness of his position would always 'stand in my way'. If he had been 'outside', free, on an equal footing, I could have given him up and married Milan. But his hands were tied and that bound mine.

Why had he mentioned 'someone else'? Were political prisoners taunted by callous warders with their partner's real or invented infidelity? Would it be kinder to tell Pavel or to leave him in ignorance? The truth might be less hurtful than tortured doubt. In the end I wrote that I had a dear friend of whom I was very fond. He was kind and helped me with the boys, wishing to lighten my burden for a while. There was no question of a permanent relationship. 'He will fade out of my life long before you return. My affection for him has no bearing on my feelings for you or our future together.'

I loved Milan. I did not love Pavel. But I was bound by loyalty to Pavel. In jail, or released after many years' deprivation, the time to leave him would never be right.

Chapter 14

Weeks and months merged painlessly. I could not help being happy with Milan. It was my nature to be happy; without happiness life was a waste. No particular event stands out, until Eva's return to Prague. That was a reason for joy.

She phoned me immediately and I rushed round to see her. She hugged me, exclaiming: 'I have such a lot to tell you! The water's on and I've got plenty of coffee.'

I prepared for an all-night sitting.

From the notes in my diary I will reconstruct Eva's story as she told it to me with her characteristic wry humour.

The personnel officer at the mine allotted Eva a room with a former prostitute. When she opened the door she was overwhelmed by the smell of stale cabbage, burnt milk, sweat and sex. Holding her handkerchief to her nose, she dived across the room. The window had obviously been shut for years. She attacked it with both hands. It gave and some of the unpleasant odour sailed out.

She was unpacking her few clothes when an apparition walked in. It slammed the window shut, crying, 'Are you crazy? Letting in all that coal dust! This is the only place you can breathe without choking.'

Because she had lived very fast while her meagre attractions lasted, and declined slowly ever since, Kristina's age was difficult to assess but she certainly had more to look back on than forward to. The lined parchment of her face cracked into a smile. 'You new? What's yer name?'

'Eva Steinerová.'

'Eva, that's nice and straightforward; not bloody snooty

like mine. Kristina! I ask you! Some mothers should be drowned at birth. All mine ever did for me was to pick a ruddy refined name, pin it on me and leave me in a church pew. A child of God, the old geezer at the children's home called me. Don't reckon God had much of a hand in it. More like the dustman. Ever lived in a children's home? Well, you ain't missed much. Pious gibberings about being grateful to Almighty God for what you 'ave received. That's what we got in those days.' She shrugged. 'Today it's Almighty Comrade Novotný.'

At fifteen Kristina had run away and teamed up with a man.

'Me agent he used to call hisself, as though I'd feel the loss of me earnings less if we didn't refer to him as a pimp. Then I struck out on me own. I'd heard about the exploitation of the toiling masses, see.' She broke off. 'Christ, what are all them books for? Ain't you going to do any work?'

'Yes, at the washery.'

'A filthy job! What the blazes for? You don't look like a tart. You've got edication.'

Eva stammered: 'Our — our office was overloaded so I gave notice and signed on here.'

'Yer off yer rocker! Blimey, I never thought I'd end up with a loony!' Kristina observed tolerantly. 'That's a nice bit of stuff.'

She picked up a white blouse Eva had deposited on the bed. Eva snatched it from her, groaning inwardly. Kristina's fingerprints were stamped as clearly as her criminal record card. Eva laid the blouse on a shelf in the cupboard, saying pointedly: I presume this is *my* part of the wardrobe?'

Kristina shrugged, then glanced at her hands. Crossing nonchalantly to the sink, she held them under the tap and wiped off the surface dirt onto a filthy rag hanging on the waste pipe.

Eva took her lunch in the canteen. Sitting next to her was a huge pear-shaped man. 'New?' he asked in a voice that rumbled from the bottom bulge of the pear.

Eva nodded.

'I'm an old hand. Been in the mines for twenty years.'

Glancing at her neighbour's improbable proportions, Eva asked doubtfully: 'Are you still at the face?'

'Nope, not any more. I got silicosis. Was sent to a sanatorium in 1945 and then trained for a different job, with no loss of pay, mind you. I operate the cage.'

'The cage. That's some job. I'd prefer that to the washery,' said Eva warmly.

'You would?' Vašek considered a moment, then he said: 'I tell you what, if you get an okay from the Chief Engineer, I'll take you on. We were going to apply for another trainee. I get hunches about people. I'd say you'll do fine. You've got a good head. You can't let your concentration waver on the job, you know. We had a case, the cage crashed into the top landing, cracked the men's skulls. The operator thought it was on the fourth floor. You've got to keep your eyes fixed on the dial needle. If you don't decelerate at the crucial second, the cage stops with a jolt and even that can be dangerous. A good operator can feel speed, strain, movement through the lever. Not everyone's got this kind of sensitivity, but I'd stake a month's pay you have.'

Eva believed in acting on an idea while it was steaming hot. She went straight to the Chief Engineer and asked to be put down for the six-month engineering course for cage operators on the recommendation of Comrade Hamrik to whom she would be apprenticed.

The Chief Engineer turned a glazed eye upon her and enunciated slowly and softly as though the words might take the top of his head with them: 'The course is not open to women. Kindly leave quietly, close the door with care, and in future see me by appointment.'

Eva advanced upon him and, in tones calculated to rock even the steadiest of heads, cried: 'What do you mean, not open to women? All doors are open to women today!'

'Don't shout at me, woman,' he shuddered. 'Can't you see my head's splitting. It's time we abolished name days — too painful.' He swallowed a tablet, wincing at the necessity of tipping his top storey. 'I tell you it can't be done. There never have been women cage operators and there never will be if I can help it. Now go away, there's a good girl.'

Eva was not one to be beaten by a hangover. She banged her fist on the able and brought her mouth close to the C.E.'s ear. 'If I fail, the shame will be mine and the triumph yours,' she hissed.

The Chief Engineer closed his eyes in agony. 'For Christ's sake, take the form and go!' he groaned. He drew a printed sheet toward him, added a tottery signature and a blurred rubber stamp and pushed it over to Eva. She skipped out of the room, slamming the door behind her.

When she reached her room, there was no sign of Kristina but on the table was a bowl of cherries and next to it an oily piece of paper, on which a blunt pencil and an unsteady hand had scrawled:

'For Eva. You needn't be afrayed to eet them. I havent tutched them. Onest. Kristina.'

Eva felt a twinge of shame. To make amends she closed the window as soon as she heard Kristina's high heels clicketing along the corridor. Kristina, in her turn, had bought a nail brush, a strong paste for removing oil and grime and a striped Turkish towel which she treated with reverence.

Arriving home at midnight after the second shift, Kristina grumbled: 'The right to work! That's a good one! What about the right not to work? I was earning a damn sight more delivering the goods in me own department; and I didn't keep a bloody clocking machine in the room. Pay on the dot. No blasted income tax. Ah, those were the days!'

She stretched herself with a movement that was intended to be voluptuous, but contrived only to look like a crafty old rabbit slithering about inside its ill-fitting skin.

'Why don't you change your job?' Eva asked. 'You must have worked off ages ago whatever they sent you here for.'

'Parasitism's what the beak called it. Prostitution's a naughty word now, dearie. Sure, I've done me stretch. I can walk out now 'cept, where'd I go? Where else would I get this dough? What else could I do? Serve in a shop? You've got to pass in 'rithmetic for a daft job like that. At least this crummy job makes sense.' She grinned self-consciously. 'I mean, if I don't keep the blasted lamps clean, some dumb miner'll knock his block off, won't he? And anyway, you get a bigger pension at this racket. I've got to 'ave a bit of comfort in me old age. If I live that long!'

'The rate you're knocking back beers, you won't have to worry about a pension,' said Eva. 'Cirrhosis of the liver is what you're heading for, my girl. I've seen you down thirty pints at a sitting.'

'Not bad, eh? There's not many men can beat that. That's another thing in favour of this job: there's plenty of men about. And they ain't averse to a bit of screwing, especially after a beer or two. 'Course, I wouldn't take dough off me mates, even if I could. But there's no law against free beer. The men get what they want and I keep me hand in. I can't let me talents run to seed.'

Fascinated by Eva's love of reading, Kristina asked: 'Got anything I could have a go at? I ain't read a book since I was at school. *Granny* it was called. Awful crap!'

Eva smiled to herself. *Granny* was the best-loved Czech classic. She selected *Romeo, Juliet and Darkness*, a modern novel, simply and movingly written, about the tragic love of a Gentile boy for a Jewish girl during the occupation.

Kristina commented on every happening, read aloud exciting or touching passages, asked the meaning of words and Eva's opinion of the characters. At the end, sniffling audibly, she exclaimed: 'The bastards shot her, and her only sixteen. And to think that I slept with them. I'd always been kicked around. One lot or the other: it made no difference to me. The Germans treated me all right. What a lousy slut I am!'

When the time came for Eva to sit her diploma the examiner confirmed her worst fears. 'Ha, a woman!' he cried in much the same way as he would have exclaimed: 'Ha, a mistake!' in a piece of electrical equipment. His face settled into the severest lines. She would have to know the material twice as well as the male entrants. The examiner did his utmost to catch and confuse her. Eva kept her mind on Vašek and the answers came unhesitatingly. Towards the end his face relaxed. He congratulated her. 'I was doubtful when I saw you. Now I have every confidence in you.' He wrote a neat 1 next to her name and altered the masculine word *strojník* to the feminine *strojnice* on her diploma. 'The designer did not consider the possibility of a woman taking this course. You are the first woman cage operator in the country.'

Eva bought a cheap frame and hung her diploma over her bed. Kristina teased her: 'You really are cracked, Evička luv! You go into a bloody trance when you look at the thing.'

When Eva's name was posted on the board as cage operator for the morning shift, the miners went on strike.

'Fetch Vašek, he'll convince you,' she pleaded.

He rolled up red from the shower and indignation. 'You

won't trust your miserable hides to Eva! Who have you just voted the safest and smoothest operator? Me, you mugs! And who was operating half the time while I was having four hundred and forty winks? Eva, you clots!'

'That's good enough for me,' said a cultured voice. Eva looked at the man. An intellectual who had probably been sent there on a six-month brigade by some institute anxious to 'fulfil its obligations to society'. He walked toward the cage. The rest followed sheepishly.

Eva made her way to the cabin. Suddenly her confidence shrank. The possible consequences of error crowded upon her. She daren't start. She sat there, paralysed.

A memory from the concentration camp took shape in her mind. She was too ill with typhus to move. The Russians were drawing near; the Germans were liquidating the old and the sick in the camp. She had to get from the hospital to the block where her friends would hide her. It was night. Forcing her limbs to obey her, she crawled, it seemed for hours, and saved her life by accomplishing the impossible.

Strong once more, she grasped the lever. At the end of the shift, she knew she had never worked with such precision.

She completed her first week without criticism. The men still brandished lucky charms when she was on duty, but this was merely to cover their retreat.

In a free moment she sought out the tall, thin miner and learnt that he had been a defence lawyer at a regional court. The presiding judge had been directed 'from above' to bring a verdict of guilty and pass sentence of death in an alleged case of sabotage, for which the only evidence was the man's confession. The judge had refused, and had been arrested for 'obstructing socialist justice'. A more compliant judge had been appointed. Unable to save his client, the defence lawyer had resigned and volunteered for the mines.

When a block of miners' flats had been completed Eva was offered a single unit. As a parting gift, she gave Kristina the coveted white blouse.

Kristina observed lugubriously: 'Heaven knows what low type they'll send here now that the bed's vacant again.'

For the first time in weeks there was no meeting, no overtime, no friend coming to supper. Eva looked forward to a good read, but the phone rang. The personnel officer's voice vibrated in the receiver:

'Can you go to the central hospital? Your old roommate is asking for you. Yes, Kristina. The poor girl collapsed in a pub. Couldn't stand the flow. You'll go along, won't you? Bye — oh, let me know how the old dear is. Save me ringing the hospital.'

Eva put on her coat with trembling hands. She had seen Kristina only once since she had moved into the flat. On the way she bought a large bunch of carnations. The hospital was indistinguishable from the prison, the police station or any other of Ostrava's blackened buildings. She went in. A professionally cheerful nurse showed her to Kristina's bed. Eva stared in consternation at the parched, saffron skin, the colourless eyes, and the streaks of white in Kristina's brittle, orange hair.

'Hullo, Evička,' Kristina croaked. 'Does me good to see yer. Will yer do something for yer old Kris? Bring along me lipstick, next time. It's on the table in me room. I can't bear not to 'ave a bit of colour on me dial.'

Eva took her own lipstick and mirror out of her handbag. 'Here's mine, keep it, and the mirror too.'

Kristina held up the mirror to her face: '*Ježíšmaria*, what a sight! No one can look that awful and live!' She applied the lipstick. The shaking fingers produced only a ragged smear which added the final touch of tragi-comedy. Eva handed her the flowers, too distressed to speak.

Kristina brightened. 'All them carnations for me? No one's got a bunch that big!' After a moment she gasped: 'Evička, what a place to be in! All these ruddy women! Will I be glad to get outer here! . . .' Her voice died away and a tear oozed from one eye. She gripped Eva's hand. 'Yer said it'd be the end of me. I always planned to die in the arms of a man on a couch of sin. Now it looks like one of these sterilized females'll get the benefit of me dying breath. What a fate!'

'Kristina, don't talk like that, you'll get better.'

'No, I won't. I know by the way the doctors gawp at me and then go to the winder and mutter together. It won't be so bad for you when it's your turn to kick the blistering bucket. Yer'll know why yer've lived. I'm just a bit of waste, due for the scrapheap.' More tears rolled down the side of her nose.

Eva wiped them away gently. 'You didn't get much of a chance, but you've done all right. You've never harmed anybody.'

Kristina rallied. 'Eva luv, next time you come, bring me a book.'

'What sort?' asked Eva in surprise. 'A novel? Are you up to reading?'

'No, I feel too lousy, but I'd like to have a book here. When they lay me out, they'll treat me with just a bit of respect. They'll know I've read books.'

Eva nodded. The nurse came in and announced the end of the visit.

'I'll be back tomorrow. Be good!'

'I ain't got much choice,' said Kristina with a touch of her old spirit.

Then Eva vowed to make it up to her. She would visit Kristina every day and get the Works Committee to send her to a convalescent home for six months. And when she returned Eva would see to it that she didn't slip back into her old ways.

Eva was changing after the shift, when the call came from the hospital. In a matter-of-fact voice the nurse told her that Kristina had just died.

Eva hurried home, picked out her prettiest nightgown and one of her new novels and went to the hospital. She begged the nurse on duty: 'Please see that Kristina is laid out in this and that this book is put in her coffin. She was in the middle of reading it.'

The nurse accepted the parcel and asked briskly: 'Are you her next of kin? Will you be taking care of the funeral arrangements?'

In Auschwitz the 'arrangements' had been only too simple. Eva had forgotten that in civil life, although the state footed the bill, someone had to organize the transition from death to oblivion. 'Yes,' she said, she would be responsible.

Kristina's was a bleak story: abandoned at birth, loved grudgingly in life, alone in death.

Eva gripped my hand. 'I was inconsolable; I felt I had failed her.'

'But you didn't,' I exclaimed. 'You gave her what no one else had given her — a little self-respect.'

Eva considered this. 'Well, perhaps I did,' she conceded after a pause.

Eva was a mixture of romanticist and realist. In a conflict the realist won on points. I was glad to have her back in Prague. She bolstered my own wobbly conviction that a collective reason would eventually solve the riddles that confounded our society.

Chapter 15

The unravelling of conundrums began far sooner than I had expected.

Jan, now ten, was convalescent after jaundice. I was working at home so as to look after him. The Czechoslovak Press Agency supplied me with regular articles. Being desperately short of translators, they avoided screening freelance associates too closely. In any case my position as a *projektantka* had become untenable without an engineering degree. The Ministry was checking on qualifications.

It was evening. I closed my eyes to the bucket of washing soaking under the sink and the pile of ironing under the window. What a mess everywhere! And my hair needed washing; it was as lank as seaweed. But there was no one to see it. Milan was away for a few days. I'd catch up on everything tomorrow. I exhorted my younger son to eat up the semolina he was pushing disconsolately round his plate. I had ten pages to translate before morning. The bell rang. Who the hell was that?

It was Karel. 'Get your coat quickly. I've got a surprise for you,' he cried.

He would say no more but drove us to his flat. He opened the door. There stood a strange-looking creature. Closely cropped hair, no tie, and no socks, in December! It grinned and said: 'Hullo, remember me?'

'Pavel!' I gasped incredulously.

'Tati!' With a rush the boys were upon him. No questions. Three-and-a-half years ago he had gone away unexpectedly; he had returned unannounced. He lifted one on each arm and they planted a kiss on each cheek.

'He's our Christmas present. Let's wrap him up and put him under the tree,' Jan chanted.

We had coffee at Karel's while Pavel eased himself back into our lives. Then we drove home. My mind hovered over the disorder. He'll think this is the way we've been living all the time he's been away. I had planned his return so differently. The flat tidy, flowers, my hair newly set, the boys (or would they be men?) in freshly ironed shirts.

Pavel stepped self-consciously into his new home.

'I've nothing in. If I'd known.' I murmured.

'I couldn't let you know. I've been in solitary again for the past five months while investigations were being conducted. There was a hasty re-trial *in absentia*. This is all I have to show for it.'

He handed me an incredibly flimsy piece of paper. I read that the Supreme Court had abrogated the original verdict and that Pavel Kavan was acquitted of all charges. I could hardly believe it.

Pavel laughed. 'It's genuine, all right. Oh, this is marvellous. I haven't had semolina for years.'

He was home, the husband you cooked for while he played with the kids. We were an ordinary family again. He'd had no warmth or comfort for nearly four years and I was worried because I couldn't lay on a pork chop.

I cleared the table and got out my translation, but I couldn't keep my mind on the travel-worthiness of Pilsen beer. I snapped the typewriter lid shut. I'd have to phone the press agency in the morning and explain the special circumstances.

Having said goodnight to their father for about the fifth time, the boys at last went reluctantly to bed.

'Now we can talk,' I said. 'First of all, are you all right?'

'Yes. At the moment. Those summer months working in the open air set me up.'

'Start from the beginning, from the moment you left the flat.'

'As soon as we'd driven out of our road, the police handcuffed and blindfolded me. Inside Ruzyně prison I was ordered to take off my clothes and was given prison rags — shirt with no buttons, trousers with no belt and wooden clogs. My small cell had a chair, a table and a Turkish lavatory. There was a small aperture in the door and that was an eye. The colour changed, the expression varied, from mocking to sadistic, from hostile to indifferent, but there was always an eye.

'A young officer came in and told me to write my curriculum vitae. I pointed out that I had recently written one for the security police. He snapped that orders were to be obeyed. I started writing. It took me three days. I wrote carefully — my motives for my war work, my reasons for joining the Party. Every detail of my work at the Ministry, the Embassy, for the Party.

'A slightly older officer appeared, Doubek[35], one of Ruzyně's key men. He disclosed that a treacherous faction, in league with the CIA, was threatening the very existence of the Party. The police knew the identity of many of the conspirators, but they needed further evidence before they could bring a water-tight case. They were counting on me to help. He questioned me: Didn't I think Clementis put Slovak interests above the Party? Had I discussed Zionism with Goldstücker? Whom had Margolius contacted in London? Why had I cultivated Klinger's friendship, knowing he was a Trotskyist? And so on.

'Believing I was serving a higher purpose, I tried to give reasoned answers. I pointed out flaws in the police assumptions, which caused Doubek to remark that my eagerness to shield enemies of the state cast doubts on the veracity of my statements and the innocence of my activities. I began to experience a growing feeling of unreality. Anxiety and strain were beginning to tell on me. I was increasingly disoriented. I began to wonder whether the comrades, on whose integrity I would have staked my life, had become involved, knowingly or not, in a scheme to overthrow our socialist state. The prison clothes, the regulations — standing to attention when an officer or warder entered the cell — produced a psychosis of guilt. Somewhere I, too, had failed the Party, but where? This psychosis undermined my ability to think rationally. When the questions narrowed to my part in the "conspiracy", I realized with a jolt that I was no longer regarded as an innocuous witness but as a guilty accomplice.'

His voice shook with agitation. I took his hands to still their trembling. He went on to describe how sentences in his cur-

---

35. Bohumil Doubek was the chief of the Investigation Section of the security forces in the late forties and early fifties. He was arrested in 1955 and sentenced to 9 years in 1957, but was released a year later. After this he was appointed Director of the state travel agency Čedok, while many of his victims remained in jail.

riculum vitae were extracted from their context and twisted. His father had been a partner in a small wholesale clothing firm; this proved that Pavel had been brought up in a bourgeois capitalist family, although his father had died, bankrupt, when Pavel was twelve. Pavel's attendance at a German secondary school (because it was the nearest and his mother couldn't afford fares) made him anti-Czech. On the other hand, leaving his country in 1939 for patriotic reasons made him into a nationalist. As a student he had belonged to the Czech Socialist Party (albeit the left wing): this proved he was an anti-communist. His parents had changed their name from Köhn to Kavan to disguise their real sympathies which lay with Zionism.

'In short,' Pavel said, 'I was given a new identity.'

They brought him papers to sign — statements in which questions that had been put to him were presented as his spontaneous testimony. He discovered that any fresh information he had given the police in his attempts to throw light on the situation had been turned against himself and others. I recalled Cardinal Richelieu's words: 'If you give me six lines written by an honest man, I will find something in them to hang him.'

'I refused to put my name to documents that were not of my wording,' Pavel went on. 'It became more and more apparent that they were trying to trick me into an admission of guilt. Their methods of cross-examination were not very subtle. "Did Zilliacus ask you to send a letter to Slánský?" "Yes." "You abused your position at the Embassy to pass on espionage material?" "No, that's not true." Doubek shouted: "We are not interested in the truth! Here, there is only one truth, our truth!" That was the terrible moment of revelation. They didn't want the truth; they wanted only a confession — to a bundle of lies.'

Pavel clenched and unclenched his fists; his voice shook. 'Doubek told me that Goldstücker and Margolius had already confessed. They had provided enough evidence to hang me, but if I signed a confession I would get a lighter sentence. That was a mistake. I realized that those two, and all the others, were in the same position as I was: it was a frame-up. I was relieved to be able to believe in my friends again. There was no conspiracy to overthrow the Party, only a plot to liquidate certain comrades.

'At least I knew where I stood with the interrogators. There was no longer any question of cooperation.' Pavel's voice was firm again. 'As I hardened, so they hardened. They set about to deprive me of my humanity. There are several ways of reducing a man to an animal. One is hunger. My food was cut down almost to starvation level. It was mostly soup made from mouldy potato peelings. Besides debilitating the body, it weakened the mind. Humiliation is another effective weapon. The door would open a crack, a hand would put the food can on the ground. I had to kneel and consume it like a dog.'

I felt physically sick with horror.

Pavel went on, like a man forced to exorcise the past by describing it. 'Our underwear was changed infrequently. The same pants were issued to men and women. I often got ones with menstrual stains. We were given anti-hormone drugs to deaden our sexual desires. I was blindfolded and led like an animal to the interrogations. At the beginning I found it difficult to use the Turkish lavatory. Squatting is an undignified position in a man's own eyes: in front of another person, often a woman, it was degrading. The combination of solitary confinement without a moment's privacy was nerve shattering.

'Worst of all was the mental torment. I had demanded permission to write to the Central Committee and Gottwald, and had been told that the Party leadership were convinced of my guilt and that of all the other members of the conspiracy. What was the answer to that riddle? Either we were in the grip of an anti-Gottwald faction who were lying to the Central Committee or we were being framed with Gottwald's connivance. In either case, I was in prison at the instigation of communists, and my communist friends outside would be branding me as a traitor. All the warders and interrogators wore Party badges. That was the hardest thing of all: to be treated as an enemy by people who purported to be in the same Party, to be fighting for the aims to which one had devoted one's life.'

He struggled for control, then went on: 'The last factor was physical exhaustion. The table and chair had long since been taken away; my bed was a steel slab that was pulled out of the wall at night. I was forced to walk up and down the cell for sixteen hours a day. In wooden clogs with no socks my feet were soon bleeding and the pain was agony. My legs began to swell; they were like columns.' Pavel broke off. 'But I do not want to distress you with these details.' He gently wiped a tear from my cheek.

'No, please go on. I want to hear everything. I must know what you had to suffer in order to understand — '

'Why I confessed to crimes I had not committed?' Pavel

interrupted bitterly.

'No, no, to understand what you had to endure so that I may better appreciate the miracle that your spirit survived; so that I may be proud to have married such a man. I want to know.'

'The interrogations were very frequent; the interrogators alternated and always repeated the same senseless questions. They tormented us with our powerlessness; the Party had deserted us, our families had abandoned us. One told me you had left the country with the boys. Another threatened to imprison you and send the boys to an orphanage, so I knew the first had lied. During the interrogations I had to stand under a strong light for forty-eight hours; then they would shut me up in a small room in absolute darkness; then back to the light or my cell.

'I'd drop onto the bed; but there was no rest. The cell light was burning. Every few minutes a warder would wake me with the excuse that my hands had not been outside the blanket.'

This had gone on for weeks. He was weak from hunger and cold and the pain of his swollen legs. His pulse was throbbing and his heart pounding. The prison doctor taunted him: 'You're a sick man. You're shortening your life. Your heart cannot stand the strain. Give in and you will receive treatment.' Doubek urged: 'Why prolong the agony? No one escapes us. Some last days, some weeks, some months, even a year, but in the end they crack up.'

'While I could still think, I resisted; but weeks of no sleep reduce the mind to a brute level of consciousness. Concentration becomes fluid, memory jumbled; one has no sense of date or time. There's no reality except light and darkness. A prod in the back, a dash of cold water in my face cleared the haze for a moment, then it closed in again. Voices were shouting at me — I knew that from their resonance, but the words were wrapped in wool. I wanted to cry: 'No, it isn't true. I deny everything!' But my nervous system was beyond my control. Before I could frame a reply, the thought had fled. The only all-absorbing reality was the craving for sleep.

'Involuntarily, I put my hands to my head. Constantly interrupted sleep drove me to despair. To withstand total deprivation seemed to me humanly impossible.'

Pavel's voice rose: 'I suffered hallucinations. I saw my mother and father pleading with me to save my life. I had visions of you being tortured in the next cell. I heard your voice cry out. My greatest fear then was of insanity. One could recover from physical maltreatment, but once the mind snapped, there would be no recall.'

Looking at Pavel's strong face and smouldering eyes, I could not visualize him in these degrading circumstances, terrified of losing his reason.

After a pause Pavel concluded flatly: 'I didn't believe they would leave any of us alive. At this stage, death was preferable to life as a mindless idiot. I gave in.' His voice faded away.

I finally knew how the confessions had been extorted. No medieval tortures, just twentieth-century techniques of a horribly effective kind.

Pavel mused: 'I don't know everything they did to us. We were refused proper medicines yet given frequent so-called calcium injections. I don't know what they really were. They may have been drugs to induce disintegration of the personality or permanent chemical changes. My interrogator used to boast: "We can reduce you to any state from impotence to idiocy. If you escape the rope, you'll be as we want you."'

I shuddered: even now he was not free. He was haunted by the possibility of terrible after-effects.

Pavel did not remember actually signing the confession that the interrogators had written out long before. He knew only that he was allowed to sleep, was given better food, and permitted to write to me. Doubek was friendly again. Pavel was given a script — questions and answers that would be used in the trial — to learn by heart. A young officer was appointed to rehearse him.

'As soon as I recovered my powers of reasoning, I became more cheerful,' he said. 'Once in the courtroom, I intended to revoke my confession and tell the court that the trial was a frame-up. This was naive, of course. My jailers realized my intention. They threatened that if I altered one word, the proceedings would be halted and I would be sent back to Ruzyně where the procedure would begin again. I was still optimistic. I figured that if all the charges were as transparent as my own, members of the Party would recognize that the trial was phoney and would demand an investigation. To draw attention to the fact that the trial had been written beforehand, I answered one question before it was posed.'

'Yes, I know. I heard you on the radio. But the *Brown Book* published the script with the complete question.'

My senses were aching for sleep, but one thing I had to know! Who was behind it? Who instigated the trial?

'Who? Why Stalin, of course,' Pavel replied.

'Stalin?' I repeated in disbelief.

'Stalin and his chief of police, Beria.'

After Lenin's death Stalin had gradually built up a position of absolute power. The Soviet Union was surrounded by enemies. Stalin had used the threat from outside to cement the Soviet people behind him and to impose sacrifices. He had explained all mistakes as the work of external forces. When this became untenable, he had developed the theory of the sharpening class struggle after the revolution: the greater the strides towards socialism, the more desperate the enemy became; infiltration of the Communist Party would be the penultimate weapon. Having created the theory, Stalin had to substantiate it, first in the Soviet Union, then in the so-called People's Democracies. If no real enemies were found inside the parties, they had to be invented. Russian advisers at Ruzyně had instructed the Czech security police in methods of extracting confessions. Stalin believed war with the West was inevitable. By getting rid of people who had been in the West he was eliminating a potential Fifth Column. He also liquidated everyone who might advocate a non-Soviet model of socialism, especially thinkers capable of action in defence of their ideals, like the Spanish war veterans, resistance heroes and people who had supported Gottwald's pre-1948 Czech road to socialism.

'If it hadn't been for Stalin's paranoia, these crimes would never have been committed,' Pavel said. 'Stalin rose out of a historical situation. There can never be another Stalin, because the same situation will never be repeated.'

This was an over-simplification. Subsequent events were to show that as long as the Soviet leadership insisted on hegemony in the socialist bloc, every attempt to embark upon an individual model of socialism would be relentlessly suppressed. The Czech trials had been more drastic than those in the other socialist countries because the Czechoslovak Communist Party — the strongest and most deeply rooted of the East European communist parties — was the greatest potential rival to the Soviet Party. This was to be demonstrated in 1968.

Pavel held the alarm clock towards the window, into which a full moon was gazing with a cool, wise and friendly smile. 'It's two o'clock. We ought to get some rest.'

Sleeping together was going to be embarrassing after such a long separation. However, by the time I had finished in the bathroom, the warmth and softness of an ordinary bed had overwhelmed Pavel and he was fast asleep. I slipped in beside him. Tired as I was, I could not drop off. Pavel had turned on his back and was snoring softly. I bore it for an age, then I nudged him gently.

'Prisoner 2645 reporting,' he mumbled and started to get up. I put my arm around him.

'No, no, Pavel, you're home. Everything's all right. Go to sleep.'

He sank back with a grateful sigh. I would not risk waking him again, even if he were to snore all night. Towards morning I fell into a fitful sleep.

The next day, the first of the Christmas holidays, Pavel played with the boys and talked to them about their lessons and interests. They did not stir from his side for a single moment. When they were in bed Pavel continued his prison saga.

'I was kept in solitary after the main trial with no books or writing materials.'

'For how long?'

'Eleven months altogether.'

'How did you keep sane with nothing to do?'

'I worked out a strict programme for myself. I washed all over with cold water as soon as I got up, and spent about fifteen minutes in physical exercises. Then I did Russian for an hour.'

'You mean in your head?'

'Yes. I revised my vocabulary, then I translated passages from Czech literature into Russian. Next item was a walk. My feet had healed and I was now wearing shoes, but without laces. I walked from one particular place to another. I pictured the landmarks on the way. If there were castles in the vicinity, I related their history. This was followed by mathematics. Maths was never my strong point so this required an enormous effort. I think only in prison, cut off from all distractions, can one achieve such a degree of concentration.

'Then I had to keep up with my English. I composed stories or articles in Czech and translated them into English. For relaxation I went through Czech books, films and plays slowly and in great detail. I made miniature chessmen out of soap and used to play with the chap in the next cell by means of the Morse code. The main thing was to spread these activities over the day, leaving no blank periods.'

Pavel was speaking with his customary vigour. Now it was easier to picture him as a prisoner; resourceful, fighting back. My old admiration for him surged over me. I took his hand.

'Tell me about your own trial.'

'It lasted two days. It was similar to the main one. We learned our lines. At the trial we discovered that we four — me, Eda, Dufek and Richard Slánský — had formed a conspiratorial group at the Ministry. I had spent one week in the death cell. That was the worst time of all. I really believed they meant to hang us all.'

After the trial Pavel was detained at the Pankrác prison for some inadequate medical treatment. Several months later he was declared fit and sent to Leopoldov. He was excited at what he thought would be a step toward normal life. But Leopoldov was hell, especially for communists. They were harshly treated by the warders, because they were traitors, and by the other prisoners because they were communists. The warders delighted in putting communists and fascists together and never interfered when the fascists beat up the communists.

'The food was lousy: watery soup, potatoes, a few times a week a tiny piece of gristle. We stole meat intended for the police dogs and ate it raw. The work norms were so hard we rarely had anything over to buy extras,' he said.

'Yet when you did earn something you sent it to us. I told you to keep the money and buy food.'

'I know, but I felt it might come at a crucial moment when you had nothing. My first job was plucking feathers. After a few weeks my fingers were calloused and bent. If I kept hard at it, I earned 25 hellers[36] a day. Then I went on to making ropes and sacks. About this time I managed to smuggle out a letter to Zápotocký, describing the methods used to extract confessions and demanding a re-trial. I never received a reply.'

Karel had ascertained that a letter from Pavel had reached Zápotocký's office, as had my letter appealing for clemency.

'Then they must have been concealed from him.' Pavel was

36. 25 hellers equals about half a penny.

loath to believe that the popular Zápotocký, who had succeeded Gottwald as President, could have known and ignored the truth.

'Then I was moved to Bytíz. That was heaven compared with Leopoldov. I worked on a building site. You should have seen how handy I became with a hod of bricks. I was with a mixed group of politicals and common criminals. There the code was: if you're a good con, you're okay; your politics are your own affair. For instance, the governor brought out a new ruling forbidding prisoners to use the open space in their free time. The cons decided on a hunger strike. I was the only communist in our room. At lunch time the others asked: 'So what, Pavel?' 'So we don't go,' I replied, and that was that. I was one of them. We won the strike.

'On Sundays we managed some recreation. Four of us — all of different political convictions — used to play bridge. Cards were forbidden but we kept a pack under the floorboards. A con kept a look-out outside the prison house.' He smiled in reminiscence, then observed seriously: 'Prison teaches you surprising things about human nature. When I had a bad attack of angina pectoris, one of the cons attended me with great gentleness. He was a murderer who had killed his own mother and brother! A man whose company I found most stimulating was a Nazi. Another was a Catholic priest. One's values were turned topsy-turvy.' Pavel smiled ruefully. 'Prison is a university of life but as Soukup, a Czech Socialist, used to say: 'I'm not so stupid as to need fourteen years of it!' Nowhere else do you explore your own resources so thoroughly or make such lasting friendships. Comradeship is the only nourishment a man's body and soul receive: without it he would wither within a year.'

Pavel fell silent. Many of those friends were still inside. I touched him gently. 'You still haven't told me how your release came about.'

'I smuggled out another letter. This time to the Central Committee, and that reached its destination. Two younger members came to see me. They were distressed at my revelations. I would swear that they, at least, had no inkling that justice had been violated.'

We found out later that a Politburo commission had been set up at the beginning of the year to investigate the political trials. Its policy, however, had been to admit only to certain distortions of facts, otherwise to confirm at least the partial guilt of the accused. In the cases of Pavel and Eda and one or two others the Commission had been forced to find all the charges false and order their acquittal. Another possible factor in Pavel's release was that Konni Zilliacus had been invited to Moscow. He was to pass through Prague. Enquiries about his fellow spies in quod would doubtless have embarrassed the authorities.

Pavel ended his narrative on a confident note: 'Now that some of us are out, we shall be able to secure the release of others.'

Chapter 16

After Pavel's legal rehabilitation, we fondly imagined that political and public rehabilitation, as well as compensation, would follow automatically. In fact, the only confiscated articles we retrieved immediately were the wristwatch and fountain pen that had been in the custody of the Smíchov National Committee. The two comrades fell on Pavel's neck when he looked in and proudly presented him with two little packets neatly labelled 'Dr Pavel Kavan'. They had not even deleted his academic title when sentence had been passed. In their own way they had dissociated themselves from the trial.

Pavel never set eyes again on the Soviet watch his Soviet-run trial had deprived him of. In lieu he received a few crowns, the amount for which it had been sold at an auction of confiscated items held by the Central National Committee for their friends. It took an eight-month battle to re-possess the Minx, sadly the worse for wear. Re-housing was to take much longer.

Pavel was itching to get back to work but the Party had not yet okayed a job. This left him with a lot of unconsumed energy which he directed at putting right what had gone wrong while he was away. He went through the boys' report books. Zdeněk's passed without comment. At Jan's he tore his hair: 'A two for history, a three for geography and a four for maths. The boy's a dunce,' he exclaimed tragically.

'He's not a dunce,' I said soothingly. 'He's missed a lot of schooling, that's all.'

'Why? Is there something seriously the matter with him?' Pavel demanded, now as alarmed as he had been outraged. (Pavel's abrupt changes of mood were going to take some getting used to after a long break.)

'He had all the usual children's illnesses. Then he started getting septic tonsilitis, and inflamed adenoids and middle ear, which led to bronchitis and pneumonia several times. He's allergic to dust and changes of temperature, and suffers from constant colds.'

'Why didn't you have his tonsils out?' Pavel interrupted.

'Because he was never well long enough for the doctors to agree to the operation.'

'He was a healthy enough kid before I went away.' This was a fact, but Pavel's tone implied that my neglect had been to blame. I bit my lip.

If Pavel had had his way he would have kept Jan studying an extra three or four hours a day in an attempt to catch up four years' backlog in as many weeks. I remonstrated that Jan was still convalescing from jaundice. Some marks improved, but continued low marks for maths produced another outburst:

'Hasn't the boy any ambition? He's so phlegmatic about his school work.'

'Nonsense,' I retorted. 'He's over-anxious. He works himself into such a state about what you're going to say about his damned marks that he can't think straight.'

For poor Jan, the novelty of having a father was proving two-edged. I, too, came in for a share of criticism. Why hadn't I coached Jan or found someone else to? I protested that I had done my best in my limited time. A neighbour had helped with Czech and handwriting; I hadn't been able to find anyone for maths. Why had I left Zdeněk with Vlasta for some months after I'd recovered from my illness? I explained that he'd been better off there. The headmistress was a friend of Vlasta's and had treated him kindly. He had also had better food in the country than I could afford.

'Why didn't you ask Karel for money if you were short?' Pavel demanded.

'I figured if he didn't offer, he didn't have any.'

'Nonsense, of course he did. You could have borrowed from him, I would have paid him back when I got out. It was wrong to be too proud to ask where the boys' health was concerned.'

I was silent. I couldn't say I had asked and been given advice instead of cash. Karel had helped in other ways.

I felt myself slipping into my old role, on the defensive,

blameworthy. Yet the one transgression of which I was technically guilty Pavel did not hold against me. He said: 'It's over
now. Let's not discuss it. But if you see him again, I'll divorce
you and get custody of the boys.'

Pavel had suffered: Pavel deserved recompense. I desired
above all that he should be happy. I hoped that I would be able
to disguise my own aching emptiness. I had my memories to
give me strength and Malá Strana for solace. I had my children;
I would never have given them up for Milan. I immersed myself
in my family. Life was bearable.

For a time we managed on my earnings. Then for two weeks
the supply of agency articles dried up and Pavel became frantic
with anxiety. His old prison fears for our security welled up. He
was convinced this was another form of political discrimination.
I assured him the hiatus was temporary. Unconvinced, Pavel
undertook some reconnaissance and came up with a 300-page
volume on high-tension circuit breakers to be translated into
English. I commented that the title was appropriate to our
situation but the content somewhat out of range.

Pavel protested: 'All you need is a Czech–English technical
dictionary. It's no problem.'

I smiled to hear Pavel's old slogan, and pointed out that no
such thing as a Czech–English technical dictionary existed. My
vicariously dauntless husband was equal to that too. He had a
friend who was an electrical engineer and knew some English
terminology. We would compile our own glossary of terms. I
was still dubious.

Pavel exploded: 'I find something that will keep the wolf from
the door and you find it too difficult before you've even tried.
Oh well, I might have known.'

I swallowed the bait. With my usual thoroughness I studied
six English books on electrical engineering at the university
technical library. Soon after I'd got my teeth into the circuit-
breakers, straightforward translations which, as the Czechs say,
I could have done with my left leg, began to flow in and had to
be turned down. By the time I'd paid my collaborator and a
typist, and had stuck at the translation for ten or twelve hours a
day for nearly six months, my earnings worked out at the
equivalent of a few pence per hour. But the translation was
awarded an Honourable Mention at the Brussels Expo; where-
upon I received a letter addressed to Monsieur Casanova from a
French publisher asking me to name my fee for translating

technical literature from Czech into French. Pavel drew a breath. I forestalled him.

'If you say: "That's no problem; all you have to do is to brush up your French," I'll knock you unconscious with the honoured circuit-breakers!'

A more positive result was an offer to translate a book of fairy tales for the Czech publisher Artia. Pavel, inconsistent as ever — he either expected too much or too little — asked discouragingly: 'Do you think you're up to it? That's very different from technical and political stuff. For that you need real literary talent.' (He was genuinely astonished when I made a success of the translation and was given another commission — a hitherto unpublished story by Karel Čapek.)

While I had been struggling with electric currents, Pavel had been negotiating the sordid matter of compensation for unjust imprisonment. He finally announced that he was to be paid half of his lost salary.

'You agreed? You let them get away with robbery?' I demanded. 'One injustice does not rectify another. Either you are entirely innocent and therefore are entitled to full back pay or you are partially innocent and deserve only half pay.'

Pavel demurred that the state could not afford such a large sum.

'Bullshit — I mean rubbish.' (My enriched vocabulary was not to Pavel's taste.) 'Fair damages can't ruin the country: the Prime Minister has just announced an appreciable growth in the economy. I suggest all Party functionaries contribute a percentage of their salaries until this debt of honour is paid.'

Pavel muttered that he thought that his freedom would mean more to me than money.

'Of course it does, but . . .' I gave up.

The ultimate exercise in cynicism was the deduction of thirteen crowns fifteen hellers per day for Pavel's 'keep' in prison.

He, and the other released communists, still had no job and no proper status. The leadership was protecting itself by shrouding the show trials and their victims in silence. However, it was forced to take nominal action by the 20th Congress of the Soviet Communist Party and Khrushchev's revelations of Stalin's personality cult. A second commission was appointed to investigate the Slánský trial while perpetuating the thesis that Slánský was the Czechoslovak Beria. The Central Committee was informed officially that Pavel Kavan, the three others released with him and Artur London had been acquitted of false charges and reinstated as Party members. No public announcement followed.

Pavel badgered the commission, in particular over a former cell-mate who was seriously ill. The man died in prison while the commission was debating his release. Pavel grieved for his friend and raged at the commission's slowness.

Now that his political rehabilitation had been carried a step further, Pavel was offered a post. His appointment as assistant to the editor of the State Publishing House of Political Literature came as a surprise: the other ex-prisoners had been tucked away in libraries and such innocuous corners where they could have little impact on the public. Pavel, of course, would have made an impact on an institute for deaf mutes. It was not in his nature to feel his way. He plunged head first into controversial waters.

Enthusiastically, he expounded his project to me: 'A series of paperbacks giving our — Czech — commentaries, analyses and immediate reactions to international events without waiting for Moscow to formulate its attitude.'

I goggled. True, the Soviet Union and Yugoslavia had recently stated that roads to socialism might differ according to conditions and that any tendency to impose its own model was alien to each of the parties. But to take the declaration at its face value when the Czechoslovak leadership had ominously ignored it and, moreover, to interpret it as a green light to independent thinking struck me as dangerous, if laudable, lunacy.

Pacing up and down, Pavel happily developed his scheme. 'The series will be written for the man-in-the-street, giving him the background, causes and possible effects of developments. No jargon. Plain facts, clear statements and graphic style. The only problem is: who can write in that way? Who can still use his own political judgement?'

'Only your friends who've been in cold storage for the worst of the brainwashing period,' I suggested.

'Yes, yes, of course. Evžen Klinger and Vavro Hajdú. They're foreign affairs experts. Then there's Jiří Hronek. He can turn out a political book in a fortnight. And Heda shall design the jackets.'

Three weeks later a haggard, unshaven Evžen staggered in.

'That husband of yours certainly stirs things up,' he

complained wrily. 'You start off by firmly rejecting his crazy ideas, and before you know where you are, you're in them up to your neck. We survived clink but he'll be the death of us! I've had about three hours' sleep a night since I started this damn thing but the job's finished.' He drew an MS out of his brief-case. 'Pavel thought a book on oil, the key to the Suez crisis, leading to the question of liquid fuel replacing solid, would be a useful publication.'

The next series came out after the drastic events in Hungary. *The Drama of 1956* was written by Hronek in December under the pseudonym of Politicus, Pavel's latest idea being that his collaborators should write under the same name. The book, in an edition of 12,000, was out in February, a miracle for Czech printing. The Central Committee was alarmed. Here was a group reaping political success — a faction. A faction, moreover, that consisted of cult victims who would rise to prominence once the truth about the trials was made public.

'Policy is made here, not in the Publishing House of Political Literature,' the Central Committee told the chief editor and the series was banned.

'It was fun while it lasted,' Hronek sighed.

In ordinary circumstances they would have made a name for themselves. They suffered from being men of ideas at a time when original political thinking was anathema.

Prison had given Pavel time to think: he had emerged with open eyes. He re-appraised society and discovered how far it had deviated from original socialist concepts. He was forced to admit that he, too, had become sectarian after 1948. Party discipline had clouded his judgement, as it had that of others. He saw that only the restoration of inner-Party democracy would guarantee social progress and the prevention of further miscarriages of justice. He became convinced that a movement towards change could be initiated only by a politically aware rank and file able to take a share in decision-making. This would never come about without free discussion within the Party and a re-interpetation of Marxism. He concluded that only enlightened Marxists could create enlightened socialism. This kind of thinking was adopted by other Party reformers many years later.

Pavel didn't wait for a change of heart in the apparatus. He was impelled by a sense of urgency. He himself turned to the rank and file. He directed the Party school for the publishers' employees and put across his ideas to them. He addressed the wider public through the non-Party Society for the Dissemination of Political and Scientific Knowledge.

Paradoxically, he was now a greater threat to the apparatus than he had been as a prisoner.

He had become not only a more flexible Marxist but a more open-minded human being. He no longer divided people into sheep and goats; he cultivated non-communists as well as communists as friends. He also erased the division between a man's and a woman's work, which he had applied rigidly until then. While out of work he tackled shopping and cooking. (Incidentally, the boys were far more tolerant of his culinary disasters than of mine.) Above all, Pavel valued family life more highly than before he went to prison. Even when he was working again he found time to be with the boys, taking them to football matches, teaching them chess and discussing history, literature and politics with them by the hour.

In many respects, though, he was still the same impractical Pavel, as our first weekend in Kytlice was to demonstrate.

On arrival at Kytlice Pavel organized his team. Jan was to gather up the pieces of tarpaulin that had fallen off the roof. Zdeněk was to weed the flower bed. I was to rake off the dead grass from the meadow behind the house. This proved surprisingly difficult, but I plodded on, determined not to mar our rustic idyll by provoking complaints.

In his role of foreman Pavel came to inspect our progress. He set light to my biggest pile of dead grass. In a second he was prancing like the proverbial cat on hot bricks as flames licked around his feet. My laughter was stillborn, for a wind sprang up and carried tongues of fire over the field toward the forest. I seized a spade and flayed the burning stubble. Then I heard an ominous sound behind me, like the splatter of bullets on armour plating. I wheeled. The little nursery of firs that flanked the forest was alight.

Trying to stay calm, I shouted to the boys to bring water. The firs were now burning with a fierce white brightness, scattering a rain of golden needles. Pavel and I wielded our buckets with unabated energy but the odds were against us. The boys gallantly ran to and from the well, which was thirty yards away. It was a losing battle; until the wind veered. That gave us a breathing space in which to put the firs out of action. I took toll of the casualties: ten trees mortally damaged and a score of lighter cases. We then subdued the meadow. A forest fire and a further jail sentence for sabotage had been averted.

Jan hopped about, crowing: 'A real fire! Wait till I get to school. That'll really be something to tell 'em!'

'In that respect,' I observed gravely, 'your father will never fail you.'

The boys clamoured for a camp fire. I protested faintly that we'd had enough of the Promethean element for one day.

'We'll do it ourselves,' Jan promised. 'We learnt how to make a base to stop it from spreading at our Pioneer meetings. Tati was never a Pioneer,' he excused his father kindly.

'All right.' I went indoors to wrestle with the stove which when fed with the self-same dry grass, produced only smouldering blackness. The chill had just about been taken off the room when the boys called me to supper. We sat on our haunches eating toasted sausages and all but incinerated potatoes. The meal, we all agreed, was indescribable.

I awoke in the middle of the night with my gastric juices in turmoil and prodded Pavel into consciousness.

'Quick,' I gulped with my hand to my mouth, 'Pass me that vase.'

'But it's hand-painted!' Pavel protested.

'This is not the occasion for an appreciation of the arts.' A momentous heave brought Pavel to my side without further argument. At the same time Zdeněk burst into our room with the cheering news that he had puked all over his bed.

While I gathered up the soiled sheets and pillow-cases in the morning, I pondered the cause of the disturbance. It could not have been the sausages because Pavel, the only unafflicted one of us, had eaten some. But he had declined the potatoes. I asked him carefully what they had burnt on the fire.

'Pine cones and wood,' he replied. 'Then I threw on some of the creosote paper from the roof. It made a lovely blaze.'

That explained it. The ash on the potatoes! Creosote! Coal tar! A mixture of phenols and their ethers. Phenol, commonly known as carbolic acid, was caustic poison!

'A touch of arson, followed by attempted familicide! It'll be a miracle if our children live to a ripe age,' I teased him.

Still groggy from the nocturnal upheaval, I suggested an early departure. Pavel filled the tank from his reserve can and the Minx trundled happily downhill. At the road she came to a dead halt. I had an undeniable feeling of *déjà vu*. Pavel trudged off to the village and hauled the local mechanic out of the once-a-week cinema. After tinkering for hours he had not diagnosed the trouble. Stragglers returning home from the pub joined us. At length one more perspicacious than the others perceived that the tank did not contain petrol but diesel oil, to which the Minx's British innards were not adapted.

'All out and push!' Pavel cried. This was another pre-jail slogan I could cheerfully have given a miss.

We pushed and rolled the car to the village where the National Committee chief obligingly got out of bed, in a long night shirt, and found us the only spare can of petrol in Kytlice.

We reached Prague at 3 a.m.

The old promise was still operative. Life with Pavel was anything but boring.

Chapter 17

'Sit down, I have something to discuss with you,' said Pavel grimly on the first evening of my return from a fortnight's course of lectures to teachers of English. I probed my memory for some failing on my part.

He took a deep breath and announced: 'I've lost my job.'

I sighed with relief: the fault was not mine. 'Is that all?'

'All?' he squeaked. I poured some more coffee. 'Don't you want to know why?' he demanded.

I hardly expected a concrete reason: I had put it down to the political weather vane.

'For being drunk and seducing a married colleague in working hours!' Pavel declared dramatically.

'You? Oh, no, I don't believe it! Darling, you haven't been brainwashed again, have you?'

'No, this time the charges are true,' he admitted glumly.

The dear man certainly had a flair for unusual predicaments! 'Tell me about it,' I invited him, leaning comfortably against the cushions with the air of one about to plunge into a salacious novel.

'You don't sound the least bit scandalized,' he grumbled.

Now he was shocked because I was not shocked. 'Let me hear how it came about and, if you deserve it, I'll throw a fit of righteous indignation.'

'Well,' Pavel swallowed hard. It sounded as though this confession was going to be harder than the one in court. 'It happened on my birthday. I bragged about my capacity for alcohol in our diplomatic days, and the girls decided to test it. They mixed my drinks, poured me doubles and spiked my brandy with paprika. I had a blackout.'

'Not surprising after four years of abstinence,' I put in quickly.

Pavel went on. 'I don't remember a thing till the next morning when I woke up with a head full of church bells and a tongue like mouldy cheese. At work Prokopová told me that after the drinks a young woman and I had gone into a small, unused room which, unfortunately, could be viewed from across the yard. Some zealous soul had reported our activity to the Party CC, with the result that she was instructed to give us immediate notice.'

'Normally such a thing would have been settled on the spot,' I protested. 'It's nothing to do with the Central Committee. This is a clear case of political discrimination. What a chance, though, for the CC to wag a moral finger at a trial victim.' I stifled a giggle.

'I don't see anything funny about it.' Pavel sounded aggrieved.

'I'm sorry, darling, it's my distorted sense of humour. You, who never have time even to look at another woman, caught *in flagrante* by your lady boss, the formidable Prokopová! I only regret that having made such a colossal idiot of yourself, you didn't get any fun out of it. But only Pavel Kavan could be sacked for seduction in a coma! Cheer up! We've survived tougher situations. I'll tell you what, I'm rich at the moment. I'll invite you out to dinner on my earnings, and then you can seduce me. How's that?'

Pavel grinned in spite of himself. 'All right, if that's the way you feel.'

A mood of sadness seized me. From the back of the bathroom cupboard I took out the remains of my diplomatic cosmetics, I watched my face changing under an art as ancient as Egypt; lines and wrinkles faded, hollows filled, bloom returned, eyes widened and lips retrieved the fulness of untroubled youth. I studied the picture I had painted. Gratifying, but it wasn't me. It was a deception, a gentle fraud. Would I dare to take it with me this evening? Defiantly I added a suspicion of eye shadow.

I went to my wardrobe and under an old maternity smock I found the shocking pink dress my sister had sent some years before. The neckline did not exactly plunge but it did reveal a few inches of chest bone and the skirt was slightly less severe than a Doric column.

'Why darling, you look lovely!' Pavel's unfeigned surprise was hardly flattering. 'Funny, I never thought of you as good looking. I took to you immediately we met but that was because of your honesty. And I knew you'd be a sticker. But I didn't notice you had looks.'

'I haven't; it's a genie out of the bottle,' I said lightly.

Pavel selected a wine tavern he had known in his student days and to which he had taken me during my first year in Czechoslovakia. I rubbed my eyes. Where were the dark walls and ponderous furniture? Here was a harvest of colour! Opaque tear drops, suspended from a cobalt ceiling, cast diffused light on magenta wall panels. Elegant contemporary chairs splashed emerald, purple and black patches about the room. The women were dressed in Chinese brocade, flowered silk and billowing taffeta, flashing with Jablonec jewellery. Here and there tanned shoulders gleamed.

Pavel muttered something about encroachment by the West.

'If you mean that only the West knows how to enjoy life, you're wrong,' I retorted. 'By all accounts the Russians and even the Poles do. The Czechs are too strait-laced. They confuse gaiety with licentiousness and luxury with licence. Or is it only our generation of communists? These young people don't look as though their socialist consciences are suffering for a night out.'

I ordered an aperitif, a three-course meal and wine. The heady Tokaj gave our tongues a brilliance that startled us both. From the antiquity of our austere youth we dug up fragments of poetry. I quoted Byron's *Prometheus* in English, Pavel recited his *Sons of Greece* in Czech. We contrasted the two humourists, Hašek, the Chaplin of literature, and Shaw, the intellectual clown. We were talking more freely than at any time since Pavel's return. A barrier had been dissolved — Milan. The score was even. Pavel was able to forgive. I would never be able to forget but I pushed Milan's memory onto a lower level of consciousness.

A friend whom we hadn't seen since Pavel's release joined us from another table; he had been in Bratislava. He raised his glass in belated congratulations.

'Aren't you proud of Rosemary and the way she managed while you were away?'

'What? Oh, yes,' muttered Pavel in confusion. It was obvious the thought had not occurred to him.

'Well, dammit, it was harder for her than the other wives,' his friend insisted. 'She gave up family, country and decent code of behaviour for this madhouse. We are subconsciously conditioned to tragedy. The English are so normal they don't even have a subconscious.'

'Hmm.' Pavel grew pensive. He seemed to be thinking this over.

On the way home, as I was dozing against his shoulder, he whispered: 'Of all possible ways of spicing middle age, falling in love with your own wife is the most satisfying.'

Probably never again would the combination of wine and circumstance induce my unsentimental husband to articulate his feelings. That night was like picking up a well-loved book after many years and discovering that the pleasure was as deep as the first reading, or rather had deepened with the intervening experience of life.

Now that the label 'family of a traitor' had been removed, I was permitted to take the boys to England where they had a joyful reunion with their grandparents.

We came back refreshed and refuelled. But the flat was a scene of monumental disorder. Pavel had used up all the crockery, as well as his smalls and shirts, intending to have a good clear up before we arrived. Instead he had had a coronary, and he was only forty-three. I had been sure that once he was out of jail he would have no further trouble. He looked pale but his eyes were bright. Papers were strewn all over the floor, the chairs occupied by Klinger, Hronek and Arnošt Tauber.

'He's supposed to be resting,' Evžen complained. 'He's got a heart attack because he thinks he can translate *Ten Days That Shook the World* in a month on coffee and cigarettes. When he is discharged, instead of obeying doctor's orders, he comes up with . . .'

'A political dictionary,' Pavel burst in. 'I've checked with the bookshops. There is an absolute dearth of comprehensive but concise reference books. We'll supply one within a year.'

Hronek's small, wary face cracked in a lopsided grin. 'It's a bloody nerve, really, four people taking on such a huge enterprise. Tauber is covering economics; Pavel diplomacy and foreign affairs; Evžen will do Slovakia; and I'll be handling everything else. Pavel will compile and edit the whole thing as he's unlikely to find regular employment in a hurry after his latest fiasco!'

Pavel flung himself into the work with renewed energy, stopping only to take a pill when his constitution protested. His output was high, but offset by emotional ups and downs. When he was in the depths, he would come to me, stating: 'I'm depressed. Cheer me up.' When he was out of the trough, riding the crests once more, he would resent his interim dependence upon me. So, he alternately clung to me and rejected me. This was unsettling though understandable; for he was haunted by his old fear that his life would be cut short before he had accomplished his aims. A less ambitious man would have attempted less, a more philosophical man would have suffered less.

Encompassing the whole political scene, however concisely, required space. Pavel spread the whole world round our flat which would have more comfortably accommodated one ageing person of limited interests. His reference books were piled on the floor or stacked in boxes. Not an inch of floor or furniture was free of paper.

'Italy,' Pavel roared with double strength, as befitted a two-tailed Czech lion, at eleven o'clock one night. 'I've lost Italy.'

'You'll wake the house,' I cautioned him. 'And stop prowling, or you'll tread on Trotsky or Khrushchev or somebody and they'll go to press with footprints over them. I'll find Italy for you. Go and make yourself some hot milk.'

I located Italy under 'Abyssinia,' one of the cross-references.

Lebensraum was now a most acute problem. We should have to acquire our rightful quota before we went beserk. The authorities were still passing the buck. Coercive action was indicated. Equipped with a thermos flask and blanket, I ensconced myself in the office of the housing manager of the Ministry of Foreign Affairs.

'It's positively disgusting,' I told him. 'A man has been unjustly imprisoned and he still can't get justice. This Ministry owes us a decent flat.'

'We have no flats available even for our own employees,' the official stated. 'May I point out that your husband no longer works for the Ministry.'

'That's not his fault. The Ministry turned us out of our original flat. I'm not leaving until you've found us equivalent accommodation.'

He shrugged and returned to his work. After an hour I poured myself some coffee. The official fidgeted but said nothing. Another hour passed. I poured another cup. The official had been chewing gum steadily since I arrived.

'I should have thought this country could have imported more useful commodities from America than chewing gum,' I remarked conversationally.

He snorted as though bitten by a persistent horsefly. Surreptitiously, under cover of blowing his nose, he removed the gum. I took out my knitting, dropping a needle on the floor with a clatter every few minutes. With a groan, the man suddenly reached for a sheet of paper. I watched with bated breath while he wrote a statement authorizing our re-housing. He signed it and handed it to me: 'Now go away.'

Two years after Pavel's release from prison, we moved into a three-roomed flat in a panel block on the outskirts of Prague. Work on the dictionary proceeded more smoothly after that. It was completed within a year. Its authors were exhausted but satisfied. Experts reviewed it and recommended publication. The publishers were about to hand it to the printers when the wheels ground to a halt. Pavel Auersperg[37] of the Central Committee had sharply criticized the dictionary's political concept.

'It's strange that none of the other political authorities discovered these shortcomings. Auersperg's reservations are directed not at the dictionary but at its authors. It's enough that the name Kavan is among them,' Pavel exclaimed bitterly.

I sighed. It was clear that until the truth about the show trials was published and the socialist bloc made up its mind about Yugoslavia, Pavel's position would remain precarious. Neither prospect looked hopeful. The two commissions had been wound up, a few cases had been reviewed and re-tried. The activity of Slánský and his co-defendants had been redefined as anti-Party rather than anti-state. All the blame for inadmissible police methods was laid on Doubek and one other investigator who were then tried and convicted, and released after serving a few months. The cover-up was complete; both the Party rank and file and the general public were left in the dark. Titoism — now

37. Pavel Auersperg was the head of the ideological department of the CC CPCz in the '60s, and in charge of the working group which drew up the reformist Action Programme for the Party in early 1968. However, later that year he openly welcomed the Soviet invasion.

re-christened revisionism — was again a term of political abuse.

My own recent experience had confirmed that the name of Kavan was no asset when job-hunting. Artia had a vacancy for a representative to deal with the English publishers of books printed in Czechoslovakia. My Czech was almost faultless, I could claim to understand the English. I seemed perfect for the job and the job for me. I was turned down as a security risk. Why? On account of your husband. But he's been rehabilitated. That makes you an obvious recruit for the British Secret Service. English wife of wrongfully jailed Czech; bound to be bitter. Not true. We know but . . .

'In any case,' I interrupted impatiently. 'The Secret Service would suss out in a moment that I'm far too transparent to be of any use. I couldn't fool anyone.'

The director shook his head regretfully. 'We cannot be too careful.'

Pavel came in angry and strained. 'The publishers refuse to publish the dictionary,' he stated flatly. 'Of course they're too cowardly to give the reason.'

The crushing weight of his disappointment bore down upon me. I sank on to a kitchen chair and dropped my head on my hands. After all that work, to break their contract; it was too cruel.

Pavel declined supper and said he would go to bed early. Suddenly he doubled up in agony; his face was grey and sweaty. I phoned for an ambulance. 'Please hurry, it's a coronary. I know the symptoms.'

The voice at the other end asked for details: name, date of birth, description of symptoms, dates of previous attacks.

'Can't you complete the form later and just send the ambulance,' I pleaded. 'My husband's life is at stake.'

I paced the room between Pavel's divan and the window for half an hour. I phoned again and was told sharply that as soon as an ambulance was available it would be sent. Another agonizing half hour passed.

'My husband's a heart case, he might have died before you got here,' I reproached the big ambulance man.

'Sorry lady, all the hospitals are short of ambulances,' he apologized awkwardly.

I held Pavel's hand all the way. 'You'll be all right. People have four or five coronaries and get over them. There are statistics to prove it.' I was telling myself as much as Pavel.

He squeezed my hand gratefully. 'I haven't been much good to you, but I have always loved you.'

'I know,' I gulped, a lump in my throat. Pavel might be exasperating, but he was also brave, indomitable and loyal. A very special person.

Pavel surprised everyone: he recovered quickly and, what's more, found an employer.

'Not a political job this time,' I hoped.

'But of course, what else could I do?'

'Anything else. A nice quiet job where you have no say and can't be accused of getting out of line.'

But Pavel would rather drown in the treacherous eddies of the political current than look on in safety from the bank.

'Don't worry, it's not a front-line post this time. My title is Political Head of the Recreational Club for Employees of the Ministry of Fuel and Power. The club has not been very active up to now. It needs injecting with new ideas.'

The old glint was in his eye. Nothing would really change Pavel. He would no doubt find a way of working himself to death even in a recreation club. The recreation club's thousands of users welcomed the new activities he introduced. But the 'old men at the top' were less enthusiastic. They mistrusted change. They sought ulterior motives for excessive zeal. No one but a lunatic or an enemy agent would do more than his work contract stipulated.

Pavel raged: 'It's not only the country's leadership that needs changing, but the managers and functionaries all the way down. I'll give you one small example. I discovered a workshop of poster painters a few streets from us. I wanted the club to take them over. They could have earned us 100,000 crowns a year, and the club isn't paying its way. But the management dithered. They haven't had to take a decision for so long they can't give a prompt answer to the simplest question. It was a two-headed coin: nothing to lose. But they brooded so long that the Municipal Enterprises got wind of the nest egg and snapped it up. Now the chick has hatched and it's a gold mine.'

Pavel and Hronek collaborated on one more disastrous venture. Pavel was asked to arrange a programme of entertainment for construction workers at a power station. Hronek wrote a satirical revue that took the mickey out of everyone on the site from the director down to the workers. Pavel thought it wildly funny and the two friends enjoyed rehearsing the performers. But the local Party bosses were not amused. The authors were reprimanded for their 'lack of understanding of the working class'. Again, Pavel had been over-optimistic in reading the signs. The current liberalization of the arts did not extend to satire served neat to the workers.

For Pavel this was the final disillusionment. Change would come too slowly: he would not live to see it. He succumbed to black pessimism, trapping us all in a thick layer of gloom.

The boys complained: 'Tati's always grumpy, and now you're sad.'

I rallied because the family atmosphere depended on me, the mother.

Pavel was rapidly becoming isolated. His friends avoided him because of his unpredictable behaviour. He had quarrelled even with Karel and Eva.

I do not remember whether any particular event or outburst brought on Pavel's next attack. I do remember my sense of hopelessness when I visited him in hospital, grey and drawn, an old man. I left the hospital choked with pity, for Pavel, lonely and friendless for myself, exhausted and bewildered by his reproaches and reminders. He had forgotten that I now had a full-time teaching job, as well as part-time translations.

When Pavel was discharged from the hospital he was put on a full invalid pension. At the age of forty-five he had been thrown on the scrap heap. The terrible indictment 'unfit for work' eroded his being. I was witnessing the slow disintegration of a dynamic personality. It was worse than his prison sentence: that had contained an element of hope, because the verdict had been phoney. This sentence led to a slow but inescapable death.

After four months, Pavel announced his intention of going back to work at his own risk. 'The doctors on the commission are a bunch of old women. They don't see that nothing will kill me as surely as doing nothing.'

It was foolhardy. His doctors had told me: 'With his constitution, he may live for another five years, or he may go suddenly.'

I tried to deter Pavel but he was resolved. Daily I expected a fateful call from his office. I rushed home after my evening lessons sick with dread. I sank into a chair, weak with relief, each day that he cheated the grave. I was beginning to feel the strain; I began to suffer attacks of migraine and complaints from my gall-bladder. I slept badly and woke up several times a night bathed in sweat.

Fear and frustration drove Pavel to a state bordering on hysteria. The very sight of Jan, who was going through the awkward adolescent period of breaking and bumping into things, infuriated him. Zdeněk was the only one who could manage him. His calm, steadfast gaze quelled Pavel's rages. He would hand Tati his tablets, sit by him and talk quietly, wise beyond his years. Pavel recognized in his younger son an equal in stubbornness. There had been many scenes between the two since Pavel had returned from prison. One thing Pavel would not tolerate — especially after years of nauseating scraps — was fussiness over food. He made an issue of every leftover. On one occasion Zdeněk went without food for forty-eight hours rather than give in over a cup of cold tea. They were the best of friends immediately after the crisis was over, their mutual respect strengthened by their battle of wills.

I was finding it more and more difficult to get through to him. He had become pathologically suspicious, interrogating my movements if I arrived half-an-hour late, insinuating that I had a lover. He accused me of spending money for bills which he, himself, had forgotten to pay, of hiding books and papers which he had mislaid, of setting his friends against him. Old resentments welled up; he seemed to hate me.

When pain seized him, he cried: 'It's all your doing! Can't you see your very presence aggravates me? Do you think I don't know that you're waiting for me to die so you can marry again? Get out and leave me in peace.'

'You mean you want a divorce?'

'Yes, yes, of course. What else?'

After repeated assertions that he could not bear the sight of me, I began to believe him. If we parted, it might prolong his life. I had heard that one of the nurses at the hospital was fond of him. Were he to marry someone trained in handling heart cases, he might enjoy his remaining years in serenity. After Pavel's next outburst, I observed quietly: 'You don't have to put up with me if you'd really rather not. I've seen a lawyer who tells me that we can be divorced without any fuss within a few weeks.'

Pavel nodded.

Before the first hearing, he announced: 'I can't go through with it. It would be the death of me!'

Again there was accusation in his eyes. What was I to do?

I told him: 'We'll call it off. I thought you said you wanted . . .'

I stumbled out of the room. I sat down at my desk. What *did* Pavel want? If we stayed together I might involuntarily provoke an attack, if we separated it might hasten his end. I was caught in a terrifying trap. Whatever I did would be wrong. There was no way out. My head was about to burst. Instinctively, I put up my hands to prevent it from flying apart. I craved a break from responsibility, complete unconsciousness. But I had work to do. The letters danced before my eyes as I struggled to finish a short translation. I strove to rally my failing senses. I had never let anything beat me before. Common words eluded me; the dictionary was too heavy to lift. I had yet to prepare my lessons for the next day. I reached for the *Daily Worker* to select a passage for discussion. I read words that conveyed no meaning. I would not be able to face my class. I had not the will to go on. I admitted defeat. I fetched a glass of water and lay down with a bottle of sleeping pills.

I had not provided myself with enough liquid. I swallowed only ten. That would not suffice to keep me asleep for ever. My legs were leaden. I could not drag them to the kitchen for more water. I would have to wait until tomorrow night.

I awoke midway through the afternoon, sick and dizzy. I had no wish to return to reality. Towards evening Margot, an English friend several years my senior, called. She took one look at me and said strangely: 'I know what you have in mind. You're coming with me. You need looking after.'

I had no will to resist. I submitted to her instructions, relieved of the burden of my identity.

Margot put me into a large bed with cool, sweet-smelling sheets in a cool orderly room. My mind slipped from my grasp and floated away on the lavender air. A doctor came. I could not focus. He was a blur with a pleasant voice. Name, date of birth? Date? I never could remember dates. Never mind, later will do. He left, and I drifted back into timelessness. Margot was a calm, gentle presence that came and went noiselessly, dosed me and let me lie down again. She kept the curtains drawn: day and night merged. Occasionally a faint buzz penetrated the haze that enveloped me. The phone. Margot spoke in low tones; the words hovered beyond the radius of my hearing.

Then one day everything that had floated away began flowing back; senses, memory, appetite. I sat up. My head felt steady. I was no longer afraid it would explode or roll off. Apart from a not unpleasant physical languour and an inability to concentrate, I was on the road to recovery.

Margot announced: 'The doctor has asked me to bring you to his surgery this afternoon, if you are fit enough.'

Outside the clinic, Margot stopped her car and laid a hand on my arm. 'Rosemary, I have bad news for you. It's Pavel.'

'Not another attack?'

She nodded.

'Please take me to him — now.'

'He's gone.'

Gone, gone where? Oh, not that! The whispered telephone calls. He had been dying and I had not been told!

'He's dead?'

'Yes. It happened on Thursday, in the hospital.'

'Oh, poor Pavel! I wasn't there when he most needed me! I failed him!'

I burst into uncontrollable weeping. Pavel had died alone. After all that I had suffered with him and because of him, I, his wife, had not been there to share his last moments, to sweeten them with the reminder that he lived on in his sons.

Before my nervous collapse I had been too exhausted to think logically, to realize that Pavel, cheated of his life, had needed a target for his bitterness. He could not have denied his faith and blamed the Party. That left only me. But his accusations had been merely a safety-valve. Why had I given in? I should have hung on just a little longer. I could have been there at his deathbed to make our final peace. I buried my face in my hands. I would be haunted by guilt for ever.

A psychologist friend assured me: 'We cannot change people or hold ourselves responsible for their lives. A misplaced belief in our power to influence another, or inability to come to terms with our failure, is a kind of arrogance, or at least a lack of humility. To survive, we must accept our limitations. This Pavel was unable to do. He destroyed himself.'

Now, when it is all so far away, I see that we were both guilty of concealment; we were not open and honest with each other.

Our misunderstandings went deeper than differences in nationality, race, temperament and upbringing. It was only too simple to blame such things. But the fault lay in ourselves. We shared aims, ideals and disasters. We did not share confidences; we were incapable of baring our true feelings to each other; we never had a serious discussion about marriage, our relationship or the complexity of our feelings for each other.

Why didn't I reveal my true needs to Pavel? Why did I never demand my own space in our marriage? Because I was afraid of him? Afraid of his ridicule? Because I was so concerned with keeping up a brave front, getting on with the job, living down my middle-class background, not complaining, not being thought trivial and weak-minded? Why did Pavel never disclose to me his needs and the real reasons and motives for his behaviour? It's easy to say that he wasn't given to introspection; he was a man of action. But why did I never probe to the roots? Why was I satisfied with conjecture?

Why does it take a lifetime to learn that you have to understand yourself before you can understand another; that to succeed a relationship must constantly be brought out into the open and overhauled, and that this requires mutual trust, courage and honesty?

Margot soothed me: 'It was very sudden. There was nothing you could have done, especially in your weak state. I consulted your doctor. He thought the shock would be dangerous until you had recovered a little. Pavel has gone; we have to think of you now. You will need all your strength to carry on alone.'

Margot led me, still weeping, into the surgery. The doctor gave me a tranquillizing injection. Back at her flat I tried to pull myself together. I asked who was looking after the boys.

'Your brother-in-law and his wife have moved into your flat. They'll stay until you're better. The boys are coming to see you today.'

They looked pale and lost. Life had dealt them its most tragic blow. Though grieving deeply, they maintained an outward composure.

A colleague of Pavel's dropped in and told me: 'Pavel was at work before his attack. We told him to go home as we were moving offices. He insisted on staying, and pushed tables about and carried chairs. He swore he felt fine. Heart cases are often like that before the end. Exuberant, they feel like flying.'

I recalled something Ostrovsky had written: 'Man's dearest possession is life. And since it is given him to live but once, he must live so as not to be seared by the shame of a cowardly and trivial life; live so that dying, he may say: All my life and strength were given to the finest cause in the world — the liberation of mankind.'

That might have been an epitaph to Pavel — a tragic and heroic man.

Chapter 18

Pavel's story did not end with his death. His fate moulded his sons' lives: Jan became an activist and reformer; Zdeněk withdrew into the protective shell of a thinker and observer.

I am often asked why I didn't return to England when Pavel died. There were many reasons. The boys did not want to move. They spoke little English and they had been taught to regard England as a bastion of imperialism — the enemy. Czechoslovakia was their home. Though I longed for the freedom, courtesy and orderliness of England, the practical realities dismayed me. Rents were high; we'd have to live with my parents. This would create problems. My father was obsessed with tidiness and discipline, whereas Jan was untidy. The boys quarrelled incessantly and both argued with me. In any conflict, my mother would undoubtedly take my part against my father. Our presence would cause a rift in their peaceful marriage.

In Prague I was my own boss, I had a centrally-heated flat and social security. Now that I was getting well-paid literary translations and a small widow's pension in addition to my salary, I would be able to get the boys through university unaided. And there were other reasons for staying. Pavel had been the prime force in my life. He would continue to be so even after his death. My loyalty to him and the ideals we had shared made me want to carry on the struggle. Yet I still had to come to terms with our relationship. Pavel had swamped me: I needed to rediscover my identity in the milieu where I had almost lost it. I had made friends who were too precious to give up (Heda, Yvonne, Hanka and many others). Furthermore, I was committed to the Czechs and curious about the next chapter of their story. Lastly, there were the mystical bonds that linked me with Prague.

I did not regret my decision. The following years, especially from 1963 onward, were a fascinating period of hope and frustration. Economic, political and cultural pressures toward reform were building up under the surface. A modicum of liberalization would be achieved and hopes would rise. Then the leadership would get cold feet, or at a tap on the shoulder from Moscow, the initiators would be punished and the liberal trend suppressed. Hopes would sink. After a hiatus, the process would be repeated, the progressive gaining a little ground each time.

I became closely associated with two forward-pushing streams: the student movement, and writers and journalists, which made this a hazardous but optimistic stage of my life. It climaxed in 1968, which brought to fruition Pavel's ideas and those of other reform communists.

The boys had buried the shock of their father's death deep inside them and refused to talk about it. Months later fourteen-year-old Jan burst out: 'It was the trial that killed him: the execution was only delayed. And we still don't know the names of his murderers.'

There and then Jan vowed that he would unravel the truth, even if it took a lifetime.

I told him that his father had been a victim of the abuse of power. 'Tyranny is imposed from above, but fear is generated from below. If the man on the lowest rung refuses to be intimidated by the man above him, it is impossible to build up a pyramid of terror. Your generation is not bound by false loyalties as ours was. You will be less blind and more outspoken than we were. You will combat wrongs as you encounter them. That will prevent distortions of socialism in the future.'

An open invitation to trouble that proved to be!

Zdeněk was the first to suffer. His class were asked to write an honest assessment of the ČSM, a Czechoslovak Youth Union modelled on the Soviet Komsomol movement, under direct control of the Communist party. As a result of his essay Zdeněk was threatened with expulsion. I asked him why. He told me that he had written that the ČSM served no useful purpose; it solved no problems and the only thing it provided were well-paid jobs for its functionaries. Young people joined it only as a passport to university and jobs.

'The Head told me that if I was against the ČSM, I was against socialism and for capitalism, and did not deserve a place in a socialist secondary school. I said that that was sophistry, and that it was dishonest to ask for an honest opinion and then use it against me. Most of the class felt as I did but had not risked putting their views on paper. He said he'd give me another chance. If I recanted, he'd forget all about it. I said I'd rather sweep roads; what I'd written didn't become less true because he was threatening me. That shook him. He mumbled something about looking into the ČSM and dismissed me.'

Jan confirmed Zdeněk's view. His classmates, too, were unresponsive to the ČSM. Inept political indoctrination was self-defeating. Combined with the constant re-wording of history books, and the cult revelations, it had created a contempt for authority and scepticism about any political organization.

Jan's reforming zeal began with the ČSM. As an elected leader he set out to pump life into it by introducing visits to the theatre and camping at weekends. Even that was a battle: the *apparatchiks* frowned on the mildest forms of entertainment; any non-political activity initiated from below was *ipso facto* politically negative. Moreover, Jan persuaded controversial public personalities to address his class and held open political discussions.

The school staff exhorted their pupils to join the Youth Union en masse, as proof of their own political reliability. Jan objected to this bloodless rubber-stamping.

'Membership is supposed to be an honour conferred on those who have shown an interest in current affairs and a willingness to work for the community,' he explained to me. 'If we automatically enrol all those who think non-membership will harm their prospects, we shall merely acquire a lot of useless ballast.'

His form-master regarded Jan as a threat to his own position. For years no one had taken the ČSM seriously, and now this crackpot was trying to turn it into an association of avant-gardists. He hinted that Jan's chances of a university place would be jeopardized if he didn't conform. Jan refused to trade his principles. Fortunately, the Head thought highly of Jan. Had he not intervened, a damaging report, classifying Jan as 'a dogmatic individualist unsuitable for higher education,' would have been sent to the university.

Anxious to secure his father's approval, Jan had worked hard to catch up with his lost schooling, surpassing even Pavel in dogged perseverance. Though plagued by ill-health, he excelled at the secondary school and scored high marks in the final examinations. However, his acceptance at university was by no means certain. His political background was in doubt. Some cautious members of the admissions board were checking his father's past.

Zilliacus was once more in disgrace. Rehabilitated or not, Pavel's reputation was not safe. Jan wished to study foreign policy and foreign trade but was explicitly told that as Pavel's son he should not even bother to apply. However, after weeks of suspense, Jan was enrolled at the faculty of journalism and social science. One of the interviewers, impressed by his knowledge of international affairs, had fought hard to get him accepted. He was only sixteen.

Jan continued his efforts to reform the ČSM at university and to turn it into a genuine political organization of the students. He was soon elected ČSM faculty president. Here too he encountered indifference. Not that all students were apolitical. On the contrary, Jan said, some accepted the basic tenets of socialism, but rejected its official interpretation. They were eager to use their critical faculties and form their own opinions.

'They simply don't see the ČSM, or any other existing organization, as a platform for their views,' Jan told me. 'They see it only as a sieve through which the Party filters resolutions to youth, and as the ČSM stands today they are on the whole right but the majority won't risk their necks by saying so publicly, let alone try to do anything about it.'

Shortly afterwards, Jan joined the Communist Party, thinking that in the Party he would eventually have access to the secret documents on the trials and the chance to use this knowledge. But he soon realized what he was up against. He found no one who shared his political views in his CP faculty branch. His first clash with the Party occurred three months after he joined.

However, he did find some kindred spirits in the ČSM with whom he could work for political change.

As his briefcase bulged and his brow furrowed I became concerned that his immersion in meetings and minutes would blind him to the human condition. I need not have worried. Even at school, the Headmaster had asked his help in dealing with various problems ranging from truancy to deflowered virgins.

As a student, Jan's first protegée was a six-year-old orphan, Marie, whom he met through a foster-aunt, a trainee nurse. Marie was a timid and unsociable little girl. The orphanage hoped that contact with the outside world would help her to relate to people. Men were a rare and hence terrifying phenomenon in her life. With kindness, Jan was able to win her over. She became passionately attached to him. One weekend when the foster-aunt was on duty, Jan brought Marie home with him. She clung to his hand all evening. Only he was allowed to bathe her and put her to bed.

In the morning, when Marie came into the kitchen, Jan, Zdeněk and a student friend who had stayed the night were having breakfast. Her eyes widened apprehensively and she ran to Jan. He took her on his lap and introduced her. The three boys vied with each other in amusing her; they performed card tricks, animated glove puppets and made paper boats and rabbits. Gradually the female in her awoke. She went from lap to lap, enjoying her power and her popularity. When she left in the evening with Jan, she sighed ecstatically: 'So many uncles!' Marie occupied many of Jan's weekends after that, and the orphanage reported 'a marked improvement in her social adaptability.'

His next case was Milena. I arrived home from work one day to find the phone ringing. To my amazement, an irate male voice accused me of abducting his daughter. He threatened to call the police. I told him he was out of his mind, I had never met his daughter, and was about to slam the receiver down when a sixth sense prompted me to find out more. I asked him to hang on for a moment and went into Jan's room. He was in earnest conversation with a weeping girl of about sixteen. She was unhappy at home he explained, and had run away. Somewhat crestfallen, I returned to the phone and invited the father round for a drink.

In the meanwhile, I gathered something of Milena's background. Her father, a widower, was a jealous guardian of his daughter's virginity. She was not allowed to have boyfriends or to go dancing and had to be in by nine o'clock every evening. He resorted to the old-fashioned punishment of locking her in her room if she disobeyed him. For Jan, who had taken full responsibility for himself since Pavel's death, such tyrannical behaviour was indefensible. When the girl's father arrived, the evening turned into a family counselling session. Unable to communicate directly, father and daughter ironed out their differences with Jan and I acting as mediators.

Milena was followed by Dela, a fellow student of Jan's. He brought her home at 3 a.m. saying, 'She's dead drunk. I couldn't let her go to the hostel in this state, she'd get sent down.'

He dumped Dela onto my double divan and withdrew. With crumpled dress, dishevelled hair and smudged mascara she presented a sorry spectacle. I bathed her face, brushed her hair and helped her out of her dress. I made her drink some hot milk, placed a bucket handy and got back into bed. Dela burst into tears.

'My dear Dela, what is it?'

'He's married someone else,' she sobbed.

'But Dela, it's not the end of the world. There'll be others. You're always surrounded by admirers.'

'Spongers! The boys invite me because I can always get places for us in full taverns or wheedle an extra round of beer out of the waiter. They don't care about me.' She hiccoughed. 'They wouldn't care if I dropped dead.'

'Jan would.'

'Yes, perhaps Jan would. He's a real friend. But no one loves me. No one's really close. Jan's lucky, he's got you.' The words tumbled out. 'I've no mother and I hate my step-mother. She nags me. That makes my father unhappy but he doesn't dare to stand up for me.' She swallowed a sob.

'If he's that weak he's not worth bothering about.'

She rolled over on her side and clutched my hand. 'I really loved Peter, even if he was fifteen years older than me. Now what have I got to live for?'

'Everything, at your age. Young people believe there can be only one true love in their lives and that when that fails, everything is finished. This is a romantic fallacy. The human capacity for love is infinite, and every love is special in its own way. We can love as intensely at sixty as at twenty; perhaps more so because we love a real person and not an idealised image.'

Dela hung on to my hand, trying desperately to understand. I stroked her hair.

'I'll tell you something from my own life, if it will help.'

She nodded hopefully.

'When I fell in love with my husband I was sure he was the only kind of person I could live with. Years later I fell deeply in love with a man who was his exact opposite. When we parted, half of me died. I thought it would never come to life again. But it did, in time. I'm sure I shall find someone else to love some day.'

Little did I know how true this was to prove.

'But you're an exceptional person. I haven't got your strength of character.'

'Rubbish! I've nearly given up a score of times. But every time, a little voice reminds me that over the next hill something marvellous may be waiting, and I should hate to miss it.'

The light from the street lamp fell on the sad face beside me. A wan smile flickered over it.

'Cultivate good friends, Dela, especially one or two close women friends: they'll last you a lifetime; men friends rarely do. They either boil up into a passion or cool into indifference.'

It was 6.30. I crawled out of bed. 'Have a good sleep and help yourself to coffee when you get up. Borrow any make-up you need from the bathroom, and come and see me soon.'

I tucked her in and she put up her arms like a small child. I bent and kissed her.

That evening Jan came in with a small bunch of violets. 'From Dela with love.'

'How is she?'

'She'll be all right, especially now she's found a refuge here.'

Dela often dropped in for a chat. She talked about her childhood, her parents, authors and politicians she approved and disapproved of. Dela had strong views on every topic.

She recovered in her own colourful way. She neglected everything for a period of exhaustive promiscuity. Then she flung herself with renewed zeal into work. A series of successes in freelance journalism brought her back to sanity, ready for a deeper relationship. When I did not see her, little notes kept me informed of her progress.

'Mamulinda,' Jan began. This was his pet name and a warning signal. What was it this time? An advance on his allowance or a loan of the cottage for the weekend? 'We must help deserving cases, mustn't we?'

'Another broken heart or casualty of the generation conflict?'

'Yes. It's Zdeněk Pinc[38], from the philosophical faculty. He's good looking and brilliant but he suffered from polio as a boy and it left him with a withered leg. He's convinced his girl ditched him because of his handicap and says he's going to chuck his studies. If he could stay here for a time, I think we could get him over his depression. And you could talk to him.'

'A middle-aged female may be the last person he'll want to confide in.'

'Oh, everyone talks to you,' said Jan. 'Once he's here, we'll make him feel wanted.'

The second evening after his friend moved in, Jan phoned to say he'd be late. 'Talk to Pinc till I get in; don't let him brood,' he ordered.

Pinc chatted freely about student affairs, particularly their efforts to secure a bigger say in university management and the Youth Union. The apparatus had been forced to grant a concession: the students had been allowed to set up their own committee, VOV,[39] within the Youth Union. Pinc saw this as the thin edge of a wedge which might eventually topple the political monolith.

I steered the conversation round to the young man himself. His father was a miner, his mother a cleaner. His parents had never had time to ponder what politics was about. He'd joined the Party to find out. He objected, though, to the title 'comrade'. He did not feel indiscriminately comradely toward all its members, he said. His friends, therefore, called him Pan (Mister) Pinc. Pan Pinc's interests were wide but the overriding factor in his life was his physical disability.

'At first I tried to pretend it made no difference,' he said. 'In the classroom it was easy: I was always top. But I had to excel at a sport as well. Swimming was the answer. I practised for hours a day. For a time I beat the healthy boys. But later, as they grew bigger and stronger, I got left behind. I couldn't improve my

38. Zdeněk Pinc was one of the student leaders in the late sixties. He signed Charter 77 in 1977.

39. VOV Prague (Vysokoškolský obvodní výbor) — Prague University Students' Committee.

speed beyond a certain point. That was the bitterest blow. From that moment I knew I was marked for life.'

'Forgive me, but I find your standpoint irrational. People who suffer from claustrophobia don't go potholing. All our ambitions are limited by our abilities. At least you have an excellent brain.'

'What's the good of that?' he muttered. 'The girls I go out with are flattered to be seen around with Pinc, the brilliant student leader, for a time. Then they drop me because I'm also Pinc, the cripple.'

I persisted: 'You take it too personally. Student love affairs rarely last. A boy can't afford to marry the first girl he falls in love with during a five-year study course. Why should the reasons be different in your case?'

'I don't insist on marriage,' he protested. 'But I need a steady girl friend. My whole attitude to life is bound by my ability to retain a girl's love. Failure in that signifies failure in everything else.'

'You have so much to offer, you'll find the right girl one day, I promise you. In the meanwhile, a degree is not a bad thing to have. You'll be in a better position to keep her when she does turn up. If I were twenty years younger, I'd accept you like a shot,' I added warmly.

Pinc laughed for the first time. 'In three years' time I'll hold you to that. I'll be Jan's stepfather. Then we could team your Zdeněk with my sister and that would make me his brother-in-law too. I would be both grandfather and uncle to their children.' He was still gaily working out absurd relationships when Jan came in. He smiled with relief and kissed me.

Pinc rallied and philosophical volumes began to appear on the bookshelves in Jan's room. Hegel and Descartes were exerting their fascination again.

'Pinc is getting married,' Jan announced three months later.

I choked on a slab of bread and dripping.

'He's only known the girl a fortnight and they're utterly incompatible. His friends have laid bets that the marriage won't last. But it's probably the best solution at the moment. Pinc will have proved his normality to himself. If the marriage ends in divorce, well, there are hundreds of divorces. He'll be one of the many, not a freakish exception.'

The wedding was a noisy affair of one happy man, a momentarily glowing bride and a hundred worried guests, including me, the only member of the older generation to be invited.

The marriage lasted six months. As Jan had predicted, Pan Pinc took the divorce philosophically.

Chapter 19

Journalism was another outlet for Jan's social conscience. Students of journalism were required to publish a number of articles by the end of their five-year course. Jan seemed set to achieve the lowest score while causing the greatest commotion round each assignment. Taking Jan on as his part-time assistant, an ex-worker columnist on *Mladá fronta*, the youth daily, observed: 'A journalist is either a knave or a fool. He either sells his soul or beats his head against the wall.' Jan's detailed investigations of letters of complaint — usually cases of individual versus institution — invariably provoked the anger of authority. The columnist asserted that he had acquired a wall-beater to beat all.

For example, investigating an eleven-year-old boy's suicide, Jan found that one interested human being could have saved the boy's life. He wrote an impassioned indictment of indifference. The paper's censor banned it: officially there were no suicides under socialism. Countless other papers and journals took the same view. Eventually a Slovak weekly accepted it, the Slovaks, under First Secretary Alexander Dubček, being less hidebound than the Czechs.

On another occasion, Jan took up the case of two long-haired youths wrongfully accused of hooliganism. He commented bitterly to me: 'Not so long ago anyone who spoke foreign languages was a cosmopolitan and hence an enemy agent. Now we have a faculty of linguistics, mainly for Western languages. Today everyone with long hair is a delinquent. Is there no objective justice — if not in the courts, then at least in public thinking?' In this instance, however, justice prevailed. Jan, who had witnessed the incident, not only wrote about it, but spoke so convincingly in the youth's defence in court that they were acquitted.

Jan had not forgotten his pledge to publicize the truth about the rigged trials. Those that had been held in the other socialist countries had been revised. Khrushchev had pressed Novotný for a clean sweep in Czechoslovakia. Novotný had appointed yet another commission of inquiry. Its findings were submitted to the Central Committee in April 1963. The documents, which recommended a complete reassessment of the trials, were accessible only to top Party functionaries. They remained a dead pigeon in the Party archives until 1968. Months later, largely as a result of Slovak pressure, the Czech press admitted that charges of treason against Slánský and his confederates had been inaccurate but that most of the accused had committed serious offences against the Party. A few Party chiefs were demoted. The matter was closed. Or it would have been if the Slovaks hadn't published articles vindicating the 'bourgeois nationalists' Husák and Novomeský, and elevated Clementis to a national hero victimized by the Czechs. Jan got hold of a copy of *Unfinished Chronicle*, a Slovak publication containing Clementis's letters from prison to his wife Lída. This, he felt, was the love story of the century. He visited Lída in Prague and came home deeply moved.

'She suffers from constant pain in her feet,' he told me. 'When she was in prison she was forced to walk many miles a day on a stone floor in an unheated cell for two years. Now the frost-bite makes her feet bleed. She looks very frail but her memories give her strength. Her room is a shrine to Vlado. His photos, pipes and books are preserved. She talks endlessly of his goodness and their love.

'She described their last meeting. They had been exchanging love letters written actually in adjacent cells, but she had pretended she was outside, not wanting Vlado to know she was in prison. Before the meeting she was given infra-ray treatment, a perm and make-up. Vlado's last words were: "In ten years' time you will greet a socialist Europe for me." He believed that one day the archives would be opened up and his innocence established. And so they shall! Lída must live to see his name cleared publicly and with honour by the highest authority.'

Jan presented his interview with Lída to *Universita Karlova*, a liberal journal published by Charles University. A dozen variously emasculated versions were rejected by the censor's office. In the end one of them got into print through a mis- understanding — contrived by Jan — between two censors. It was the first piece about a trial victim to reach the Czech public.

'It's a beginning,' Jan remarked. 'One day I'll publish the full, uncensored article.'

Jan did not write only on political and sociological themes. He wrote also about subjects close to youth — pop and rock, hiking and camping. He published humorous and touching stories about individual patients and ward life inspired by his frequent periods of hospitalization. So too, he published one or two poems and wrote a television play on the theme of moral courage. This would have been staged in 1967, had political events not intervened.

Although the trials remained taboo and other political issues tricky, 1963 inaugurated one of the laxer periods in the pattern of loosening and tightening. I therefore applied for a job that would bring me closer to events and allow me to write about them. This time I was lucky. Despite my — habitual — lack of experience, I was taken on by *Czechoslovak Life*, a monthly magazine presenting Czechoslovakia to the world in four languages: English, French, Italian and Swedish. What a widen- ing of my horizons. I had the company of a multinational staff, access to foreign newspapers, contact with visiting celebrities and delegates to international conferences, and the whole spec- trum of life in Czechoslovakia was opened up to me.

I approached my first assignment with an empty head and a stomach full of butterflies. My target was an artist who made puppets for advertising and for educational films. He was curious both about English life and about my own situation. A bottle of duty-free Cinzano maintained me in top gear for an hour. We then got through a second bottle and the latest political jokes. In the evening I floated airily into the street, and only when I reached home and comparative sobriety did I realize that the topic of socialist advertising had remained unbroached. I conducted the interview by telephone the next day. Photographs were selected over a flask of brandy and the finished article was toasted in Bull's Blood. I was won over to journalism!

My search for material made me even more aware of the contradictions of Czechoslovak society. There was no lack of achievements in science, medicine, technology and culture. Czech films and experimental theatre were earning international reputations (and much needed hard currency!) Yet nearly every success represented the tenacity of an individual or small group in the face of bureaucratic bloodymindedness, and had required miracles of improvization. I interviewed many remarkable people, such as cinema director, Miloš Forman; Ladislav Fialka, founder of the Prague Mime Theatre; Jiří Srnec who introduced the Black Theatre; Alfred Radok, inventor of the Laterna Magica, a combination of live actors and multiple screens; Jiří Suchý and Jiří Šlitr, composers of satirical sketches and revues; Dr Nan Žaludová, Scottish wife of a Czech scientist, who had built up a department of quality control and mathematical statistics from scratch on a shoestring, and Marta Kubišová, singer and former student of Indian philosophy. At our interview she said: 'I hope I shall know when it's time to leave the stage.' Unfortunately, she was given no choice. After singing her famous *Prayer for Marta* for her invaded country in 1968, she was banned from the stage for life.

In each issue of our magazine we printed a story or novel-extract by a new young Czech or Slovak author. We also ran a series on modern Czech artists. I learned that many of these writers and painters had rejected socialist realism from the start. They had recorded a picture of the time according to their own conscience and had stored their works in drawers and attics until the official screw was loosened.

Cultural brinkmanship persisted throughout my five years on the magazine. Non-conformist writers, artists and film-makers continued to stretch the bounds to the limit. Those at the fore were proscribed and we were obliged to shelve our reviews of their work. The second line stepped up and eventually found themselves at a new brink, farther forward. The earlier prohibitions were lifted and we were then able to publish our reviews.

In spite of the hazards, my enthusiasm never flagged. Each month I became engrossed in the subject of my article, whether it was mental health, co-axial cables, pollution, preventive medicine or demographic trends. (The latter, incidentally, were alarming. The current pay policy, whereby a navvy earned more than a neurologist, together with the housing shortage, was causing a sharp decline in the population and its IQ. Statisticians predicted that by the year 2000 every fifth Czech, or Slovak, would be either a gypsy or an imbecile!)

I plunged boldly into controversial topics, such as legal abortion, female emancipation, provisions for unmarried mothers, care of the aged. After some time I received an invitation to call upon the Party Central Committee man responsible for foreign language journals. Expecting to be congratulated on my work in these new areas, I sailed confidently into the room. Behind an impressive desk sat a lugubrious gentleman in a well-cut suit draped over an ill-cut body. He greeted me in the heavy tone of an overworked undertaker. My exuberance evaporated as he said: 'The Language Institute recommended you for candidature to the Party. On this basis you were admitted to the honourable profession of journalism. Journalists are privileged to defend the revolution through their medium and to chronicle the glorious achievements of the working class. I have followed your articles closely. They show an unorthodox approach. I have, however, let them pass — to date. But here is an article I cannot tolerate. It claims to be a candid view of the factory floor. You give a lot of irrelevant detail about our workers' lives and opinions and much less about socialist competition and the political aims of the working class. You make socialist production sound like a struggle against tremendous odds. This is tantamount to sabotage of our propaganda.'

'Not at all!' I exclaimed. 'My point was that, presented as flesh-and-blood people, our workers would be closer to our foreign readers than if they were just cardboard figures fulfilling production targets.'

'Ah, but what section of our foreign readers? This sort of objectivism plays into the hands of our opponents.'

'On the contrary, propaganda driven home with a sledge hammer loses us readers, even readers of the Left. I know the Western mentality. If I never mention problems, no one will believe me when I praise accomplishments. I'm trying to present socialism as an ongoing process, a continual search for solutions.'

The custodian of the revolution remained unconvinced. He recited stiffly: 'Comrade Kavanová, you will have to broaden and deepen your knowledge of Marxism–Leninism and the decisive role of the working class, or we shall be obliged to terminate your contract.'

For two years I was denied the pay rise due to me on grounds of 'political immaturity', and my second nomination as a Party candidate was conveniently lost.

Reprints of some of my articles in Western communist journals, and letters of appreciation from their editors spiked the CC guns for a time, but victory was never unconditional. Our readership, however, increased, and I rejoiced in my international mail and the conviction that I was winning friends for Czechoslovakia and converts to socialism.

Journalism and our commitment to writing the truth formed a strong bond between Jan and me. It transformed our relationship from one of mother and son to one of very close friends. We discussed our articles together and provided each other with background material.

Jan used to quote a current aphorism: 'A window onto the world can be blotted out by a newspaper.' He found that to get articles on foreign affairs or domestic policies past the censor, the content had to be disguised.

Jan had become one of the two assistants to the editor of *Universita Karlova*. After a year the editor decided that further collaboration would cost him either his job or his sanity. '*UK* has the honour of being the most-banned journal in the country,' he complained to Jan. 'The censor informs me that the largest number of banned articles are either written by Kavan or supplied by Kavan!'

Like Pavel, Jan was undeterred by failure. If an article was tossed out of a daily or monthly, he tried to get it into his faculty magazine or a VOV bulletin, sometimes inserting it on the way to the printers. He filed away his banned articles for future use.

In my job I continued to pinpoint specific aspects of social progress. I visited the newly established Sexological Institute. I spent a day and a night at the phone-in or drop-in Crisis Centre. I talked to people who were concerned with training in the use of leisure.

At the same time, however, events in the student world proved that political freedom was still an illusion.

Jan was reading *Buchar*, the engineering faculty's magazine. 'Listen to this.' He read aloud: 'Students assess actuality in terms not of what it is but of what it ought to be, and by this yardstick it falls short of its potentialities.'

It was a quotation from Jiří Müller[40], the editor, whom Jan had met through Pinc. Müller, three years Jan's senior, was to play an important role in our lives. Jiří's sense of justice had been deeply shocked by his uncle's imprisonment and the judicial murder of eleven innocent men. As in Jan's case, it was to shape his life. His parents had insisted he study engineering so that he might be assured of a steady job under the regime. But Jiří was a thinker, not a technocrat.

Jan was a strong supporter of Jiří's programme for the reform of society and the ČSM, which he saw as an extension of Pavel's and his own ideas. It was based on wide public participation in decision-making and the creation of concepts, the right to minority views, a re-evaluation of censorship, a democratic political system, a greater exercise of political power by the trade unions and other social (non-Party) organizations, and democracy within the Communist Party. It also set out practical proposals for the scientific management of society and the economy.

Jiří presented his programme at a students' conference in December 1965, together with his ideas on the role of youth. He maintained that, without a degree of independence, the young would be unable to lead socialism ahead. While supporting the Party's socialist aims, they should form their own views on the methods employed. He suggested that the Youth Union should, if necessary, act as a corrective to Party policy. This, Jan told me in the evening after the conference, had been a bombshell.

Jiří was strongly opposed to the imposition of unity: true unity, he claimed, could exist only if it was based on common interests and common values. He urged decentralization of the ČSM into industrial, agricultural and student unions, serving the specific interests of the different social groups while allowing a co-ordinated approach to common problems through the central organ.

Similar reforms had been discussed, unofficially, by Party reformers, but Jiří's was the first to speak out on a public platform. Serious problems were inevitable. The *apparatchiks* accused him of advocating opposition to the Communist Party. No Czech citizen was credited by the regime with the ability to

40. Jiří Müller (1943–   ) was the best-known of the student leaders of the late sixties. He was arrested in 1971 and sentenced to five and a half years. He was one of the first Charter 77 signatories.

form his own opinions: it was assumed, therefore, that he had been briefed by the West German Intelligence. The usual corollary to 'pro-Western imperialism', i.e. 'anti-Sovietism', was thrown in, supposedly substantiated by Jiří's visits to the Chinese Embassy in search of authentic information. Jiří defended himself vigorously but to no avail. The *apparatchiks* were out for his blood. Their combined pressure culminated in his expulsion from both the Youth Union and the University, and his drafting into the army, just a year after his conference speech.

Jiří wrote to his mother from the army: ' . . . Naturally I should have preferred to have remained at the University, but not at the price of renouncing my ideas (I don't mean all of them, of course, but the basic issues of freedom, justice, man's rights and duties and so on), that is to say, of disavowing myself. I truly rate spiritual values higher than material, and derive greater happiness from them . . .'

Chapter 20

Jan was incensed by Jiří's expulsion. 'In a clash of opinions,' he raged, 'the authorities pick the most articulate individual and make an example of him, hoping to scare off the rest. This time they have miscalculated. Ten of us have pledged to get Jiří reinstated. We need a quiet place for our meetings. The University's no good; we can never be sure which students are police stooges. You won't mind if we meet here, will you?'

I was in a quandary. I admired Müller's courage; I supported his views. But I knew from experience how the system worked. A few critical people worked at the same place, drank at the same pub or met at the same flat and, *voilà* — a 'faction', a 'conspiracy'. Up to now my role had been to keep our somewhat disorderly home going. My part in politics had been determined by Pavel. Now I was being asked to make a political decision of my own. Brave words about combating the wrongs at one's door step rang in my ears. The choice had already been made. 'Of course you may meet here.'

Jan hugged me. 'The other parents refused; they were too scared. I knew you wouldn't be. I've arranged the first meeting for tomorrow evening.'

Pan Pinc arrived first.

'Well, Mrs Ferdinand, I see they have disposed of Müller!' he observed[41].

The others came in twos and threes. Karel Kovanda was a

---

41. This is a pun on the first line of *The Good Soldier Švejk* which opens with a charwoman, Mrs Müller, telling Švejk: 'And so they've killed our Ferdinand' (meaning Archduke Franz Ferdinand assassinated at Sarajevo).

frequent visitor — with a different girl each time. For Karel, falling in love was as easy and necessary as breathing. After the end of an affair he would drop in and recite Romantic poetry with appropriate Slav melancholy. Then his natural buoyancy would assert itself and he would respond eagerly to the next pair of shapely legs or languishing eyes.

The rest of the group was unknown to me. There was only one girl, Jana, a slim, elf-like creature with an alert, humorous face, poor skin and astonishingly large violet eyes. She was an anthropologist whose concern for people had led to political involvement. She was to become as dear to me as a daughter. She arrived with a tall, handsome young man, Jirka Holub. (The possibility of a romance did not occur to me at the time.) A fair-haired young man with an obdurate mouth and a steely glitter in his eyes introduced himself tersely as Laštůvka[42]. A slight youth with a guarded expression turned out to be Luboš Holeček[43] who had collaborated on Müller's programme. His enemies called him a fanatic, his friends an absolutist. He was certainly a moralist who demanded of society the same ethical standard he set himself. When he moved into our flat I discovered qualities which a casual acquaintanceship did not reveal. One of them was courage. Nearly blind in one eye, a skiing accident deprived him of the sight of the other for quite a time. He never complained or demanded special treatment, but swotted for his examinations from notes tape-recorded by his friends, and passed them at the first attempt.

I served wine and sandwiches, wished them luck and was about to withdraw.

'Aren't you going to drink a toast with us?' Karel inquired.

'Why, yes, if I'm invited.'

'Sit down then,' said Pinc.

Evidently I was not considered a security risk. We toasted the success of the venture, then Pan Pinc opened the meeting. 'This is a matter of individual conscience. None of us knows who will be next. If anyone wants to back out, no one will blame them. There is everything to lose and nothing to gain. But to carve out

42. Vladimír Laštůvka (1943–   ) is a nuclear physicist who was arrested with Aleš Macháček in 1977 and then sentenced to two and a half years for distributing literature from abroad.

43. Luboš Holeček was a well-known student leader in the late sixties, who was killed in 1976 in a hit and run accident.

one path to freedom is to act as though we were free and thus force the milieu to respect that freedom.'

'Okay, okay, wise chief, we wouldn't be here if we hadn't thought that one out,' remarked the irrepressible Karel.

Those of the group who were Party members — Pinc, Jana, Laštůvka, Coufal and Jan — were the most vulnerable, for the apparatus had given them a clear-cut choice: 'Either with the Party or with Müller!' None of them had wavered. The group's ultimate aim was to secure Müller's reinstatement; their immediate aim was to publicize the views for which he had been expelled. The daily press would not touch Müller with a barge pole. Jan suggested that a special Müller bulletin be printed by an enterprising student who had managed to acquire an antique press.

The bulletin was duly produced but it was seized by the ČSM *apparatchiks* before it could reach the factories. The 'Prague radicals', as they were now called, settled down for a long siege.

Our household became known as the Kavan Commune. Everyone in the group had a key. They came and went as they pleased and shared the shopping, cooking and clearing up. The appearance of a bunch of flowers, box of chocolates or bottle of wine addressed to the 'mother of the regiment' indicated a windfall or simply the collection of a grant. The grapevine that hums so efficiently in all totalitarian states warned us that our phone was tapped, and we were under police surveillance.

My younger son sometimes left his chess problems and appeared at discussions, listened, came to his own wise conclusions and withdrew. He wanted to understand, not make, history. He too had been admitted to university. He would have preferred to read psychology. As he said: 'With two lunatics in the family, it seems a practical subject.' But that year enrolment was closed at the re-established department of psychology. Rather than be drafted, Zdeněk had switched to law. In view of Jan's activities, this too seemed a practical choice.

The radicals were determined to win over workers for their programme. This was no easy matter. If there was one thing that Novotný had achieved it was the depoliticizing of the workers. He had sown among them distrust of the intelligentsia. A further obstacle was the sheer physical difficulty of contacting workers. Just as unofficial meetings were forbidden, so were unofficial and horizontal contacts between social groups. It would have been illegal for students to enter a factory in order to talk politics. The last thing the workers' state wanted was for the workers to get ideas!

The whole social structure was pyramidal: orders came down from the apex, proposals went up from the base. Occasionally such proposals were blessed and sent back down through the various layers. More often they got stuck at the tip — in the case of youth the ČSM Central Committee — and were never heard of again.

A two-day Prague City ČSM Conference offered an opportunity for communication. There students and workers were actually under the same roof. Even so, there were problems. The students had no chance in the conference hall; but during the breaks they managed to get into conversation with workers in the corridors. Hearing for the first time views other than official ones, a number of workers continued the discussion late into the night. This immediately bore fruit. The next day Luboš Holeček, Pinc, Jan and Laštůvka were elected as delegates to the National Congress. This was a triumph indeed!

The *apparatchiks* launched a counter-offensive. Congress delegates were ordered to reject student proposals out of hand. Standpoints to be adopted by Party members on all issues were laid down.

A communist faculty lecturer warned Jan of the consequences of disobedience. Despite precautions, the radicals waylaid other delegates at lunch and in the corridors and deluged them with Müller's ideas. In this way, they successfully divided the congress.

Jan arrived home shining with triumph and celebratory Risener.

'Imagine, Mama, not a single unanimous decision was taken! And over a hundred delegates voted against Zavadil's re-election!' Zavadil was the ČSM chairman who had been responsible for Müller's expulsion.

To have broken the spell of unanimity was an unprecedented achievement. It signified the first crack in the political monolith. A further encouraging sign was that some courageous Party members among university staff quashed the disciplinary proceedings instigated against Jan and other disobedient students.

One night not long after the congress, Jan mentioned casually: 'I sold you for six hundred crowns today.'

'How so?'

'I owe a friend six hundred. She agreed to waive the debt if I would try to win you for her father.'

'Really Jan, marriage broking, and with your own mother as object! What will you be up to next? Your friend doesn't even know me.'

'Yes she does. She was in that group of girls Dela and I arranged for you to interview for your population article. She liked you very much. Her father's a widower. He's engaged to some woman who's only interested in clothes. She and Alena don't hit it off. Alena's going to work on her father; then we'll arrange for you two to meet. You could do worse, Mamulinda, he's tall and good-looking and clever. He works in foreign trade which means he travels about a lot, and he isn't a bit stuffy.'

'But what about Arnošt?' I managed to get in at last.

I had been going out with Arnošt for some months. He was a middle-aged divorcee, a prudently progressive communist and a kind and devoted man.

'He won't last,' my son prophesied. 'I mean, he isn't your type, really, is he?'

'He's a very good man. A woman has to be sensible at my age.'

'He's much too old and dull for you.'

'He's fifty; that's not old,' I demurred.

'Well, you act like twenty; that's a big age difference,' Jan retorted. 'You're not seriously thinking of marrying him, are you?'

'I haven't promised but he'd like me to; and I've got to settle down some time.'

'You don't love him.' Jan's eyes were coldly accusing. 'You'd be marrying him for security. I'm sure Arnošt is all you say, but he's too conventional. Mamulinda, you'll be bored to death in a couple of years. You've never compromised, taken the easy way out. Some women equate comfort with happiness, but not you. Think it over carefully, Mama. Not just because of Alena's father — that's only partly serious, though it might work — but for your own sake.'

My son's tired face was full of concern. My happiness was very important to him. Though he expected me to act as nurse to his ailments and counsellor to his friends, he never forgot that I was a human being as well. He was sensitive to my moods and could not bear to see me unhappy or out of temper with him. This rarely happened. Though, I must say, he would have tried the patience of the archangel Gabriel. Absent-minded, like his father, he strewed Prague with forgotten caps, umbrellas, pens, spectacle cases and address books. For him, as for Pavel, time was immeasurable: all his obligations were fulfilled with nerve-racking haste in the small hours of doomsday. And such mundane tasks as sorting background material for articles, carbon copies, faculty notes, newspapers and letters were postponed indefinitely. If I remonstrated that his den was a breeding ground for bacteria and an offence to the aesthetic sense, he would reply loftily: 'Shaw worked in chronic disorder and he was not only a creative genius but lived to be ninety-four, or was it six?'

He was extravagant. I at least spent only what was in my pocket; Jan spent what was on the horizon. A ring on the downstairs bell at 2 a.m. would drag me to the window. Jan would call up: 'Be an angel and throw me down 30 crowns for the taxi. I'll pay you when my next article comes out.' I would be about to demur that he already owed me more than a front-page, three-column splash could cover, but the reflection that the taxi meter was ticking away further crowns precluded argument. When Jan received a fee, he would remember somebody's birthday or take flowers to a friend in hospital or to Lída, and the settlement of his debt would recede farther into the future with the consoling promise: 'If I don't pay before, Mamulinda, I certainly will in your old age, when you'll be in greater need.'

From time to time I steeled myself to deliver some home truths; but the target would elude me. Having assured me he would be in for supper, he would phone to cancel the meal for unimpeachable reasons. Or he would come home unexpectedly early and regale me with details of a political meeting or faculty discussion. His talent for mimicry and outrageous black humour — which only he and I understood — would soon reduce me to helpless laughter, in which state I could not work up steam for a sermon.

If ever I did manage to administer some overdue rebuke, Jan would hover around miserably until I had forgiven him, which I did almost immediately. It was impossible to remain angry with him. His demonstrative affection and constant need of my companionship far outweighed the anxiety he caused me.

Now I considered Jan's words. He was right. Marriage to Arnošt would be a convenience. I was not in love with him; it would be unfair to him. His offer was tempting; someone with whom to share the cost and responsibility of living. A chance to ease off, relax a little. (As though there could be any relaxation with Jan around!) Arnošt would have to move in with us. In his position, he might take exception to Jan's political activities. I might have to choose between loyalty to Arnošt and loyalty to my students. I knew what my decision would be. I had thrown in my lot with the students. I believed in them. They in turn awarded me special status. 'We always think of you as one of us,' Jana said. 'You are, after all, only a grown-up child.'

To which Jan added with a grin: 'She doesn't mean you're mentally retarded but that you haven't lost your youthful enthusiasm.'

I thought of Milan. Arnošt had not really assuaged the ache. With Milan I had known real love. I still believed in it. I remembered my words to Dela. It might happen again. Nothing less would do. It took me three months to summon up sufficient courage to break off with Arnošt. Every time I screwed myself up to the point, he brought me steaks or theatre tickets and I postponed the discussion. For weeks I was tormented by remorse. A year later Arnošt was happily married. Alena's father was still engaged and I was unattached.

I was not lonely; my life was too full for loneliness. Time and energy seemed to flow from magic cups: the more I drained them, the more remained. I still had a job and a half, a home and children, yet I squeezed in theatres and concerts, swimming and tennis, and an ever-increasing social life. Pre-fifties' friends were back in circulation. Colleagues from my teaching days kept in touch. My new job brought friends — on the magazine staff, in the journalists' union and among the people I interviewed. Jan, of course, continued to fill the flat with his friends (besides his radical colleagues), whom he automatically assumed would become my friends. Even Zdeněk, who was not gregarious like his brother, occasionally brought home a kindred spirit. Not all the evenings were spent in serious discussion. Some were devoted to rock and pop music, for my mother sent the boys the latest English and American records long before they were available in Prague.

Apart from my full working and social life, I was too absorbed in events to be lonely.

While I was writing about positive developments such as retraining schemes for redundant workers and improvements in work safety, the critical forces were precipitating open clashes with authority. The first was provoked by the writers. At their national congress in June 1967 they openly attacked censorship and Party control of culture as well as the leadership's failure to solve any of the basic human problems — the economy, housing, education and so on.

Pinc and Jan entered my office. 'Can you lend us a typewriter, some paper and a room where we won't be disturbed?' Jan asked.

I pulled them hurriedly into a small storeroom. 'What's going on?'

'We've got a copy of Ludvík Vaculík's speech!' Pinc stuttered with excitement. 'It's dynamite! We want to type as many copies as we can this morning, then we'll distribute them to other students who will make copies of them. By tomorrow evening nearly every student in Prague will have read it.'

I scanned the speech. It was a crushing indictment of power politics which, the author claimed, would eventually create instead of a resistant, cultured community, a docile populace, easily dominated by foreigners.

I supplied the boys with the necessary materials. Then, in summer 1967, Czech *Samizdat* was born.

The regime took harsh revenge. The most audacious writers were expelled from the Communist Party; *Literární Noviny*, the writers' openly critical weekly, was taken out of their hands. From Jan and Pinc's personal friendship with a number of writers sprang a bond of solidarity between writers and students. Protests in support of the writers were hatched in our flat. The writers reciprocated a few months later when students clashed with the police. The immediate cause was a purely practical matter. For months students at one of the technological colleges had been urging the authorities to repair the faculty cables that were responsible for frequent power cuts. When the lights went off for the umpteenth time on a dark October evening, the students' nerves snapped and they marched out in protest. Their orderly procession was set upon by the police who inflicted severe injuries with their batons. The press and the ČSM apparatus published only distorted police reports of the incident.

Jan put out a bulletin explaining the students' case. Again the ČSM *apparatchiks* intervened to prevent its distribution. After a few issues it was banned.

Nevertheless, the demo proved to be a turning point. It had brought students into direct conflict with the regime. It brought them closer to the writers and to some of the reformist politicians. The defenders of Jiří Müller, equipped with this earlier experience, set up a political structure and began negotiating with the government. Jan was elected a chairman of a committee co-ordinating activities among the university faculties. The following spring, Professor Kadlec[44], the pro-Dubček Minister of Education, referred to student activity as 'a trigger to democratization'. At the time, however, the leadership took a different view. Mamula[45], head of the Party CC's infamous Eighth Department, insisted that the student unrest was fomented by foreign Intelligence. Novotný was rumoured to be planning a trial with agents Pinc and Kavan.

Pinc chuckled over supper. 'I'm supposed to be in contact with a spy ring in Latin America. The idea probably sprang from that pair of orthopaedic boots a Mexican student sent me!'

Jan was an obvious suspect. He visited his grandparents in the West. His mail bore stamps from all over the world. Since his schooldays he had had pen-friends in several continents. In the summer months our flat was filled with foreign students whom he had met on his roundabout trips to England and generously invited to enjoy the beauties of Prague and his mother's hospitality.

I awoke to find Jan bending over me.

'Mama, do you know where my travel permit to Hungary is?'

'Are you mad? You're not going to Hungary at this time of the morning. It's only six o'clock.'

'I know, but the police are here . . .'

44. Vladimir Kadlec is an economist and was the Minister of Education in 1968. He is now a Charter 77 signatory and a regular contributor of economic analyses to samizdat periodicals.

45. Miroslav Mamula was the chief of the CC CPCz department of security in the early fifties and a loyal supporter of Novotný.

In crumpled dressing-gown, unwashed and uncombed, I donned my hostess smile and advanced into the passage, where two men were standing.

'My son is extraordinarily untidy; I'm sure it will take him hours to locate any specific piece of paper. Won't you come in?' I waved vaguely towards my room. This was a piece of bluff. My bedtime reading had consisted of several copies of *Svĕdectví*, a journal on Czechoslovak affairs published in Paris by a Czech emigré, Pavel Tigrid. The two policemen declined my offer. They did not wear shiny leather overcoats, nor did they get up so early in the morning as their predecessors of the fifties. After ten minutes they withdrew with Jan's passport, saying: 'Report to Bartolomějská at 10 a.m., Mr Kavan. If you find your other travel document, bring it along.'

What could the police want of Jan? That question blotted out everything else all day. I went through the motions of work at the office, but like a sleepwalker I had no memory of what I had said or done. To my relief Jan was in his room when I reached home.

'For Christ's sake, what was it about?' I demanded.

'They questioned me about Vladimír Andrle and my movements and contacts abroad.'

That dread phrase 'movements and contacts abroad' again! The implication was clear. Andrle, one of the ten radicals, had fallen in love with an English girl; he had remained in England after his vacation and asked for asylum.

'You didn't see Vladimír when you were in England?' It was hardly a question.

'Of course I did. He's my friend. His decision to stay was a private one. He wants to study there and get married.'

Nevertheless, the regime regarded Vladimír as a defector, an enemy of the state. Contacting him had aggravated Jan's own position.

Two days later Jan announced that he had been summoned for further questioning to Hradec Králové, Vladimír's home town where preliminary investigations were being conducted. I nodded, not trusting myself to speak. He left. I felt sick with anxiety. The fifties had come to life. Pavel had also had preliminary interrogations. Would Jan's similarly be followed by arrest and conviction? I pictured Jan being subjected to the same treatment as his father. How long would his health hold out before he confessed to whatever was required of him?

Novotný had a bad conscience: that would make him hate the victims of injustice. He would be only too happy to prove their 'guilt'.

Momentarily, I weakened. I longed for Jan to give up the struggle. The price was too high. We had suffered enough. He was gone all day. The evening dragged on. Zdeněk chatted to me to take my mind off my worries. He always emerged from his shell to support and console me when his brother was in hospital or in trouble. At midnight I went to bed, but not to sleep.

At one a.m. I heard the front door open. I gave Jan time to fall asleep, then I crept into his room. Moonlight slanted across his face; he looked innocent and vulnerable. Tears of relief trickled down my cheeks.

Jan was unusually uncommunicative over breakfast. He said only: 'The investigation was supposed to concern the Andrle case, but secret police from Prague interrogated me for hours about Müller et al.'

My fears were confirmed: the police were indeed trying to pin the label 'hostile faction' on a group of friends.

A nice little trial with some fresh agents of imperialism might have rallied the workers and united the Party behind Novotný, but he wavered, uncertain of Party support and public reaction. Opinion had swung round in sympathy with the students after the police brutality. A few broken heads had lost Novotný the chance of 'legally' disposing of others.

They had also proved to be the last nail in the ČSM's coffin. Students resigned from the Union en masse. Jan and Jana, convinced now that the ČSM was beyond reform, initiated a referendum for or against the creation of a separate student organization. Considering that Müller (and later Holeček) had been expelled for advocating federalization of the ČSM, this move illustrated well the extent to which the students were able to put the regime on the defensive.

In the meantime, the philosophical faculty anticipated events. On the initiative of the radicals, the faculty elected a student micro-parliament to run its affairs. I attended the inauguration ceremony. My presence at student meetings was never questioned: someone always recognized me as 'the mother of the regiment'. In addition, I was collecting material for an article on student aims. A solemn hush descended on the large lecture hall as the ČSM representatives handed over their authority and funds. It was a thrilling and symbolic moment: the first act of abdication by the power apparatus.

Other faculties followed suit. By this time the ČSM leadership would have accepted federalization — as preferable to separatism — but the tide had swept ahead. The whole student movement decided to build up a new organization from the faculty parliaments. This was the climax to the long struggle inaugurated by 'my' students. This time the authorities dared not take revenge.

To the West it might seem a matter of indifference whether students belonged to a national Youth Union or to a separate and independent student union. But in Czechoslovakia it had tremendous significance. In Jan's words: 'We students have proved that the power structure can be undermined and ineffectual leadership removed by pressure from below. In this sense it is important for the nation as a whole.'

And, indeed, all sections of public opinion — consumer, worker, intellectual, economist, Slovak, and Party rank and file — were expressing dissatisfaction. The new economic model introduced half-heartedly in early 1967 was being throttled by political absolutism. Party reformers were demanding democracy within the Party and the public democracy within society. But under its present leadership the CP was as incapable of change as an arthritic octogenarian of swimming the Channel. Something — or someone — would have to give.

Chapter 21

In the end it was Novotný who gave in. On 5 January 1968 the Slovak Alexander Dubček, unknown to the Czech public, was elected Party leader in his place. But we could not yet feel safe. Everything was still in the balance. Dubček took no decisive action. However, after two months of wavering and marking time he abolished censorship. The radicals had already stepped up their campaign to get Müller and Holeček reinstated. The editor of *Universita Karlova* asked Jan for an article on Müller, analysing the principles involved. Other stories on Holeček and student views followed. The public rallied to the support of Müller and Holeček. The new Minister of Education was open to reason; finally, even Zavadil, the chief ČSM *apparatchik* retracted his accusations, blaming the 'general atmosphere of the time'.

A few days after Novotný resigned the Presidency, Jiří Müller phoned to say he was being released from the army, discharged from the military hospital and re-enrolled at his faculty. Luboš had already been released and had moved into our flat. It was natural that Jiří too should spend his first days of freedom in the Kavan Commune.

I was curious to meet the young man who had caused a major upheaval in the state. That evening I resolved to prepare a special meal. Unfortunately I was detained at the office. I caught a hare at five minutes to closing time and roped in some vegetables as the shutters were going down. I still had to call on Paula, a journalist friend, to collect some material on young people's emotional problems. Paula ran an agony column in a Czech daily. I settled down to a last-minute translation while my precious dish cooked in the oven. The ringing of the door bell sometime later brought me down to earth with a jolt. My hare! I rushed into the kitchen. It was obliterated by blue smoke. The bell rang again, more insistently. Dazedly clutching the tin, I went to open the door.

'Hello, Rosemary, we've brought you the notorious rebel!' Karel Kovanda bent to kiss my cheek. 'What on earth have you got there?'

'Supper!' I groaned. 'Good God, how many are there of you?'

'Only Luboš and me and Jiří. Jirka Holub and Jana are on their way.'

'Oh well, come in, all of you,' I gasped.

'Delighted to meet you, Mrs Kavanová.'

It was a soft, low-pitched voice. I looked up to meet a round, guileless face lit by an angelic smile. Jiří had a slight squint that in no way detracted from his good looks. He had a sensuous mouth, a firm chin and a polite, modest manner. He did not look like the born leader. He merely appeared to be an agreeable, charming youth. His light grey eyes had the steadfast gaze of a high-principled, uncompromising nature. The clear, broad brow indicated a mind capable of profound analysis and original thought.

Karel had taken the tin from my hand and was prodding its unrecognizable contents. 'It was going to be jugged hare in honour of Jiří,' I explained. 'But I forgot it while I was working. We'll have to fall back on spaghetti. I expect you're all hungry.'

'You bet,' Karel said cheerfully and followed me into the kitchen.

'Don't get under my feet when I'm agitated,' I begged him. 'Make some Nescafé and take it into Jan's room. Where is he by the way?'

'Proof-reading at *Mladá fronta*. He'll be along.'

I discovered a tin of spam and some tomato juice and an old knob of cheese. I boiled a huge mound of spaghetti, added the tomato juice and chopped meat and sprinkled grated cheese over it. It was a far cry from the fatted calf but it disappeared in record time. Jan exploded with laughter when he saw the charred animal. 'I've heard of a dish called blue hare,'[46] he cried, 'but not black. Mama, you're the most eccentric cook in Prague!'

46. A traditional Czech dish.

In the morning when I went to dispose of the carcass, only a thin, ebony shell remained; it looked as though it had been cleaned out by vultures. Perhaps, though compared with army cooking, it would not have been so bad.

Once back in circulation, Jiří was expected to lead the new students' union. Unity in opposition had been easy to achieve. To combine the freedom of differing ideas with a positive programme was proving more difficult. The student body as a whole was as yet unused to independent political thinking. It counted on Müller and his friends presenting a ready-made programme.

Jiří declined, explaining: 'We radicals have not struggled for freedom from a programme dictated from above in order to impose our own. If our group were to stand for election in the present union, we should all be elected. As the politically most experienced students, our views would carry weight. We should, in fact, become a monopoly power group, and we should find ourselves representing even those who disagree with us. That would be at variance with our principles.'

Jiří was nothing if not consistent.

The radicals had achieved their initial aim — to rectify the injustice done to Müller. Jan turned his attention to another of his objectives — to write freely about the trials. Through long interviews with Heda Margolius, Marian Šling, and Lída, he was able to reveal the political background to these personal tragedies. He also quoted from the Central Committee's memorandum of April 1963 on the trial commission's findings. This document still had not been published in Czechoslovakia but extracts had appeared in *Le Monde*. *Le Monde* was inaccessible to the Czech public but my enterprising son had obtained a copy. From it my sons learned the identities of many who had been responsible for the death of their father and of other honourable men: Soviet advisers and their Czech and Slovak collaborators in the Ministries of the Interior and Justice, the Prosecutor-General's Office and the Supreme Court.

More and more was disclosed in the press. We learned that besides the main Prague trials, other phoney trials had been staged all over the country, that political prisoners had numbered tens of thousands, and that nearly two hundred death sentences had been carried out.

Emerging from a bookshop on Wenceslas Square I collided with Sláva whom I had not seen since I left the Ministry of Transport. We went to a coffee bar to catch up on the intervening years. I was astounded to hear that in 1960 he and Mr Němec had been framed on a charge of over-pricing. The charge had been fabricated by an ambitious but incompetent subordinate — a confidant of the secret police. By an ironical twist of fate, during his three years in prison, Sláva had executed designs for the Škoda plant at inflated prices which, he said, had gone straight into the prison governor's pocket.

Jan brought the news that a student at the philosophical faculty had tried to commit suicide after learning of her father's role in the fifties. In many homes young people were asking their parents: 'Why did you do nothing, say nothing?' My two sons had suffered, but they had been spared disillusionment in their father. We could not know how Pavel would have acted had he not been a victim. Would he have raised his hand in dissent? Or would Party loyalty have silenced him?

This was a time of good will and optimism. Neither the afflicted nor the public called for vengeance; they demanded only rehabilitation and recompense, and removal of the guilty from office.

At last, twelve years after his release, Pavel's name was publicly cleared and I received the residue of his compensation. Sixteen years after Rudolf's death, he too was unequivocally rehabilitated and the authorities settled their debt with Heda, in so far as a debt of that nature can be settled.

Dubček appointed a commission to uncover the full extent of responsibility for the trials and the subsequent cover-ups. The trail led right up to the Politburo and the inner Political Secretariat and included Presidents Gottwald, Zápotocký and Novotný. The publication of the Commission's report was prevented by the Russian invasion. It was subsequently smuggled to the West where we finally caught up with it, and ended our twenty-year-old quest for the whole truth: it was only poetic justice that I should be one of the translators of the English version.[47]

Meanwhile Pandora's box, opened by Dubček, was revealing other long-hidden truths about chicanery, inefficiency and

47. This is a reference to the publication of the Piller Commission's Report as 'The Czechoslovak Political Trials 1950–1954', Stanford University Press, 1971.

indifference at all levels of the power pyramid; about factories that had gone on producing obsolete goods that went straight into salvage; about Czechoslovakia's economic exploitation by the Soviet Union; about stifled research and shelved innovations. Nothing was sacred, not even Czechoslovakia's membership in the Warsaw Pact and Comecon.[48]. No stone was left unturned; from underneath crawled out monstrous scandals. Journalists were having a ball; censors were playing *mariáš*. So eager was the public for news that the once despised dailies were sold out by eight o'clock. But people were confused by the explosions of truth in the press. Meetings with activists, writers and journalists cleared up much of what had been unsaid. The public turned up hours beforehand and fought to get in. Hundreds had to be turned away. After years of generalities and anonymity of views, public figures voiced their true opinions. For the first time the population was in position to decide whom to trust and whom not. Every citizen had become a politician.

Jan was often among the speakers, representing youth. In March 1968 he shared a platform with Pavel's old friend, Eda Goldstücker. If Pavel had been alive, he would have been there, next to his son, elaborating with Eda the Party's new aims which were published the following month in a best-selling Action Programme. This remarkable document brought pie down from the sky and offered it as daily fare. It pledged to restore and guarantee basic human rights and freedoms. It promised the people a genuine voice in public affairs. Decision making would be shared with freely elected trade unions and social organizations. Workers' councils would be established. The Party would cease to control every aspect of life but would strive to win public support by persuasion and example. (The Programme explicitly admitted the 'incorrect policy of direct Party control of the ČSM'. This was the final blessing to the rehabilitation of the student radicals.) The Party itself was to be more democratic: votes would be secret and every member would have the right to act according to their conscience. By removing political restrictions, the Programme gave grounds for hope that the new economic system based on flexible planning, market relations, profit-sharing and a degree of competition

48. The Czechoslovak government did not express any wish to leave either Comecon or the Warsaw Pact during 1968.

would function efficiently. The programme reinstated the intelligentsia: it recognized science and technology as essential to progress, and culture to human relations.

Ideas similar to those for which Jiří Müller and others had been persecuted were now accepted Party policy. The younger generation had their own ideas. At this meeting Jan, and particularly Holeček, made it clear that youth's support for the new leadership was conditional. Youth rejected the leading role of the Party and insisted it gave up its monopoly on information, concepts, etc. Holeček called upon young people to form their own interest groups and through them to formulate a political programme more radical than the reform communists'.

Holeček stressed that youth was sceptical toward all political parties and believed in democracy rather than democratization.

Later he affirmed: 'The Czechoslovak crisis was part of the system of universal manipulation. That is why we young people wish all concepts to remain open. Ours is an anti-programme programme — an antidote to manipulation. We are anxious to avoid the mistakes of our fathers. We shall continue to probe. We shall return to the classics and seek the cultural values created by our nation in the past, regardless of the praise or censure of present-day politicians. There must be no closed doors, either on to the past, present or future.'

Jiří Müller had specific doubts about the Party's intentions toward workers' councils. The Action Programme's wording was ambiguous, he said, and would permit the authority of the technocrats to outweigh the power of the workers.

While Jana concentrated on the student union, Jiří, Jan and Karel Kovanda visited factories to discuss the setting up of workers' councils, for as Jiří said: 'Only when the immediate producer enjoys full and democratic rights will the intelligentsia have the right to speak about their own freedom.'

For the first time students had access to workers. They were listened to politely; but the workers' attitude to their ideas, as well as to Dubček's Spring, was one of wait and see.

The atmosphere reminded me of 1945. People allowed themselves once more the luxury of enthusiasm. They were willing to tighten their belts and pull their weight. They contributed some of their hard-earned pay to a Fund for the Republic.

There is a saying in Prague: 'If you walk the length of Wenceslas Square, you are bound to meet someone you know.' I can vouch for the truth of that. Shortly after my encounter with Sláva, I was hailed by Mirek in the main thoroughfare: 'Ježíšmarjá! Rozmarýnka! This calls for a glass! There's a small place over a delicatessen store near here. Come on.'

Mirek, who had always been a slow walker, plunged energetically through the crowd, dashed across the shop and dragged me up a narrow staircase. He ordered two glasses of wine and made his way to an empty table. 'We'll make a date for a proper celebration. Saturday okay? Fine! I've only got time for a quick one now.'

Mirek, who always had unlimited leisure for booze!

'You're not married are you?' I asked.

Mirek laughed. '*Sakra*, no!' He patted his briefcase self-consciously. 'I've got some figures to work out for the Works Committee by tomorrow morning. I'm a member now, you know.'

I spluttered helplessly on my wine. Mirek had never entertained a political notion in his life except in derision! I couldn't have been more surprised if he'd converted to Buddhism.

When I had recovered my breath, Mirek explained: 'We elected an entirely new trade union committee — by secret ballot — and I got on. Formerly I would have turned it down as a bloody waste of time. But now the committee can really get things done for the ordinary people, it seemed worth having a bash. Gives you a different angle on work, you know. You'd never credit, Rozmarýnka, the time I spend thinking up ways of saving money on bloody projects!' He tapped his forehead and grinned sheepishly.

Mirek politically activated! That was all *I* needed to prove the viability of the new democratic course!

A poster greeted my eye in the tram. 'Don't be inconsiderate!' read the caption over a drawing of a man pushing past a female passenger and catching her stocking on a sharp object in his string bag. Opposite was a drawing under the caption: 'Be considerate!' This time a young man was offering his seat to a middle-aged woman laden with shopping. Here was concrete evidence of socialism with a human face. The living payload was also showing its human face. There were no snarls as corns were trodden on in the packed vehicle. Instead of browbeating her hapless cargo, the conductor coaxed them sweetly to squeeze into yet smaller spaces. Twenty-year-old complaints about Prague transport were no longer uttered. The nation of grumblers had ceased to grumble!

The new face shone in the shops. Polite requests for a specific piece of merchandise until now had been greeted with a surly, unadorned No! Now the smiling assistant either produced the item or informed the customer regretfully that it was not in stock but would certainly appear shortly. In the meanwhile was there anything else he . . .?

Giorgio, our Italian editor, feigned a state of shock.

'I've just come from the shoe shop. You'd never believe it: the assistant didn't expect me to buy the first pair she stuck under my nose! She brought several pairs but none of them was really comfortable. In the old days I wouldn't have had the guts to walk out without buying anything. Can you imagine: this girl didn't try to convince me that half a size too small is a perfect fit! She said: "No good taking them if they aren't comfy. We're getting some more stock next week. Why don't you come back then?" What's the world coming to?' He shook his head in mock dismay, adding: 'I was so amazed, I nearly invited her for a coffee on the spot.'

Churlish distrust had gone out, exit permits for all had come in. Mile-long queues of prospective holiday-makers formed outside Western embassies. Even bureaucracy wore a smile. It seemed to have changed its shape too: it was less square and intractable; it had grown taller and slimmer and had flexed its muscles.

It had been a long road to the democratic socialism Pavel and I had envisaged in 1945. For me the Prague Spring was a justification for sticking out the years of disillusion. Our new leader was not alone in his naivety. I believed that once Dubček got rid of the hawks, he and his team would ensure that the reforms went through. True, neither the promised free general elections nor the Fourteenth Party Congress which was to elect a new Central Committee had been held, but I was convinced that popular pressure would bring these about in good time.

Intoxicated with the new freedom, I attended every public meeting. I talked to people in pubs and restaurants; I joined groups that formed spontaneously in the squares and streets and discussed present and future policies. Faces were eager and open; no one threw a glance over their shoulder.

In spite of shocking revelations about the Communist Party,

non-Party friends assured me that it had never enjoyed such confidence. Even the newly-founded KAN, an association of non-party people, and the 231 Club, composed of ex-political prisoners, were willing to co-operate with the Party, provided it was on terms of equality. In the absence of censorship, I wrote freely about these organizations and their programmes and demands before they were officially registered.

After work or a meeting, I would rush home to the telly. Jan and Zdeněk, who had also been activated and was helping to formulate statutes for the new student union, would join me. Sometimes Heda, now living round the corner in a newly allocated flat, would drop in. We would sit glued to the box drinking in every word of an astonishingly open political debate or address by a political leader. Heda and I spent exciting hours interpreting the news and filling in the background for foreign correspondents gathered in the foyer of the Alcron hotel or introducing them to the wine taverns of old Prague.

The eyes of the world were on Czechoslovakia. John of Luxembourg's[49] belief in the Czechs' special mission seemed to have been justified. If members of my generation — those who had suffered — needed to believe in Dubček and the new course, there were others who viewed developments with alarm. My chief editor (who must have been the only Jewish communist to have fought in the West and remained unpurged since 1945) complained that the Party reform programme had been turned into a mass movement which was recklessly heading for disaster. Unlike Dubček, he did not trust the Russians. Dubček, nevertheless, returned triumphant from discussions with Soviet leaders in Slovakia. I set off on holiday, confident that all would be well.

49. John of Luxembourg became King of Bohemia in 1310. He died in 1346 at the Battle of Cresy. He was the father of Charles IV.

Chapter 22

I was staying in Paris with a friend of Jan's when I heard the devastating news.

François rushed into my room waving his shaving brush and shouting: 'Rosemary, wake up! The Russians have invaded Czechoslovakia!'

Stunned, I tottered after him into the bathroom to hear the radio blast: 'Warsaw Pact armies . . . tanks . . . barricades in Prague . . . firing at the Radio building . . . Wenceslas Square . . . a blood-stained flag . . . the first dead and wounded . . .'

We looked at each other in anguish. Tears were running down our faces. François had visited us in Prague several times and had fallen in love with it. To me, of course, it had been a beloved home for twenty years.

I left for London immediately to find that Jan was in the States attending a U.S. National Student Association's conference; Zdeněk was in bed with a London bug. After a few days I cut short my holiday and prepared to leave.

'It's madness to return,' English friends told me. I had not heeded similar warnings in 1950; I did not heed them now. I returned to occupied Czechoslovakia.

My heart cried out when I saw Prague, my beautiful Prague, desecrated. The Museum pitted, a block next to the Radio building gutted. On its broken wall the words *ex oriente lux* could still be read. Street names had not yet been restored. Tanks had been withdrawn from the centre but were still stationed in a field near our house. I looked with loathing at the young crews. If I had had a gun I think I would have been capable of using it.

Friends were eager to relate their experiences, to re-live that terrifying, yet wonderful, week of national solidarity.

Her eyes shining, Eva cried: 'You who have suffered so much with us, who have seen our nation on its knees, you missed our finest hour! The invasion brought out the best in us. No one panicked and bought up food stocks as they did during the Cuban crisis. People helped each other. Youngsters took food to old age pensioners; citizens provided meals for the radio and television broadcasters; car owners ran free taxi services. For the first time in many years I was proud to be Czech.

'In some ways the invasion set us free,' she went on. 'Now we owe the Russians nothing. When I think how we looked up to them!' Her voice shook. 'We looked up to them. For years I cherished the memory of riding into Prague on a Russian tank in May 1945. But they're barbarians. Their troops shot our people quite capriciously. Russian officers shot their own men for trifling offences. The soldiers stole everything they laid their hands on. They drank a bottle of perfume belonging to a girl in our office; the cups smelt of it. They left excreta on the floor. Elsewhere they wilfully destroyed expensive laboratory equipment; and they did two-million-crowns' worth of damage to the Museum.

'The Russians know nothing about socialism. They know only dogma. Yet they came to destroy our socialism.' She sighed heavily. 'Given the way things are, I suppose we were bound to fail. Yet we had to try.'

It was the Czechs' fate to introduce new designs for living far in advance of their time: the Taborites had founded a classless society; King George of Poděbrady had tried to form a league of nations, five centuries before it was actually created. How long would we have to wait for another, successful, Prague Spring?

Karel Kovanda was still fired by the activities.

'Boy, you missed something, Rosemary! Twentieth century Hussites sitting in the path of tanks. Žižka routed the crusaders with farm wagons and women's petticoats. We confounded the invaders with paint and ink. We produced clandestine papers, printed leaflets in Russian describing developments here, and mixed with the troops explaining our political attitudes.'

Yes, I thought, the parallel with the Hussites is appropriate: they tried to explain their faith and their programme to the invading Catholic crusaders.

'New slogans appeared every day,' Karel grinned: '"One step forward is enough to find him who was at our side behind our backs", or "Go to blazes, or at least go home!" or "Soviet paralysis the most progressive paralysis in the world!" And the jokes! Have you heard this one? Brezhnev is standing outside a big gate. Brezhnev begs to be allowed in. Kosygin cries: "No, don't come in!" "But this is heaven," exclaims Brezhnev. "That's what I thought," says Kosygin, "But those bloody Czechs have changed the signposts!"'

To Paula, the invasion was a tragedy. She had spent many summers working in the Russian virgin lands. She had wept to see a young man with whom she had tilled Russian soil driving a Russian tank. She mourned for the young Russians who committed suicide when they discovered their leaders had misled them: there was no counter-revolution in Czechoslovakia. Sadly she had written to wives, mothers and sweethearts at the request of soldiers who feared they would be sent to Siberia on their return and would never see their loved ones again.

I wandered through the old city, my thoughts in turmoil, consumed with a rage and hatred I had not thought myself capable of. I felt a personal betrayal. *My* hopes had been dashed; *my* dreams shattered. From a loyal friend I had been converted into an implacable enemy. I understood what millions of Czechs were suffering. And for what? The Czech reforms had not threatened socialism. Indeed a report of 20 August had shown that only 5 per cent of the population would welcome a return to capitalism. The Soviet Union could compromise with its enemy America, yet crush its ally Czechoslovakia. It *had* to crush Czechoslovakia because she was a direct threat to Soviet hegemony in the socialist bloc. Hussitism had overflowed into the neighbouring countries and the people had revolted against tyranny. Socialism with a human face would have proved equally contagious. Freedom of expression and genuine workers' control were the last things the Soviet Union wanted in its satellites. They had to be erased at the source. Czechs characteristically fight with their wits. But what, I wondered, had become of the Hussite will to take up arms in defence of one's beliefs?

'The army was ready for action,' Vladimír Laštůvka, fresh from his military service, told me when I ran into him in a wine tavern near the faculty of journalism. He had just completed his military service. 'The lower ranking officers and men were wholeheartedly on the nation's side.' He added bitterly: 'We're about the only European country with two years' conscription, yet we are never allowed to defend ourselves.'

The young Pavel's voice echoed down the years.

'The Russians have wanted to station their troops here for years,' pronounced another youth at the table. 'They negotiated with Novotný in the autumn but he fobbed them off. Having led the nation into conflict with the Soviet Union, Dubček should have acted consistently and fought.'

After the euphoria of the week in which they prevented the Russians from taking full control of the country, people listened in a state of shock to Dubček who, tears in his eyes, explained on television that he and the other Presidium members kidnapped by the Red Army on 21st August signed in Moscow the so-called Protocols which will ensure a return to 'normalization'. Although the precise content of the Protocols were not immediately known, the unmistakable impression was one of capitulation. The general gloom deepened as the government began making more and more concessions to the invaders. In our flat the atmosphere was less despondent. The students were planning resistance.

Jan returned to Prague but left a month later to take up a year's scholarship at Oxford offered to him before the invasion; Zdeněk had remained in London for a course in English. Jana had moved into Zdeněk's room. Through her I shared the excitement of the first student action, of which she was the prime mover. This was a three-day sit-in to back the students' petition to the government demanding fulfilment of its pre-invasion pledges.

Jana was enthusiastic when she returned: 'Most of the lecturers and some of the public supported us. Factories sent us funds, some held token strikes and scores endorsed our petition.'

Now that the foundations had been laid, Jiří Müller quietly pressed for further co-operation. He travelled the country talking to workers.

He was popular with the workers. He spoke their language and understood their problems, having worked in a factory for a year during his studies.

The workers had been slow to get off the political mark during the Prague Spring, but the invasion had acted as a spur. Now they were receptive to new ideas and found common cause with the students. Jiří's first achievement was a contract signed by the Czech students' union and the metalworkers' union. This supported Prague Spring policies, specifically workers' councils, and demanded general elections and withdrawal of foreign troops. It also established forms of cooperation between the two unions.

Jan turned up in Prague some six weeks before Christmas. His trip had been legal, so he was permitted to come home for the holiday. He and other students followed up Jiří's success and the results were further student–worker solidarity pacts. I attended some of the meetings and came away immensely cheered. It seemed to me that something from those eight months of promise might still be salvaged.

Jan's colleagues stumped for a spokesman with both good English and guts, asked him to address the coming Budapest conference of national student unions on European security. I smelt a rat. Jan tried to reassure me in vain: 'Don't worry. It's a perfectly sound speech, condemning imperialism, Portugal, Greece and all that.'

When he got back from Budapest the secret police again began taking a solicitous interest in his welfare, and his passport. This strengthened my doubts.

'I gather your speech referred to the invasion,' I remarked.

'Well, yes; one can hardly talk about European security and ignore what happened in the heart of Europe a few months ago. I condemned the invasion in the name of our union and I quoted National Assembly and Party documents to prove that there had been no counter-revolution, but admitted that some mistakes had been made.'

'You could get into serious trouble for using the term "invasion" now that it has been explicitly banned,' I observed. It was not a reproach, merely a statement of fact. Jan had been out of action for several months. It was inevitable he should pitch himself head first into the trickiest waters.

In the light of Jan Palach's supreme sacrifice shortly afterwards, this seemed little enough.

The student who burnt himself to death as a protest against Czechoslovakia's fate and growing public apathy became a national symbol. To dispel this aura certain officials imputed sinister political motives to his death, inferring that Holeček and 'other ruthless fanatics' had been the instigators. Palach asked to see Luboš just before he died. He did not know Luboš personally but trusted him as a student leader. He told Luboš he was convinced by public reaction that his sacrifice had not been in vain but he did not want others to follow his example. His dying message was: 'Tell them to join you in a living fight!'

The police interrogated Luboš several times. He had been living with us for nearly a year. I had grown very fond of him, respecting his integrity and enjoying his flashes of dry humour. Disquieted, I waited up every night until he came home, though it was well past midnight.

Palach's funeral, organised entirely by students including Jan, was attended by hundreds of thousands. It became a focal point around which the nation could rally in a fresh burst of solidarity.

Unhappy the nation that needs heroes, said Brecht. This small nation, surrounded by enemies, did indeed need heroes to preserve its identity and its self-respect. It had needed Hus; it needed Jan Palach, as it would need Jiří Müller and Jan Tesař.

Years later I was to see a re-run of the *World in Action* film of Palach's funeral with a commentary by Jan, looking young and earnest. It brought tears to my eyes again. By then Palach's grave had been removed by the authorities but his memory could not be erased.

The Budapest affair was duly filed for the time being and Jan's passport was returned. He postponed his departure by a few days so that he could help with the organization of the funeral and take part in the negotiations with the government over the wording of the student union's appeal to Palach's anonymous followers which Jan eventually read out on the radio. He was therefore still in Czechoslovakia when Ralph Schoenman arrived in Prague, looking for speakers to attend a preliminary meeting of Bertrand Russell's tribunal on Czechoslovakia. I begged him not to go. Stockholm on top of Budapest would really be pushing his luck. The Kavans never know when to draw the line. Jan completed his article at midnight and left early in the morning.

Returning from town in the afternoon, I opened Jan's door. My heart gave a disbelieving thud. His luggage was there. He hadn't flown! I dropped onto the divan. Jana looked in and gasped: 'Oh God!' She went out and returned with the vodka bottle and two glasses. (My nervous system was beginning to show signs of wear. I now kept a bottle of spirits handy for our not infrequent emergencies.) 'Here, you'd better drink this, Rosemary; it'll pull you round.'

Jan slunk in later. Too angry to speak without exploding, I cooked supper in silence. At last he could bear it no longer.

'Don't you want to hear what happened?' Pavel's voice and Pavel's question. Genetics had done a good job.

'Your passport was confiscated yet again. You may not get back to Oxford at all. Your thesis will not be finished. Shall I go on?'

Jan sat with his head down, a picture of dejection. I relented.

'Here you are, here's your supper. Now tell me the whole story.'

'The airport police searched our luggage and discovered my pounds and dollars — '

'Pounds and dollars?'

'The pounds were from my Oxford grant, the dollars were a fee for an article I wrote on the Prague Spring and the invasion in the States in the summer. I was as surprised as the police to see my wallet and a copy of the article at the bottom of the case. I thought I had left them in Oxford. The day I left for Prague I only had about ten minutes to get ready in. I'd been at the dentist all the morning and was feeling groggy. I just pushed a few things on top of the clean shirts that were still in the case from the summer. Of course the police didn't believe I'd brought the money into the country unwittingly and was taking it out equally unwittingly.'

'You can hardly blame them. After all, travellers usually know what they have packed, and they usually unpack when they reach their destination. So I suppose the customs officers impounded the money?'

'Yes,' Jan admitted miserably.

'I see there is more.'

'Well, yes. I had about 300 political documents with me which I wanted to present at Stockholm.'

'So I presume you are once more under investigation?'

Poor Jan, he was only partly to blame. He was the victim of stress. His organism had reacted to Pavel's imprisonment with severe headaches. Psychologically he had adapted to continuing tension, but once the pattern had been set, he seemed compelled to create unending stress situations.

A few courageous people who still remained in high places spoke up for him. The police, however, took their time. Finally, Jan was told he was free to travel. Besides his grant, he had lost a whole term at Oxford.

Chapter 23

In the meanwhile I had lost my job. Journalists were the first to be sacked for 'political unreliability'. *Czechoslovak Life*, like the rest of the media, was expected to applaud the invasion and current policies. (Ironically, owing to our long production time, my articles on KAN and the 231 Club came out when these organizations had already been banned, and one on students and their programme for social reform appeared in September, after the agreement on the stationing of Soviet troops in Czechoslovakia had been signed.) One or two members of the staff hurriedly repented their pre-invasion enthusiasm in an attempt to save their jobs. Our cautious boss survived, of course. Giorgio stuck to his Prague Spring convictions. He and I and many good friends were among the hundreds expelled from the journalists' union.

Here I was, unemployed and rooting around for translations again. The clock was being turned back to the fifties. I fought off a crippling sense of defeat. As always when grappling with black thoughts, I crossed the river to Malá Strana. The magic began to work. Evil and tyranny shrank to manageable dimensions. I succumbed once more to the beauty of Prague. Although I now knew Prague well, she continued to surprise me. On every walk I stumbled upon some unexpected touch of bawdy humour or wistful humanity.

I made my way to U Malířů, one of my favourite medieval taverns, and thoughtfully sipped a glass of Ludmila. Whatever happens, I told myself, Prague's values remain sane. Its people still love the simplicity of Nature and the timelessness of music. They're addicted to good food and drink, to good books and company. They're civilized without having yielded to gimmickry and gadgetry. I defy even the most obdurate misanthropist to feel alienated in Prague. Whatever troubles, the individual is not alone: there are scores of others in the same plight, eager to share experiences, to comfort and advise.

These reflections were suddenly checked when I noticed a copy of *Rudé Právo* lying on the table. My own name leapt out of the small print. I quickly scanned a full-page Ministry of the Interior report, and there I learned the awful truth. I was an agent of imperialism! During the Prague Spring, I had passed on information to 'a certain diplomat', discovered by the vigilant security police to have been a British spy — after his recall!

True, I had attended the Jonsens' receptions as a representative of my magazine and had interviewed guests of honour. In 1968 I had attended film shows and cocktail parties in a personal capacity as a bilingual guest guaranteed to enliven the evening. That was the sum total of my espionage activity. I wondered, was this a new stratagem to 'prove' to the public that not the reformists but the CIA and MI6 had contrived the Prague Spring?

I wrote indignant denials to the editor and the Ministry, to which I received no reply. I waited apprehensively for the pre-breakfast ring at the door. None came. But one or two publishing houses found it impossible to commission translations from me.

In spite of the gathering clouds, life had its compensations. Zuzana Blühová, a cheerful Slovak student of drama, had taken over Luboš's place in the Kavan household, Luboš having become engaged to a wise and pretty student of engineering. Jana and Jiří Müller were feverishly trying to submit their theses before the guillotine fell. Most of Jiří's thesis was written in Zuzana's room while she supplied cups of black coffee and checked his calculations. In the next room Jirka Holub was numbering pages, retyping passages and correcting punctuation for Jana.

Jirka had moved in with Jana. Living up to Jirka's intellectual standards would have strained anyone's vitality but Jana's. He was teaching her German and Polish, and they were both attending courses in Hebrew and Arabic. Jirka did not hold with marriage and Jana was called upon to envisage their life together as a common law monogamy with seventeen children, on each of which they would practise different psychological theories and educational methods. The first was on its way.

After a complicated pregnancy and difficult confinement, Jana gave birth to a large and alert Ilja. The sight of Jirka washing the baby or its nappies with a book of Sanskrit propped over the bath drove away the spectre of the security police. Zuzana and I occupied first places in the hierarchy of 'aunts' and 'uncles', in whose eyes Ilja was the most exceptional child of his generation. Altogether, in that time of bitter national disillusionment ours was probably the most cheerful community in Prague. Jirka struggled to support his family on freelance teaching. A brilliant linguist he had been sacked by the Language Institute because of his ethical views on political consistency; in other words he had refused to condone the invasion.

When I broke the news that I would have to leave Czechoslovakia and settle in England, Jana was to say: 'The five years with you have been the happiest of my life. Your departure will be the end of an era. None of us will ever forget the fun, friendship and freedom of your open house.'

I was to lose all my possessions. Those had also been my happiest days too. I had had companionship I valued, hope for better things and faith in my young friends' ability to achieve them.

We filled our glasses to celebrate first-class honours for the two theses — in Jiří's case prematurely, it transpired.

Again we raised them to commemorate the banning of the Czech Students' Union. The reasons given by the Ministry of the Interior were Jan's speech at Budapest, his foreign policy document (prepared for the last student congress in Olomouc in April 1969 for which Jan returned from Oxford), a letter to the Bertrand Russell Peace Foundation in support of workers' councils, composed by Luboš, Jiří and Karel, and Jiří's articles on the Party in *Buchar*. The Union had been a symbol of liberty. I had watched over its conception and rejoiced at its birth; I could only grieve at its passing.

After his Olomouc speech, Jan was warned by his friends to return abroad and stay there legally until things cooled down. In their opinion, if the authorities took action he would be the worst off. Not only had he been in charge of the student union's foreign relations but he had more contacts with the West than any of the other leaders.

After his term at Oxford, Jan enrolled at the London School of Economics. This made his stay legal but meant he had to start his degree course all over again.

Unfortunately, things showed no signs of cooling down. On the contrary, they were hotting up under Gustáv Husák who had replaced Dubček as Party leader in April 1969. A week before their finals Zuzana, Jiří and Luboš were expelled from university for their 'activity in the Czech Students' Union'. I felt their disappointment as keenly as if they had been my own children. After the long battle for Jiří and Luboš' reinstatement, it was cruel that they should be deprived of the fruits of their efforts when the end was in sight. The expulsions were more than a personal defeat: they were part of a process by which all the achievements of the past five years would be whittled away. For a time none of them could find work. Eventually Jiří got a job as a travelling salesman to a group of sacked intellectuals making synthetic rubber toys in an ex-journalist's kitchen. It was illustrative of Jiří's popularity that even in this risk-fraught time, thousands of signatures were appended to a student protest at this second expulsion.

Mrs Müller, up from Brno for the weekend, swallowed this second disappointment with that mixture of pride and sorrow with which she regarded all her son's activities. 'Look at him,' she cried with tears in her eyes and a fond smile on her lips. 'At twenty-six he has no degree, no flat, no prospects. He owns nothing but a toothbrush and a briefcase.'

Jiří mildly remonstrated that possessions were a drag and that his prospects did not depend on a piece of paper.

I raged at this prodigious waste of talent; but worse was to come. As a result of Husák's 'loyalty tests', a third of the Party members were expelled and a multitude of ex-Party and non-Party people found themselves jobless or at least downgraded. (Workers were not exempt, especially those who had been members of workers' councils, now branded as 'counter-revolutionary'.)

Husák seemed bent on creating an era of mediocrity unrivalled even by Novotný's. His hatchetry echoed the fifties. Science, education and culture were axed with a vengeance. Children whose parents had been active in 1968 were barred from higher, secondary and university education. Courses in 'dangerous' subjects — psychology, sociology, philosophy and some Western languages — were banned again. Strict censorship was reimposed: agitprop realism was reinstalled.

The fringe theatres, traditionally a medium of protest, sought ways of communication through allegory and analogy. The public responded. In fact, as a prominent director confided to me: 'Audiences read their own interpretation even into genuinely unambiguous lines. They applaud eternal truths ecstatically.' Fearing the power of words, the authorities would have to abolish all media if they wished to prevent contamination.

Not content with immobilization Husák unleashed a relentless smear campaign against the reformers. Dubček's 'socialism with a human face' was described as a 'period of dictatorship and terror against the workers and peasants'. The radical students were attacked for having 'broken up the ČSM'. Jan was labelled an 'anarchist who adopted the methods of the Western New Left'. Most cynically of all, the villains of the fifties were whitewashed while their victims were blackened. Pavel, Eda Goldstücker and several defendants in the Slánský trial were depicted as parasites and cowards who had saved their own skins at the expense of others. Anti-Semitism was again cultivated under the guise of anti-Zionism. A creative genius among the 'reliable' journalists invented a group of Zionists who since the thirties had infiltrated the Party in order to influence its foreign policy in the interests of Zionism, and prepare the soil for a 1968 situation. Though at school in the thirties and dead in the sixties, Pavel was named among them. Poor Pavel, he had no peace even in the grave! The label was passed on to his elder son. Jan found that he too had become a Zionist overnight.

What was Husák's reaction to the dishonouring of his former fellow jail-birds? He had shared a cell with Pavel at one time; he and Eda Goldstücker had been at Leopoldov together for a long period. According to another ex-inmate of Leopoldov, Husák had 'formed' his future 'government' while in prison. Ambition of this calibre would hardly be affected by human feelings.

Sometimes I experienced near-despair. To have come so far along the road to freedom and now to be dragged back to a dark age! How could Husák of all people so dishonour his fellow prisoners? He and Pavel and Eda had been incarcerated at Leopoldov together. Husák knew only too well the true face of the fifties.

In one respect the seventies differed from the fifties: no one was fooled by the crass propaganda, not even loyal communists. A few people were bought by Husák's goulash-and-carrot communism which offered consumer benefits as a compensation for lost freedom. Some withstood the drastic turn of the tide with fortitude and wry Czech humour, and endeavoured by political discussion and scientific study in small groups to preserve a continuity of enlightenment. Many turned inwards to their families or their hobbies, their pets and their yoga. But inevitably time wore down their hopes. Months of fruitless job-hunting or of boredom in monotonous or arduous, ill-paid employment, with few mental stimuli in leisure hours, plus continual harassment in one form or other, began to deflate all but the most resilient spirits. A grey inertia settled on the vast majority.

One antidote to despair is action. Having supported the reform movement since the early sixties, I could not bear to view its destruction unresistingly. I was sure that if any organized resistance existed, Jiří Müller would be involved. My suspicion proved correct. Jiří told me that several underground opposition groups had been formed. Their power was words, their weapon information. Some produced regular broadsheets. These presented facts about domestic and foreign affairs and analyses of current trends. They were able to disclose top-level Party and inter-party decisions, because some unpurged comrades were salving their consciences by top-level leaks.

The opposition also smuggled into the country and distributed *Listy*, an émigré journal produced in Rome by Jiří Pelikán[50], and Tigrid's *Svĕdectví*, as well as books by authors of the Western left and by Soviet dissidents. With mounting excitement I realized that oppression was being combated — Czech-style — by maintaining the flow of ideas.

All duplicators and photocopying machines were strictly guarded, Jiří said, no one in the underground had access to one. Therefore typing was the only method of reproduction. This was something I could do. I offered my services to Jiří's group. He immediately drew from his briefcase a copy of their

50. Jiří Pelikán is a former Director-General of Czechoslovak Television and is currently a member of the European Parliament representing the Italian Socialist Party.

clandestine monthly *Facts, Comments and Events*. I fingered it with reverence. It was a symbol of courage on the part of the authors, the typists and the distributors. It comprised a dozen single-spaced, somewhat blurred sheets. It would take me hours to decipher the faint letters and reproduce ten copies. No matter. For the first time in my life I had an abundance of leisure.

I cannot pretend not to have felt a quiver of apprehension when I started to type as soon as Jiří had left. The clatter of the keys echoed in my quiet room. I imagined the neighbours would hear and wonder. The penalty for disseminating enlightenment was heavy. A minimum of two years in the cooler, Jiří had told me. But I took fresh heart thinking of Pavel. At least I had his guidelines for survival.

I had already become used to surveillance since our return from London. I was experienced in speaking in riddles over a tapped phone. I now learned to exchange written messages in bugged flats, to recognize unknown collaborators by signs, to reach destinations by devious routes and to throw off shadowers. I wore my oldest, least conspicuous clothes on delivery days. Even so, I was stopped by the police on my third errand and asked for my identity papers. One of the two scrutinized the little red book, embossed with the Czech lion, muttered 'Kavanová' while exchanging meaningful glances with the other. I waited for the familiar 'Come along with us', wondering with detachment what tale I'd think up if it came to a search. But the significant tone was merely a feature of psychological warfare against the citizenry. He listed through the pages. Suddenly he shouted: 'Ha! You have no proper employment, I see!' trying to catch me out on the parasite article.

'If you'll examine the pertinent page again,' I said, 'you'll see that firstly my last work contract was terminated according to the regulations and secondly, I am the widowed mother of two children and have reached the age at which employment is no longer statutory for that category.'

'You are a housewife, then?'

I nodded. It seemed the most innocuous definition.

'Then this document is not in order! It should specify your exact status.'

He was wrong. The document contained several rubrics for employers' rubber stamps but none for other specifications. However, the citizen was at a hopeless disadvantage in any encounter with the police. They were not guardians of the law. They *were* the law.

'I'll have the omission rectified at the registration department immediately, comrade,' I murmured meekly.

The scraggy one sniffled loudly. He had been left out. 'What's in your bag?' he demanded peevishly.

'Shopping,' I replied airily. I pulled the handles apart, revealing an earthy assortment of unwrapped, slightly sodden veg. 'And today's *Rudé Právo*. That's an interesting speech of Comrade Bilak's, isn't it?'

The stalwarts mumbled their agreement. Obviously neither of them had read the Party gospel. Uninterested in its contents (had they but known about the sheets interlarded among its pages!) they exhorted me again to correct my registration, returned my document and left.

Liaison between the underground and the West was essential. It seemed obvious that I should become one of the links inside the country, and Jan one of the links outside it. I must confess I did not feel exactly cut out for this job. It always took me some time to collect myself out of a deep sleep when Jan phoned me at 1 a.m. to deliver some seemingly nonsensical message. (At least my remonstrances must have sounded convincing to the secret police!) Then slowly the code would float into my head and I would formulate my coded reply.

Smuggling was the last of the many occupations I undertook without previous experience. There were occasional mishaps. Accepting a case of 'subversive' material on a main highway in broad daylight was something I would not have cared to repeat too often. Neither was my favourite nocturnal pastime dragging a rubbish bag of 'contraband' through Prague in the dead of night. The black plastic dustbin liner was obviously foreign. The nature of its contents was recognisable from the bulges. I felt as conspicuous as a murderer trying to dispose of a corpse. I dared not take a tram or even a taxi. Many taxi drivers were fired intellectuals, but there were also police informers among them. So I went on foot choosing narrow, ill-lit streets and hugging the houses. If I was stopped by the police, I'd had it. There was no way I could explain away the possession of new books on controversial — or even non-controversial — subjects in English, Russian and German.

We had extended our service to include books. Up-to-date information from the West enabled dissidents, at least in private, to continue their studies and research or at least keep abreast of their field. It was also a means of maintaining morale. Then there were the books by the Western Left which enabled the dissidents to follow trends of political thinking outside. My guardian angel — evidently a dissident sympathiser — got me home safely in the small hours and I would drop thankfully into bed. One morning, however, my collaborator did not turn up. I spent several anxious days waiting, alone. I had given Zuzana, Jana and Jirka what furniture they needed and was now living in a single-unit flat with a minimum of belongings; it was hopeless for concealment. Accommodating 'subversive' literature was like living with a time bomb. Eventually, I was relieved of it. My collaborator explained that he had been checked by the police, leaving another dissident's flat. He had thought it wise to lie low for a while. Jan used the *Samizdat* we smuggled to him as a basis for articles in the Western press. What happened to the material that came in I do not know. Ignorance was the best protection in dealings with the police who were stepping up their activities. I received frequent warnings to clear the deck when a dissident's flat was raided. A round-up of political suspects would be expected.

Apart from the occupational hazards of underground work, there were practical difficulties, caused by shortages. Typing, copying and carbon paper were rarely available in the shops. Fortunately some of my friends were still employed in offices and in spite of the tight stationery rationing, smuggled small amounts to us.

There were disappointments. Once-fearless friends declined to participate. Paula had returned to the fold and her column. Eva had thrown in her Party card and retired from work and the world. 'I've done my stint. Three betrayals by West and East in a lifetime are too much. I'm too old to join another struggle,' she declared.

I missed Heda sorely. She and her second husband had settled in the United States. I found an unexpected ally in Magda, a gentle, cultured woman some ten years my junior. She had aged perceptibly since the invasion. Shadows saddened her dark eyes, but her face had retained its wistful charm. After being fired from a responsible job, she had been reduced to office cleaning. Recently she had been promoted to clerk but this brought her no joy. 'Employees elbow for positions and settle personal accounts under the guise of political vigilance,' she complained. 'Mistrust is rife not only because of police informers but because nearly everyone has yielded to some form of corruption. There are no depths to which our people will not sink when political pressures are exerted.'

Mirek had put it more pithily. 'We're a sub-nation! We knuckled under to Ferdinand II and Francis Joseph. We bowed to Hitler. Then along comes Pepík Stalin and we double up to him. We put up a bloody great statue. Not even the Zhittites and Missites and all those other ites had an idol that size. It cost billions, and what did it look like? A bloody meat queue with the old butcher himself at the head! Then Nikita blows the gaff and what do we do? Blow a fortune in marble to smithereens! And now we're all licking Brezhnev's arse!'

The Czechs veer readily from national pride to national castigation, I observed.

Unfortunately, Magda had not exaggerated. Morale had indeed declined. Deceit, fraud, sloth, sycophancy and careerism were the order of the day. Everything had a price, from a university place to the delivery of raw materials. Hypocrisy was rewarded, honesty pilloried. The economy was again built on rejects, with the difference that now shoddy workmanship was, in part, a form of passive resistance. The workers refused to 'tear their guts out for the Russians.'

Magda burst out: 'We're cut off from the world and each other, we're even divorced from our own history! If only there was something I could do!'

I thought quickly. I had known and trusted Magda for several years. Her sincerity was beyond dispute. Without revealing my source, I asked whether she would like to receive, type and pass on underground journals. Her face lit up. She couldn't have looked more pleased if I'd offered her a free trip to the Bahamas. She hugged me, laughing. 'Life will have a purpose again! Here's to co-operation! And thank you. You've saved my sanity.' She put down her glass. 'I'll have to type at my mother's. My husband . . .' Her shoulders sagged.

Her husband had found the price of integrity too high. Outwardly he supported the new regime in order to keep his job. Magda felt the humiliation deeply. I reserved my condemnation for those who enforced such choices. How many Englishmen would openly criticize Ian Smith or John Vorster if their jobs were at stake and no unemployment benefit existed, I wondered.

So far the resistance groups had acted independently. In November 1971 they executed their first concerted action.

General elections were to be held. The electoral law allowing for wider representation, proposed in 1968, had not been passed. We were back to the old farce. The unwilling electorate would be herded 'joyously' to the polls to give a unanimous mandate to a list of candidates they did not know, drawn up by officials of a regime they did not support. The ideology mongers did not waste time on subtleties. Abstainers and deleters would be branded as traitors and treated accordingly. Some enterprises underscored the point by declaring that November pay packets would be issued only on the production of voting receipts.

The underground organized an audacious campaign to persuade the electorate to vote according to its conscience. The duplication and distribution of vast quantities of leaflets presented almost insuperable problems. But as Jiří, who was now a frequent visitor, said: 'If politics is the art of the possible, the possible can be achieved only by striving for the impossible.' The possible was achieved. A duplicator was obtained; about 70,000 leaflets were turned out.

The leaflet declared that to vote for the official candidates was to endorse the occupation and the current violations of human rights. It reminded the public that the elections would be rigged, all the figures would be determined beforehand. It pointed out that by law, voting was a right not a duty; no citizen could legally be penalised for not voting. It suggested that to boycott the elections or delete candidates would be tantamount to registering disapproval of existing conditions and policies.

I felt privileged to be a part of this campaign. It was the first major gesture against the regime since Jan Palach's death and proof that the whole nation was not 'a docile populace, easily dominated by foreigners'. Obviously the leaflet would not sway the vote and oust the government but its very appearance would demonstrate to both rulers and ruled the strength and resolution of the resistance movement. Public morale would be boosted both by the leaflet and the publication of the real polling figures in the underground press.

The participants were under no illusion about the risk they ran. Husák bleated from time to time that no citizen would be brought to trial on political grounds: only law-breakers would be punished. But what guarantee of legality was there when the Minister of Justice declared: 'The necessity for protecting the rights of citizens and the independence of courts is a subjectivist theory'? What chances of a fair trial were there when a third of the country's judges had been removed from office for refusing to judge according to political directives, and pliable working class cadres had been rushed through one-year law courses? If the punishment for playing a tape of Husák's August 1968 speech deploring the invasion was two years in prison, what would it be for an unofficial election leaflet?

Interrogators from the fifties were back in business. I had nightmares in which I was arrested and thrown into jail. Sometimes the dream took place in the fifties. I was fretting because the boys were ill and needed me. Pavel visited me. From the other side of the glass partition he told me I should have thought of my sons before I got involved. In another dream Pavel lay dying. He didn't know I was in prison; I heard him revile me for not coming to his deathbed. Other dreams were in the present. I was in the same cell; the warders were the same. The same interrogators tricked me into betraying my collaborators.

On 8 November leaflets were mailed or transported to private addresses, offices and factories all over the country. The next day the remainder were slipped into letter boxes or displayed in public places. There were some arrests among the distributors. Otherwise the country-wide operation worked smoothly.

After the deadline was up, I was left with a few hundred undelivered leaflets and no instructions to destroy them. Perhaps they were to be scattered near the polls on the eve of the elections, two weeks away. I looked round my bare room in despair. Where could I hide them? I stepped out onto the balcony. Nothing there. Flower pots were too obvious. Beyond the wall of the balcony reared the rooftops of other, lower buildings. In a sheltered corner in the distance I spotted a small and inexplicable patch of soil. I waited until nightfall then I climbed the wall and, crouching low, dodged among the chimney pots until I came to the spot. I removed some weeds, scooped away the earth with a tablespoon and pushed a polythene bag containing the contraband into the hollow. I replaced the soil, propped up the dispirited weeds and crawled back, elated with my evening's work.

I had had to come to some decision about my future. The Ministry of Education had refused to extend the boys' stay abroad. If they wanted to gain university degrees they would have to remain in England as émigrés. If they returned to Czechoslovakia, they would be drafted into the army or imprisoned for 'illegal sojourn' abroad. That was one reason for me to return to England. The other was my ageing parents. Visits abroad were rarely granted to Czechs now. There appeared to be only one solution: to emigrate. I therefore applied for an emigration passport.

It was months before the answer arrived. Application refused. My emigration was 'not in the state's interest'. For the same reason, I was refused an exit permit to travel West on holiday. This confirmed my suspicion that I was being detained on political grounds. There were two possible explanations. The Jonsen affair was one. Some persons had recently been interrogated on their connection with Jonsen. My name had come up. I had received messages from unknown well-wishers to get out before it was too late. Several Czechs had been tried for allegedly passing espionage information to the Dutch Embassy. A similar scandal might be being prepared with the British. The other possible explanation was that the police were aware of my other activities. They might have obtained information from a detainee; they might be planning further arrests in connection with the leaflets. I warned my collaborators of the probable implications of my rejected application.

Legal emigration being out of the question, I considered other possibilities. Though loyalty to my friends urged me to stay, concern for my mother and sons swayed me. My mother's health had deteriorated since Pavel's arrest. Another shock might prove fatal. I had a premonition that after the elections it would be too late. My two previous presentiments of disaster — fifteen months before I was bombed out and eighteen months prior to Pavel's arrest — had been accurate. I could not wait. I had to act immediately.

The resourceful Jan had planned an emergency exit for me, should all else fail. This was the moment to put it into operation. I phoned London and gave the code message. For reasons of security, I must leave the reader — and the security police — in ignorance of my escape route. Suffice to say it worked efficiently. My motto had to be 'business as usual' until the last minute. I spent the last week hammering out translations, fees for which I would not have time to collect, and my last day playing a part in a short film for a secondary school English course. In the evening I sorted papers and distributed them among friends for safe-keeping, and handed over to Magda the latest issue of the *samizdat* chronicle.

There still remained the hidden leaflets. Once my absence was ascertained, the flat and its vicinity would be searched very thoroughly: they might be discovered. There was no time to ask for instructions. I scrambled over the rooftops and unearthed the bag. Burning would be the most thorough method of disposal, but where in a centrally-heated flat did one incinerate? The large saucepan that had been used for boiling Ilja's nappies offered a solution. I placed it on the tiled bathroom floor, closed the common ventilator shaft, opened the window onto the balcony a fraction, and began to tear up and ignite the sheets of paper. The bathroom was soon a furnace. Smoke filled my nostrils and stung my eyes. From time to time I tottered out, gulped some air and checked to see if smoke or flames were visible from outside. The last thing I wanted was a visit from the fire brigade! The paper burned slowly, charred flakes remained. I flushed these down the toilet. Two hours later, throat parched, face roasted and eyes smarting, I burnt the last leaflet, washed out the blackened saucepan and threw it in a dustbin.

In the morning I had a streaming cold. From a distant vantage point I watched myself perform the necessary last-minute actions as though I were a character in a TV drama. I combed the flat once more for incriminating evidence. I re-checked my zip-bag and its contents for Czech labels. As a final act of defiance I stuck an anti-regime joke on the wall to greet the police when they forced an entry.

I stood at the door ready to leave. Strange that, like Pavel in 1939, I too was fleeing East in order to reach the safety of the West. I too was seeking freedom — at a price. I had lost everything, including twenty-six years of my life. I had nothing to show for them, except a handful of clothes — less than I had brought with me to Prague in 1945. But I had gained much. I had gained insight and self-reliance. I could contemplate calmly the prospect of prison if the escape bid failed or starting life again at fifty if it succeeded. I had acquired friends whom I would never forget and who would not forget me, even if we were never to meet again. Women in particular had sustained me. Women are geared to survival. I too had learnt the art of survival. It enabled me to combat with confidence the cancer I was to find I had brought away with me. My experiences in Czechoslovakia had challenged and finally reaffirmed my belief in love, courage, goodness and freedom.

Two hours later I said goodbye to Prague, and carried with

me an ache like the longing for a loved one who is dead or far away. An ex-lecturer of the law faculty once said: 'To be Czech is not a nationality; it is a disease.' I would add: 'It is a contagious disease; it has entered my bones; my heart is affected.' In my mind's eye I carry a picture of the Hradčany panorama. A voice whispers in my ear: 'Truth shall prevail,' appending Čapek's rider: 'But it will be an almighty struggle.'

Chapter 24

Jan met me at Victoria station. I was crushed in a hairy hug. He was wearing some mangy unidentifiable animal. He grinned: 'So we made it!' I heard the love and relief in his voice. He admitted he had not slept or stirred from the phone till he received my safe-and-sound call from over the border.

Several days later I found Jan sitting pale and hunched.

'Jiři's been arrested!' his father's voice sounded in my ears: 'They've arrested Eda!' Jan went on painfully: 'A week after you got away there was a big round-up in Prague and Brno.' He rested his forehead on his clenched fists. I knew what he was thinking: What am I doing here?

'Someone has to tell the world,' I reminded him.

That l night I tossed on my fold-up bed in Jan's draughty kitchen. Mice scampered along the wainscotting; my thoughts darted hither and thither. What had gone wrong? What evidence had the secret police found? I had warned Jiři in time. Nothing could have been discovered in his lodgings. Had I been careless over the phone? One could never be sure. An unguarded moment, an unwitting betrayal.

We learned later that Jiři had been betrayed by others during interrogations.

The taste of freedom was bitter. My only consolation was that the election campaign had not been in vain. Some genuine results had been published by the underground and these refuted the official poll of 99.8 per cent. In the capital alone, 10 per cent of the electorate had abstained, in the factory districts 11 per cent. One fifth of Prague's voters had registered no confidence in Husák. More important was the knowledge that the Party leaders knew the *full* results. (They had instructed the election commissions to draw up a secret report on the real poll and the behaviour of individual voters.) The true figures would prove to the leadership the instability of its position. All this information had eventually reached the West.

Jan's light was on. I went in to him. He was listing through old Czech magazines, articles by himself, by Luboš and Jiří, declarations of faith, of ethical principles.

Poor Jan, it was harder to be outside, alone. In Prague he would have been sustained by constant contact with his close friends. In England he waged a lone struggle to keep Czechoslovakia's fate in the news. Immediately after the invasion, as a Czech ex-student leader, he had been much in demand on the British radio and television. Then interest in Czechoslovakia had died down, superseded by other political upheavals and natural disasters. Jan had continued to bombard the English and American press with articles under his own name and a variety of pseudonyms, swallowing anger and disappointment when they were cut, quoted out of context or distorted by unfeeling editors.

Now he stepped up his efforts, writing, touring the country, talking, organising another Müller campaign and protests on behalf of all Czech political prisoners, raising money for medicines and other needs for them and their unsupported families.

'You're neglecting your studies and your health,' I pointed out. Apart from his headaches, he was suffering from dangerously fluctuating blood pressure and kidney trouble. He shrugged impatiently. He valued education, as all Czechs do, but he valued other things more highly: justice, loyalty to friends, decency.

'One must live as one would like others to live,' he muttered.

I understood. But if only he would take up yoga, meditation, ease and refresh his mind and body. Jan spurned such advice and stuck perversely to his destructive pain-killers. There was nothing I could do about it; except ease the burden where I could: correct his English, type an article, translate materials that still miraculously made their way across the border and to London.

I was finding that freedom had its limitations. Our living conditions were claustrophobic. Money was more than short. Jan lived on a shoe-string. I received a few pounds National

Assistance. After an initial flutter (a couple of interviews on the radio, two articles in *The Guardian*) London had lost interest in its returned prodigal. The employment exchange was not exactly fighting over women approaching fifty. I found that twenty-odd years doing odd jobs in Eastern Europe did not equip me for the more interesting jobs that paid enough to live on, whereas I was turned down as over-qualified for the clerical jobs usually offered to unclassifiable women of uncertain age.

In the end a young English friend of Jan's introduced me to a genteel firm of architects in need of a secretary. As regards qualifications, the interview was a replica of those in Prague.

No, I didn't know shorthand. Never mind, Sir Anthony preferred to write out his letters. Yes, I could type, quickly and inaccurately; or slowly and accurately. I was however a faultless speller. Sir Anthony looked relieved: he apparently was not. No, I had had no experience with architects but I had worked in a drawing office.

I think it was my cultured accent that got me the job. It was particularly useful when mollifying a titled client because of some delay or discrepancy. On the other hand, my equally convincing Cockney accent rallied reluctant plumbers and electricians, and frequently averted disaster.

One of our projects concerned alterations in a wing of Buckingham Palace. Minutes of discussions with members of the royal household on the shape of royal urinals and the pros and cons of mahogany or plastic seats for royal loos afforded me welcome light relief.

Having been received at the front door of the Palace in 1948, I should like at least to have got in through the back door in 1972. One of our young architects promised to smuggle me in at the end of a tape measure, but I left before he got around to it.

My new secretarial job still left all my evenings and weekends free to help Jan. 'It looks bad for Jiří.' Jan handed me a wad of papers. 'This has been smuggled out to me.'

I recognized the flimsy, closely typed sheets of a *samizdat* document. It was the indictment against 'Müller et al'. Again I marvelled at the courage and resource of the underground. The hearing had been held in camera.

'You are included,' Jan added casually.

My eyes raced over the pages. In unbugged, untapped England the events of only a few months ago seemed a hundred light-years away. The defendants Jiří Müller, Rudolf Battěk,

Jaroslav Jíra, Jean Rosemary Kavanová and Stanislav Furek were charged with 'subverting the Republic', which carried a sentence of three to ten years' imprisonment. The main charge was 'assisting other persons to organise an anti-State leaflet campaign'. I was charged also with 'departing the Republic contrary to Article 109, Section 1' (i.e. illegal emigration) and with 'damaging the Republic's interest abroad' — a reference to my two *Guardian* articles which being truthful were hardly flattering.

Jiří's trial was held in July 1972, concurrently with eight other political trials. Gustav Husák could not have enjoyed eating his own words, especially to the accompaniment of righteous noises by his old enemy, ex-President Novotný.

The trial proceedings eventually came into our hands. (I was scheduled for a separate trial at a later, unspecified date.) Two further names had been added to the list of accused: Dr Jan Tesař and Pavel Mareš. The 'criminal' activities with which some of the defendants were charged, in addition to the leaflet, were signing a ten-point manifesto protesting at the betrayal of the 1968 reforms, supporting a Short Action Programme (drawn up by Brno socialists, based largely on the 1968 programme) and distributing domestic and foreign 'anti-State publications'.

Convictions hinged on the phrase 'motivated by hostility toward socialism'.

While admitting their activity (indeed some defendants, for example Jan Tesař, tried to assume maximum responsibility and protect their friends), the accused denied opposition to socialism. The court presented proof of hostility with glib sophistry: the defendants had engaged in acts deemed by the court to be hostile (acts which could not be defined as hostile unless motivation was established), therefore they were motivated by hostility, Q.E.D.

'Jiří, of course, turned the trial into an indictment of the regime,' Jan observed.

I read Jiří's speech in his own defence, which was enough to provoke a hail of bullets.

'The prosecution has assumed that there is a wide-ranging identity of interest between society at large and the group in power . . . I can only conclude that, in Czechoslovakia, loyalty to the State and society is the same as loyalty to those in power. Furthermore, the citizen is required to demonstrate this loyalty in his every belief and action. This being so, any disloyalty towards those in power would be interpreted as an expression of hostility toward the social system.'

Jiří asserted that his activities had been based on socialism, but had been opposed to a regime created as the result of the invasion of Czechoslovakia by foreign armies, a regime whose internal policy was based not on general consent but rather on coercion, effected primarily by making prospects of employment totally dependent on political opinions.

Jiří stated boldly: 'My conviction and guilt are a foregone conclusion . . . This trial is not concerned with questions of guilt or innocence. Its real concern is to prove support for a policy which could be described as "Keep quiet and don't step out of line".

'I am convinced that this policy will ultimately be destroyed. When it is, the verdict of this particularly political trial, and others, will be reversed. My future standpoint is, I am certain, obvious to everyone.'

The verdict in the name of the Republic — how familiar that phrase sounded; how many phoney judgements had been passed in its much-abused name! — was Guilty. The sentences were high. Dr Tesař came off worst with six years; Jiří got five-and-a-half years.

'Five-and-a-half years!' cried Jan, grief-stricken.

First his father; twenty years later, his dearest friend. The show trials of the fifties had launched Jiří on his political path. Now he himself was a victim. Was there no end to this cruel and senseless waste of brains and integrity?

However dearly they had paid, their sacrifices had not been in vain. It was a needed reminder that the few were still carrying the torch of honour and national self-respect. Characteristically, Jiří refused to 'keep quiet' even in prison. He wrote a letter to the Federal Assembly complaining of his treatment not on the grounds of personal suffering but as violations of the law and the prison regulations.

Jiří was allowed to leave his cell only for a short exercise break five times a week. He was forced to work twelve hours a day sticking pins into cards in the dimly lit cell; his food ration was reduced if he failed to keep up with the very high rate. He had less light, air, exercise and hot water than the non-political prisoners, i.e. ordinary criminals, and far less than the law provided. He was deprived of all intellectual stimuli. When he was ill he was placed in solitary confinement instead of in the prison hospital and was denied proper treatment.

My thoughts went out to Mrs Müller, permitted only three-monthly visits, seeing her son in a terrible state: emaciated (the doctors had refused to operate for gall-stones, the authorities to allow a diet), going blind, losing his hair; his back a mass of running abscesses, his muscles atrophied (he had suffered from this complaint as a child; lack of exercise was exacerbating it).

If I were his mother, I would not be able to bear it, I cried inwardly. Not true, I told myself. Mothers endure everything. They see their sons crucified and bathe the wounds with their tears.

Yet Jiří's spirit remained unbroken. In a letter to his parents he quoted the well-loved Czech humorist Jan Werich: 'The struggle against stupidity is the only struggle that is always in vain, yet can never be relinquished,' and could write: 'In prison, if one is calm and not bitter and is able to concentrate, the opportunities for meditation are invaluable. In many ways I feel that I am maturing for the second time . . . Prison contributes to self-knowledge. I have come to know the exact measure of my composure, fear and courage, and I have discovered in myself a greater degree of tolerance and reconciliation than I had ever dreamt of. My nature, which evidently is not easily repressed, has acquired a field for fertilization: the creation of a full life out of subsistence.'

Jiří showed more concern for the welfare of his parents and the wives and children of other political prisoners than his own. He even remembered me. He mentioned in a letter to his mother: 'I can hear Karel Gott singing "Rosemarie" on the radio and wonder what news there is.'

My chances of returning to my adopted country were nil. Twenty-six years of my life had been swallowed up without trace, like a hamlet in an earthquake. Or so I thought. I was mistaken. Jana risked writing to me openly and sent me photos of my new adopted grandson. Other friends smuggled out little notes. Heda and I corresponded regularly. I realised that bonds of friendship forged in adversity were indestructible. Though penniless, I was rich — in love and experience.

I should have been behind bars. I had escaped by the skin of my teeth. A further miracle happened: I met a painter, Richard Haughton-James — known as Jimmy to all his close friends — at his exhibition at Woodstock. And my whole life changed.

Jimmy and I saw each other nearly every day for a fortnight. We visited galleries and museums, drove through villages, walked in the country and talked and talked. Several months later we were married in Melbourne; Jimmy had found himself an Australian citizen after serving in the Australian army during the war, and had lived there until 1956. Shortly afterwards we settled in Positano in Italy, where Jimmy had earlier decided to make his home.

Despite my marriage to Jimmy, I had not cut myself off from the Czech cause. I could not have fully enjoyed my peace and plenty if I had not been contributing something. I continued to translate documents from Czechoslovakia, and during my visits to England I put myself at the disposal of the chronically understaffed Palach Press agency which Jan had founded at the end of 1975 with the voluntary co-operation of some young English people, moved and angered by Czechoslovakia's fate. These committed young people became my friends too. Our discussions and parties rekindled the spirit of our 'commune' days.

In December 1976, Jiří Müller was freed. He had been released conditionally six months before the end of his sentence. But only a month later two other close friends — Vladimír Laštůvka and Jan's old school friend Aleš Macháček — were imprisoned and accused of distributing Czech literature published abroad.

The banning of many books and authors was acutely felt by the Czechs. In Czechoslovakia culture is not an elitist thing. Books are cheap; everyone reads, not escapist trash, but works of literary merit. The regime had had to ban books if it aimed to break the people's spirit: for a spiritless people is more easily manipulated.

The underground had produced a partial solution: *samizdat* editions of new books by proscribed authors. For technical reasons these were limited in number. Larger editions involved printing; this meant publication abroad. Thus a Kafkaesque situation had arisen: in order that the Czechs might read their own authors in their own language, numerous persons had to risk their liberties smuggling manuscripts out of Czechoslovakia and the printed article back again!

Jan was stricken when he read of Aleš's arrest. He recalled his friend's loyalty and generosity, his down-to-earth attitude to politics. A qualified agronomist, he had worked on farms, setting up workers' collectives — even after workers' councils had been banned — trying to get workers to fight, through the trade unions, for their interests and a share in decision-making. How had Aleš met Laštůvka, Jan and I wondered. Two men whom we had known and liked individually were now linked by a common fate.

A fresh campaign was born. Macháček and Laštůvka were unknown in the West. There was a danger that they would be forgotten; at best the pressure of world public opinion secured only the release of well-known writers.

Jan espoused their cause vigorously in the Western press. The Gestetner which Jan had sent in several years earlier was found in Aleš's garage, but the indictment concentrated mainly on the Kafkaesque charge of helping to supply Czech books to Czech readers. The verdict was three and a half years' imprisonment. The voice of dissent was not silenced, however.

Charter 77, an association committed to the defence of human rights, was founded three weeks before Aleš's arrest and grew into a widely-based movement. *Samizdat* developed into an alternative culture with its own literature, theatre, music and university.

Palach Press gradually grew into an institution, highly regarded in the West as an authoritative source of information. It was also adopted by many chartists as their agency; they sent their documents, articles and books to Palach Press as well as incredible shots of chartists under police surveillance. Nearly all the TV programmes involving chartists, shown in England and other European countries, were made with Jan's collaboration.

Jan was worked off his feet: his headaches persisted, his blood pressure and his cholesterol count rose alarmingly. His doctor warned him: 'You're heading for a heart attack.' But he would not let up. His friends were inside Czechoslovakia, suffering persecution. He was outside, in freedom. He could not do enough. I helped out when I could.

In May 1977 I found myself in London helping Jan to translate documents for both a BBC Panorama programme on Charter 77 and for the campaign in defence of Aleš and Laštůvka. In the hassle of the campaign and deadlines, I had almost forgotten the primary reason for my visit to London. This was a lump in my breast that had suddenly became painful. I had seen my GP and been put on the local hospital's waiting list. I was not troubled by the delay. Nothing could happen to me. Jimmy was my talisman against misfortune. Then I happened to mention my problem to my sister-in-law, Faith, herself a doctor. She was very much concerned and immediately arranged an appointment for me at the Royal Marsden.

I saw Mr White, a gentle, compassionate consultant. He did a biopsy. The results would be ready in three days, he said gravely. My confidence was shaken. The test would surely shown the tumour to be benign. There were only benign influences in my life now. So sure had I been of the outcome that I had dissuaded Jimmy, whose first wife died of cancer, from accompanying me to England.

He was expecting his grandchildren for a short stay. I would be back in time to see them, I had assured him.

The phone rang. It was Faith.

'I've spoken to Mr White,' she said, 'And — '

There was a long pause. That pause told me all I needed to know. 'Now, Faith, no euphemisms. It's cancer isn't it?'

'Yes, my dear, it is.'

My heart cringed.

Faith went on in a sad, sweet voice: 'I'm sorry to be the bearer of bad news. I — er — I took the liberty of phoning Jimmy. I thought it might come easier — from me, a doctor. He's flying over.'

'Oh, yes, thank you,' I answered mechanically. Poor Jimmy, the second time within a few years.

I continued sitting cross-legged: the only space for the phone among Jan's myriad papers was on the floor.

Checkmate.

It had started in Prague, six years ago, perhaps earlier; anyway I had first noticed it in summer 1971. Then it had been small and painless. The specialist had scoffed: 'Fatty tissue, my good woman. They come and go. Nothing to fuss about.'

I hadn't fussed; I had forgotten. But I had carried the dread disease away with me — from Prague.

I was still gazing at the phone, as though waiting for it to ring a denial. Then I remembered the translation. Whatever my fate, it had to be handed to Panorama in the morning. I rose to my feet, and the movement sent blood and optimism coursing through my veins.

Not checkmate. Only check. I am a survivor. I have to survive — to see Prague again.

I sat down at the typewriter and continued translating the voice of hope.

Epilogue

My mother never saw Prague again. The cancer proved to be stronger than she was and she died in the early hours of 1st November 1981, aged 58.

Perhaps towards the end she did become aware that she indeed faced a checkmate. No-one will ever know. I should, however, make a confession: I have replaced the 700-word epilogue my mother wrote in the autumn of 1981 with the last chapter of the 1977 version of her book. I do not know why she later decided to discard this chapter. I recall that she was then advised by a literary agent that her escape from Czechoslovakia would be the most natural end of the book. In addition, after the January 1981 reoccurrence of her cancer, she might have concluded that her optimism was a bit premature. She clearly wished to conclude the book on a hopeful note and would not have wanted to allow her own dimmed prospects to colour her belief in the Czech cause.

Her own 1981 epilogue was written when she was already seriously ill and while undergoing harsh chemotherapy. The epilogue opened with a statement: 'No story has an end. Neither Pavel's, nor mine, nor Czechoslovakia's. Others take up the tale.' After briefly mentioning the campaigns we organized on behalf of Jiří Müller and Aleš Macháček she devoted the rest of the epilogue to one incident which profoundly depressed her during the last months of her life.

On 27th April 1981 Czech customs officers discovered secret compartments in a van driven by two young French socialists. The compartments contained copies of Czech émigré periodicals, novels and memoirs by banned Czech authors, records by unofficial Czech folk singers, specialist Western academic books and a simple portable duplicator. The drivers were arrested, and deported three weeks later. The police used the incident as a pretext to detain ten days later about 30 or so human rights activists and *samizdat* writers, including Jiří Müller. Jiří and most of the others were soon released but five men and two women remained in prison for a year. A further seven were charged but remained free, including former Foreign Minister Prof. Jiří Hájek, whom my mother remembered from her 'diplomatic' days and always referred to as 'a very decent man'. At the time of my mother's epilogue they were all accused of 'subversion of the Republic on a large scale and in cooperation with a foreign power', a 'crime' which carries a sentence of up to 10 years imprisonment. With one exception they all denied that they had anything to do with the consignment of literature in the French van. The police's failure to fabricate at least relatively convincing 'evidence' of a link between the detainees, many of whom did not know each other, and the van, forced the prosecutor to focus on other 'criminal activities' such as writing essays or novels or history books. Until British Television offered him an unexpected gift which he couldn't refuse.

In June 1981 Thames TV transmitted a programme, *The Last Round-Up?*, in which the reporter, Julian Manyon, asserted that in the van there was a list of 'names and addresses of people inside Czechoslovakia; contacts for Jan Kavan's secret organisation'. Not surprisingly the interrogators used the transcripts of the programme against the defendants. I helped to produce the programme as I was led to believe that it could help the political detainees, as we had reason to believe other similar TV programmes had done. I trusted the *TV Eye* team, despite my growing disagreements with them as the filming progressed, mainly because I regarded one of them as a friend. Many years ago he even travelled to Czechoslovakia as our courier. At a press conference, held a day before the transmission, Manyon, using the excuse that the soundtrack was not yet ready, read the commentary out of his notebook deliberately omitting the incriminating passage because he knew very well that I would immediately expose this dangerous lie. Thanks to this trick I only discovered the lie, invented by Manyon to add spice to his programme — to produce, as he put it, 'a political Starsky and Hutch' — when I watched the programme with my mother and a friend. I will never forget how much this callous disregard of a British journalist for the safety of Czech civil rights activists shocked my mother. The *TV Eye*'s credits had given way to adverts but she still stared at the TV screen in utter disbelief, as if expecting an immediate retraction. Her intimate experience with injustice still left her unprepared for a stab in the back from British television journalists, especially since other TV companies had tried to be helpful to the people of her adopted country. She was also worried that my participation in the programme might adversely affect the good reputation of Palach Press for which she had worked so selflessly.

She concluded her epilogue with an expression of a belief that since the human spirit is indestructible, Charter 77 would survive the blow of these arrests and the forthcoming trial.

Sadly she did not live long enough to see her hope come true. Less than five months after she died all the accused in the 'van case' were released without trial, although the charges against them have still not been dropped. This means that they could be rearrested anytime the Czechoslovak authorities decided that their actions would not provoke another outburst of world protest.

The 'van case', known as Šiklová et al. and later as Jan Ruml et al., became a kind of official *cause célèbre* intended to deal Charter 77 a crippling blow. However, there were many other victims of the government's quite irrational fear of a spill-over of the 'Polish disease', which stepped up repression in 1981 to an unprecedented level. That year the opposition lost more people through forced emigration or imprisonment than at any other time before or after. More people were put under surveillance, house searches became regular occurrences, activists were interrogated every week. There were more uniformed police on the streets, popular bars were raided, hundreds and even thousands were needlessly harassed. The passing of a new law which even banned the waving of Czechoslovak flags at sports stadiums during matches, especially with Soviet teams, reflected the atmosphere in the country well. More ominously, the authorities began to resort quite brazenly to threats of violence and even to violence itself. Dissidents were beaten up not only during interrogations but much more violently by 'unknown thugs' in the middle of the night, in their own apartments or in parks. Others were threatened with fatal accidents.

My mother was deeply affected by the news of the use of violence. Ten days before she died I managed to publish a long article in *The Times*, 'Crisis time for the Czechs who chose freedom'. I rushed to her bedside because I hoped to cheer her up since she knew how difficult it is to get supportive articles about our friends in Czechoslovakia published in the British press. Despite being very ill, in great pain and affected by strong drugs she read the article eagerly. But when she read that Jiřina Šiklová, whom she admired, was being beaten up by other prisoners encouraged by the warders, tears filled her eyes and I felt that my attempt had backfired. Then a wave of anger swept her, her spirit rekindled, and she radiated enthusiasm and concern, characteristically, on behalf of other people.

While the repression failed to silence the movement, it inflicted heavy wounds on Charter 77. The Polish war against its own people, declared in December 1981, clearly reassured the Czechoslovak rulers. Combined with the need to project a more liberal image to the West in general, and to Austria in particular, the Czechoslovak regime became relatively lenient in 1982. That year Charter 77 entered into a dialogue with the West European peace movement. This dialogue about the indivisible link between peace and human rights, about the need to overcome the present division of Europe and to build a democratic Europe free of fear of holocaust and prisons continues to play a major part of Charter 77 activities to date. My mother would have been very happy to know that Palach Press also helped to include in it sections of the British peace movement and, more generally, that Palach Press proved able to maintain its close links with the chartists and to publicise their struggle — despite a chronic lack of funds, the Czechoslovak government's undiminished attempts to isolate its peoples from the rest of the world, the Thames TV programme and other obstacles which in 1981 seemed especially daunting.

There is no day in my life when I don't think of my mother and don't painfully feel her loss. I wish she was with me whenever I am overwhelmed with problems, sad at being let down by those I trusted or simply too exhausted to go on. Nevertheless, I miss most the joy of sharing with her the exhilaration of achievements. However small such successes may have been she was able to make us feel that they were worth years of hardships. I was therefore trying to imagine her during the June 1985 press conference I was chairing which announced the formation of a charity, The East European Cultural Foundation, and the launching of its new quarterly *East European Reporter*.

The EECF aims to co-ordinate the dissemination of information from within Czechoslovakia, Poland and Hungary. It also plans to give support to a wide range of unofficial cultural and educational activities in those countries, while its magazine will offer extensive coverage of human rights' activity in these countries as well as analyses of political, economic and cultural developments in Central Europe. Copies of the first issues are not only on the desks of Western journalists, scholars and other interested readers, they also circulate in small numbers in Eastern Europe.

I recall the numerous occasions at which my mother expressed her conviction that no substantial permanent change could be achieved by one East European country alone. The traumatic experience of events in Hungary in 1956, in Czechoslovakia in 1968 and in Poland in 1981 ensured that many people came to such a conclusion. The EECF was in fact established as a result of requests received from Czechoslovakia, Hungary and Poland and is a natural offspring of the increased contacts between the democratic oppositions of those countries.

There is, of course, another reason why my mother would have been pleased at the EECF press conference. One of the main Czech speakers was Aleš Macháček who emigrated to England only several weeks earlier. He came directly to Palach Press and offered his help. I hadn't seen him for almost 20 years but it did not seem to make any difference. Such friendships and loyalties do not rust. My mother was always interested in news about anyone from the 'Kavan Commune'. In the section of the book which was left out when she was asked to shorten the manuscript I found a brief summary: 'Luboš had been killed by a runaway car while waiting for a tram. Pinc, now happily remarried, was a Doctor of Philosophy, a nightwatchman and a Chartist. Jirka Holub and Jana were struggling to feed three children on one uncertain salary. Andrle had a degree, a job and a charming wife in England. Coufal was making money in Hamburg. The plausible Kovanda with a degree in agriculture had talked his way into MIT in Massachusetts and got himself a Doctorate in Political Science. Zuzana had embarked on a shaky marriage with Jan Šling, son of Otto Šling, a defendant in the Slánský trial who had been hanged in 1951.' Since then Pinc has become a social worker, Jana and Jirka have acquired another child and more rooms; Zuzana has got a divorce and is pursuing a busy journalistic career in London. Karel Kovanda became a successful American businessman but continued his interest in human rights issues and recently helped us to obtain a grant which will finance an unofficial educational project in Czechoslovakia.

I was always very glad that my mother got on so well with all my friends and I rarely stopped to reflect on the fact that she was closer to them than to almost any member of her own generation. It just felt so natural to everybody. After she died I was given the notes she wrote while in hospital. Some of them are brief, reduced almost to points; some cover her attitudes toward her illness, while others deal with her feelings towards me or my father; yet others refer to subjects covered in her book. Under the heading 'need to make clear' I read: 'Why were student activities so important to me? Because of Jan, because they were under my roof, because I couldn't help approving, supporting them. Because I believed they were the hope for the future. Because I needed that belief. After the invasion — my hopes crushed too — I had to cling to promise of better things in future represented by Jan, Jiří & Co.'

The hospital notes also make clear how worried she was that the 'two-way traffic in literature and information' which was temporarily halted in April 1981 would not be renewed. She understood better than many how crucially important it is to preserve this hole in the wall which the regime had built around a Central European nation which had for centuries its cultural and political traditions embedded in what is today known as 'the West'. She need not have worried. After a brief pause, many more took their hammers and chisels so as to widen the hole in the wall. Even the manuscript of this book found its way to Prague where it was translated into Czech and recently published in *samizdat* form.

She longed to see the book published. The book was to have been a gate for her, she said. A gate closed on the past and opened to the future. In her hospital notes she admitted: 'I set its publication against the whole of the rest of my life. I put it on one side of the scales, while on the other side I laid all the worries, troubles and problems I had had in my life. If it was published then everything balanced out, it would expunge the bitterness, erase the unhappiness, crushing burdens, losses, mistakes and disappointments of the past . . .' The publication of the book acquired such an importance in her eyes because she consciously used it for years to help her to survive the bad times, to sustain her through the years of non-creative work. She used to say: 'It's all experience. All grist to the mill. The meat of drama.' She did not take into account the commercial realities of the Western publishing world. Each rejection letter from a publisher, most of whom pointed out that books on Eastern Europe do not make profits, caused her a bitter disappointment. Nevertheless, it didn't deprive her of the joy of writing. She noted that 'no other sensation compares with the lightness, gladness of a day well spent in writing, when the pen has flowed, the phrases formed, the story progressed, the characters revealed themselves'. She decided to try her hand at a novel. After a fairly extensive research my mother wrote *The Night-Coloured Pearl* based on a romance between a blind girl and a deaf boy. As far as I can recall the manuscript was offered to one agent, rejected and never mentioned again.

My mother then returned to her life story. She realised that on a few occasions she 'got carried away by the act of writing and wasn't always meticulously accurate' and worked on the manuscript in her hospital bed a few days after the mastectomy. My mother paid the most scrupulous attention to feelings, 'trying to be as honest as I knew how.'

To edit the book and to prepare a new version for publication while undergoing surgery, chemotherapy and radiotherapy was obviously a daunting challenge but my mother never flinched from a challenge. In fact she argued that she functioned better in a crisis. Someone once told her that if you are a strong character life will deal blows that can actually be repelled. She clearly believed it. In her notes she boldly stated: 'Let's face it. I saw Pavel's imprisonment as much a challenge to me as to him. I took pride in not being defeated. I admire moral strength. I can't stand or understand weaklings.'

On the other hand she had little sympathy for stubbornness or foolhardiness. I, of course, knew this but it was still not easy for me to read that 'for Jan — even more than for Pavel — nothing is lost simply because it looks 100% hopeless. There is always the million to one chance that it will succeed. Even with a rope round his neck he would believe in reprieve or rescue. But I haven't got nerves for it... I shall never be free from the extraordinarily close bond I have with him. When I'm in Positano I resent the fact that I am not in London helping him and the Czech cause. When I'm in London I find I can't any longer stand the strain of constant let downs and disappointments for more than a week or so.'

This passage was understandable, if hard for me to accept. My mother came over from Italy and worked at least 12 hours a day translating the latest Charter 77 documents, which Palach Press obtained from Czechoslovakia with difficulty and at a considerable cost. She also corrected my written English in many articles only to hear that they were rejected. For many journalists the novelty of Charter 77 had worn off and what on the surface seemed like an unchanging situation of persecution and defiance had become too boring to report. Our good friends were being imprisoned or harassed and frequently the only thing we had to show for our efforts to get their plight publicised or to raise some financial help was a feeling of exhaustion and hopelessness. Whatever her own feelings were (and they are now staring at me from her hospital notes) my mother's firm conviction of the value of our work and her unshakeable optimism were my main source of renewed energy. I miss it today badly. The memory of how well she coped in the fifties in Prague would always shame me into persevering.

It always seemed to me that what made her undefeatable on the one hand and an invaluable friend, partner and ally on the other was her strong sense of humour. She always said that laughter was to her as necessary as oxygen and that wit, which she inherited from her father, drew her to the Czechs who have always used it as their defence against aggression. It helped her in her courageous fight against the fatal disease and to cope with the unpleasant consequences of her treatment. Shortly after she was told that she would lose her beautiful thick hair she was able to joke about wigs, saying that 'my life for my hair — that's a small price'. Her attitude can be well illustrated by a note she must have written down at the end of the chemotherapy treatment which proved to be unsuccessful: ' . . . face blown up like a melon from the steroid pills. At times I really couldn't recognise myself. A freak, in fact, who was also going to be bald. It is just too bizarre. I think the word bizarre is crucial. It seems in keeping with my character. A thousand times rather be bizarre than pitiful . . . I'm not exactly short of black humour. In the end humour boils everything down to size . . .'

I inherited only a pale version of her sense of humour and even that I seem to have lost since she died. Notwithstanding this I still cling to all the values my mother taught me and I am prepared to defend them with her kind of determination. Both my parents believed passionately in justice, truth, freedom and democratic socialism. Both tried in their own way, during their relatively short lives, to bring nearer a better, more just world for all of us. This is one of the reasons why I felt that this story should be published and why I agreed to share with you, the reading public, my memory of my beloved mother.

In my efforts to get this book published I was greatly supported by my grandmother, Ivy Edwards, who shared my own and my mother's way of thinking and loved us both dearly. My mother once described her mother as a 'liberal and democratic socialist, an atheist with views which were far from doctrinaire, with a great sense of justice, sympathy for the underdog and hatred of poverty and suffering.' My grandmother always tried to help as much as possible. She travelled to Czechoslovakia in the fifties, used the little money she had to send us parcels of food and other necessities, shared both our hopes and worries and was permanently on hand to offer moral support, especially to me and my mother. In the seventies she used her pension to help Palach Press, which, she said, given her advanced age, was the only way she could participate in something in which she strongly believed. It was encouraging to see how she took pride in all our achievements, however small they may have been. After 1981, when the two of us lost the person we loved most, our relationship strengthened and developed into an emotional closeness rarely seen between a grown man and his grandmother. I was able to see where my mother got her sensitivity, courage, strength of will and zest for life. I deeply hoped that the publication of the book would help to reduce my grandmother's pain at the untimely loss of her daughter, and I was aware how she longed to hold the book in her hands. It was not to be. After spending three months earlier this year holidaying in Spain, where she swam, walked in the mountains and enjoyed herself, she was suddenly struck by cancer. Her struggle was mercifully less painful and shorter than my mother's. She died on 16th June 1985, aged 87. I was glad that before she died she knew that it would only be a question of a short time before people were able to read about her daughter's achievements in the 'faraway country of which we know little' to borrow a phrase from a British politician my grandmother blamed for the fate of Czechoslovakia and thus also of her daughter.

I admit that I have a dilemma I don't know how to solve. I feel that only an author has the right to decide to whom she wants to dedicate her book. My mother did not make any formal dedication and she was still working on last-minute amendments when the deterioration of her health stopped her from writing. I have done only very limited editing work in order to prepare the book for publication. I therefore cannot make the decision on her behalf. All I would like to say is that if she were still with us I would recommend her to dedicate the book to my grandmother and to all those who help fellow human beings as selflessly as she and her mother did.

The failure to publish the book and thus realise her lifelong ambition to become a writer made my mother, given her exacting standards, question whether she had succeeded in anything at all. That questioning was probably induced by the increasing difficulties of her long struggle against the cancer. However, prompted by my brother, she reflected on the fact that so many people loved her and turned to her for strength and optimism. She concluded: 'I have succeeded in a small way as a person'. If we were still a team helping each other to formulate our thoughts I would have asked her to omit the 'small way' as inaccurate. From the first responses to the Czech *samizdat* edition of her book and from the numerous letters I still receive from Czechoslovakia about her it is clear that in her adopted country she will be remembered with affection, love and gratitude for a very long time. Only a few days before she died my mother received a letter from Helena Klímová, a writer, sociologist, Charter 77 signatory and wife of the well-known Czech writer Ivan Klíma. Helena wrote: 'When historians eventually deal with the moving fate of this nation they will reserve for you a special place full of merit and respect.'

Jan Kavan
London
July 1, 1985